THE FORGOTTEN BATTLES OF CALICUT, 1503 AND 1790

Strategy, Tactics and Geopolitics

THE FORGOTTEN BATTLES OF CALICUT, 1503 AND 1790
Strategy, Tactics and Geopolitics

Oliver Noone

GYAN

Published by

GYAN

Gyan Publishing House
5, Ansari Road
Daryaganj, New Delhi-110002
Phone: 011-47034999, 9811692060
E-mail: books@gyanbooks.com

Distribution Network
gyanbooks.com
India, USA, Canada, UK, Australia, France

ISBN: 978-81-212-8985-6 (PB)

First Published, 2023

Printed at: Gyan Press, Delhi.

THE FORGOTTEN BATTLES OF CALICUT, 1503 AND 1790: STRATEGY, TACTICS AND GEOPOLITICS
Author: OLIVER NOONE

Foreword

It is indeed a pleasure to write the foreword to a book that I believe will add significantly to our knowledge of our past. Dr Oliver Noone is to be commended for his meticulous research on a micro region, Calicut, and for throwing light on forgotten aspects of the city's past. Such research is of great importance in helping us to understand the many trajectories of India's past. The two events that he has studied, the naval battle of 1503, and the land battle of 1790, are, in a sense, indicative of two ends of the European entry and presence in India, for they mark the first aggressive arrival, and the final takeover of the country; the first involving the Portuguese and the latter the British.

As Dr Noone has said, the appearance of Vasco da Gama's fleet in Calicut was not mere happenstance, for Calicut's role in the intra-Asian world had long been known. K.M. Panikkar has spoken of the 'Vasco da Gama epoch' in his book Asia and Western Dominance, to highlight the importance of the control of the maritime worlds by the Europeans, and of the corresponding loss of access to this world by the Indians.

The competition over the trade to the 'Indies' beginning from the late fifteenth century Treaty of Tordesillas and the division of the world into two halves, one to be for Spanish domination and the other for the Portuguese, was challenged from the early seventeenth century by the northern European states. The Dutch and the English, and later the French, all challenged the Portuguese, both in conceptual terms, as seen in the work of Hugo Grotius, and in real military terms. However, such work has tended to focus on the European aspect, with Asia being merely the ground on which the Europeans fought it out. The role of the Asians is here dismissed as being merely passive onlookers, who were unable to, or uninterested in the forms and processes of the competition. This is far from being the case.

The naval battle of 1503 was one of the first in which the European method of using the ship itself as a weapon of war was seen in the Indian Ocean. As the new 'lords of the sea', the Portuguese challenged both, the reality of the Calicut control of the trade of the area, and the notions of sovereignty asserted through the use of the title of 'Samudri Raja', or Zamorin. Whose ocean was it, and how was this 'ownership' to be asserted? This was something that was manifested for the first time in this world with the Portuguese, and once established, was reinforced by the introduction of the cartaz system. We must remember that the great battle for Diu was also fought in the maritime world, and that this siege of Diu saw the coming together of probably the greatest naval armada in Indian Ocean history. Nevertheless, as Dr Noone has shown, this first naval battle marked a decisive shift in the politics of the Asian world.

As colonialism moved from sea to land, contestation increasingly became land-based and land-bound. This is the underlying dimension of the second of the two battles that Dr Noone has highlighted – that land itself, and access to this land from the land rather than the sea, had become of prime importance. Battles and tactics on land now overtook engagements in oceanic spaces; but the end result was the establishment of control over both land and sea, and of the steady erosion of the spaces of contestation by Asians, and the assigning of the spaces of action by the colonial power alone.

Prof. Radhika Seshan, PhD.
Retired Professor and Former Head,
Department of History
Savitribai Phule Pune University

Acknowledgements

I must confess that I am not a professional historian. I am a medical practitioner who spent three and a half decades with the National Health Service of the United Kingdom. Certain events and people made me interested in history and if I spent all my spare time at the British Library, it was due to the fact that I was smitten by the subject. A small incident that took place in the year 2000 led me to make these historical enquiries. While I was practicing as a physician in Norwich, Derrick Dunning, the father of my agent Sue Dunning, gave me a book written by one of his relatives, Colonel Hugh Pearse titled *The Hearseys - Five Generations of an Anglo-Indian Family*. Sue Dunning was the fifth-generation descendant of Captain Andrew Hearsey whose son Lieutenant General Sir John Hearsey had a major role in the Indian Rebellion of 1857. As the baggage-master of the 75th Highland Regiment of Foot, Andrew Hearsey had travelled through Coimbatore and Palghat and reached Calicut by the end of 1790, where he participated in the Battle of Tarvananghurry (Tervannengarry). Being born in Palghat and having grown up in Calicut, this was new information to me. It also reminded me the folk tale my aunt Alice used to tell us of the 'padayottam' (the invasion and occupation of the land of Zamorin by Tipu) which forced her forefathers to flee their home in Tellicherry, north of Malabar to the sanctuary of the Palghat Rajas. It was this knowledge which initiated me to explore the background of this conflict. Something that started as simple curiosity led me to venture into history. I was guided only by my passion for the subject.

Several people helped me to convert my interest in research to methodological precision. It may not be possible to acknowledge everyone but I would certainly mention a few. My first gratitude is to the Reference Specialists and Area Specialists at the Asian and African Studies Reading Room in the British Library, St Pancras in London. It was their initial support, reassurance and encouragement which gave me the inspiration to venture into this abyss of political and military history. Prof. M G S Narayanan, an internationally known authority on South Indian history helped me to clarify my thoughts. I had the privilege of interacting with Mr C K Ramachandran, IAS(Rtd), a founder member of Calicut Heritage Society who encouraged me to write down my findings. My friend Prof. Jaiprakash Raghaviah had gone through the earlier drafts of this book and given valuable suggestions. I am thankful to him for being with me. Dr. Dhanesh M P, former research scholar in JNU New Delhi went through the manuscript rigourously and gave his insights and suggestions. I thank him for the same.The entire editorial work was done by Radhika Samuel, a professional edotor. I thank her for her painstaking labour. I am also sincerely grateful to Prof. Radhika Seshan for providing a meaningful and significant foreword for my book.

In the course of my enquiry, I also have utilised the services of many other institutions. These include the libraries of the Bodleian in Oxford, The National Library of Wales in Aberystwyth and several local libraries, particularly in Norwich. I have also used the materials available in various museums in the Tower of London, Royal Armouries Museum in Leeds, Maritime Museum in Greenwich, and Fort Nelson in Hampshire. I am grateful to the librarians and reference specialists who helped me to wade through the plethora of information that was useful to my inquiry.

I thank my wife Dr Sheela Noone for her support and encouragement. My children Dr Mohan and Dr Padmini helped me with the technical side of computer application.

I am submitting this work to readers with a fervent hope that these essays on colonial battles would help to understand the strategies of colonial expansion.

Introduction

The heritage of Calicut, the 'Emporium of the East' as an important entrepôt of Asian commerce is well known. But the military past of Calicut as a theatre of war, in relation to a pan-Indian background, during the Age of Discovery and the period of colonial expansion is seldom explored. There are only few references to two important military conflicts that took place in Calicut: first, a sea battle in 1503 and the other, a land battle in 1790.

The appearance of a Portuguese fleet commanded by Vasco da Gama at Calicut on 20 May 1498 was not a coincidence. That there might be a direct and easier sea route to the East was increasingly appreciated in late medieval Europe and the voyages of Gama was the culmination of a lengthy Portuguese search for a sea route to Asia around Africa. The origin of these expeditions can be traced to the conquering of Ceuta in north-west Africa by Don Joao I of Portugal in 1415. Over the next 75 years, the Portuguese inched their way in the Atlantic along the African coast, reaching the Cape of Good Hope in 1488 under the command of Bartolomeu Diaz. In this complex operation, they tried and tested a variety of ships and were able to introduce the caravels and carracks which were the protagonists of oceanic voyages. They perfected navigational instruments like the astrolabe and the quadrant which enabled them to find their latitude in the high seas. They had extensive understanding of the wind and current flows of the Atlantic and could chart out their course irrespective of its direction. These factors helped them develop a lucrative trade in slaves, sugar and gold. At the same time in 1492, Columbus discovered America, adding a new dimension in transoceanic explorations.

The first journey of Gama in 1497 was more of an exploratory nature. By the time he returned to Calicut for the second time after the action-packed expedition of Cabral in 1500, the aim of the Portuguese had changed from peaceful commerce to aggressive domination of trading. The Portuguese were able to build up a large naval power in the Indian Ocean with which they were able to subdue small rulers on the West Coast of India and control trade and traffic. They also became the seller of protection to Asian seaborne trade.

There is a gap of almost three hundred years between the naval battle of Calicut of 1503 and the land battle of Calicut in Tarvananghurry of 1790. The battle was a minor conflict which took place in an obscure part of India called Tarvananghurry by the English (now called Tirurangadi, near Calicut in Kerala), between the occupying forces of Tipu of Mysore and the army of the East India Company. This attracted the attention of Lord Cornwallis, the Governor General and Commander in Chief of the English forces in India. Lord Cornwallis personally congratulated Lieutenant Colonel Hartley for his victory. What is the importance of this battle that gets the commendation of the chief? We shall discuss these complex issues here. The historic backdrop is complicated, intriguing and scattered over a vast area and period and seldom constructed into a continuous seamless event in history.

The crucial Tripartite Alliance involving the East India Company, the Nizam and the Marathas was the game changer in this whole story. How and why did the Nizam and Marathas, who knew very well that unless they were united themselves they would be decimated by the hands of the English, still ally and support them? I could not get a satisfactory answer to this very pertinent question which kept creeping up my mind. And to my surprise the same vexation has been expressed by several authors already. Unifying these different ideas, explanations, interpretations and comments necessitated the study of the two protagonists in detail - specifically in relation to the Third Mysore War. Hence the two chapters of the Nizam and the Marathas.

This book is an attempt to relate these diverse events in the annals of Indian history - the naval battle of 1500, the land battle of 1790 and the background political history of the Nizam and the Marathas leading to the Tripartite Alliance of the English against Tipu. What are these battles about, what was the background in which they were fought, who were the protagonists, and what was the significance in local, Indian and world history and politics? This book attempts to explore these extremely fascinating facts about these battles and in retrospect their role in the formation of the first truly global international system.

Contents

List of Illustrations and Maps

Illustrations

List of Maps

1

An Overview of the Period

The modern international system has its origin, it can be said, from the maritime military and commercial engagements of the Europeans with the rest of the world from the late fifteenth century onwards:

> European maritime expansion had a distinctive character in both its means and ends. The means centered on naval coercion and power projection. The ends were primarily commercial: control of seaborne trade, expansion of market access, and later, repayment of sovereign debts. Thus, the particularly European contribution to the making of the modern international system was organised maritime violence in pursuit of commercial ends.[1]

However, the formation of the first truly global international system and the firm territorial domination in Asia and Africa by the Europeans took almost another 300 years to evolve. Europe was able to subdue the Americas on a continental scale, but was unable to make significant inroads into India, Japan, or China until the eighteenth century as it was only slightly more powerful than the old Asian centres of civilisation. Dom Francisco de Almeida, the first governor and viceroy of Portuguese India, wrote to King Manuel:

"In so far as you are powerful on the sea, all India will be yours, but if you do not possess this kind of power on the sea, fortresses ashore will do you precious little good".[2] Thus, "The tools of the empire used to overthrow the Marathas, the Ch'ing and the Tokugawa were totally different from those used to subjugate the Aztecs or the Incas. Clearly, in the three intervening centuries, a transformation so profound that it must surely rank as a 'revolution'".[3] Chancey says that "[t]his transformation was effected through a variety of means—but in the literature it is the wars of the period that generally hold the centre stage—often to the exclusion of the gains made by diplomacy and political intrigue. That is unfortunate considering that more land was brought under British control through the latter than the former".[4]

Warfare at Sea

Before the middle of the fifteenth century, sea battles were waged within distinct regional domains. There were substantial commercial relationships between these adjoining realms, establishing a global network that stretched from the Sea of Japan all the way to Europe's Atlantic coast. They were the Chinese sphere, the Malay sphere, the Indo-Arab sphere and the European sphere. The Chinese sphere extended from the Sea of Japan to the Straits of Malacca. The Malay sphere encompassed the Indonesian archipelago and met the Indo-Arab and Chinese spheres in the Straits of Malacca. The Indo-Arab sphere comprised the Indian Ocean, the Persian Gulf, and the Red Sea, extending from the east coast of Africa to the Straits of Malacca. This region served as transfer points between Chinese, Malay, Persian, Arab, and African markets. Spices, notably pepper, flowed from the east to the west along with Chinese porcelain and silk. Much of this trade went to European markets, producing a flow of precious metals in return (Pliny the Elder, in 77 CE, called India "the sink of the world's gold"!).

John Ellis Jr says:

> The extent and scope of this picture of interactive emergence around the Indian Ocean had several political

> and cultural dimensions. The rise of Islam made eastern Mediterranean and Persia an area of common religion which gave a fairly unified authority, prosperous and safe for merchants. Secondly, China's economic revolutions made it a source of consumer goods that found markets throughout Eurasia. Lastly, the fine cotton and silk fabrics from India found markets from Southeast Asia to the world of Islam, from Persia to the Arab lands to East Africa.[5]

The European sphere can be separated into three sub-spheres: Atlantic, Baltic, and Mediterranean. Each had its own characteristic customs and practices and they were largely free standing and independent. According to Guilmartin:

> There was, however, a fundamental difference between their interrelationships and those that prevailed among the non-European spheres, in that there was recurrent military interaction among them. In part this was a function of geography, for Europe is not only a peninsula, and thus accessible by sea, but a peninsula of peninsulas: Scandinavian, Iberian, Italian, Greek and Anatolian, with the British Isles as an outlier. This geographic reality not only encouraged the development of seafaring, but accustomed Europeans to the movements of ships, men and ideas over long distances (Guilmartin, 2002, p. 37).[6]

The Great Asian powers were at least as capable of projecting power across the sea as Europeans until the nineteenth century. Arabs, Polynesians, Chinese, and others routinely traded across oceans for centuries before the European voyages of discovery. Yet only Europeans sought control over the high seas, key sea-lanes, and maritime trade as the end justified the sustained use of organised violence by blue-water naval forces, whether public, private, or some combination of the two, capable of operating globally.[7] For all their differences, none of the regimes of the region saw maritime trade as a continuation of naval war by other means, and none sought militarised control over trade routes, as did the

Europeans. But, despite being massively overshadowed by the power and wealth of Asian empires, the European actors such as Portugal, the Netherlands, and England managed to play prominent roles in building the international system, as Sharman articulates: "Europeans were able to build a maritime global order via gunboat diplomacy thanks to naval supremacy, but even more so because of the indifference of the Asian powers which did not regard these as worth fighting for".[8]

Sharman gives three reasons for the uniqueness of the use of violence in the seas by the Europeans. The first was the isolation of Europe and their desire for Eastern goods. This gave them a great incentive and motivation for long-distance seaborne trade. At first, the priority was for spices, but later, there was an increased demand for Indian textiles, Chinese silks, porcelains and tea, and other commodities. But for the Asians, there was little interest in European goods. So the Europeans were forced to exchange specie (coined money, especially gold or silver), the only commodity that the Asian merchants wanted. In these circumstances, one of the few competitive European exports turned out to be maritime violence. Second, right from the beginning of their regular contact with Asia, the Europeans executed their violent and militarised trade and commerce in a very skillful and professional way. For medieval ship owners, the extremely hazardous environment of the European waters forced and equipped them to fight for their seaborne trade. In contrast, the international system in Asia was more hierarchical and peaceful, especially in the organisation of long-distance trade. During the crucial period of European entry and expansion in the sixteenth and seventeenth centuries, the Mughal Empire was at its zenith, encompassing-comprising- between 100 and 150 million people, more than the combined total of all great European powers at the time. Through monetising the economy and providing a higher degree of internal peace, the Mughal rulers indirectly aided international trade. Finally, the doctrine of mercantilism shaped the mental attitude and approach of the European rulers and merchants. These doctrines were unfamiliar to Eastern rulers, who supported the belief that war was the concern of the state and trade as the pursuit of private merchants: "Importantly, mercantilism saw the economic underpinnings of military power in control of trade more than territory. Chartered companies such as the English and Dutch East India Companies were in many ways the perfect institutional representation of these new ideas".[9]

The Dominance of the Sea Lanes

The Portuguese were the pioneers in establishing gunboat diplomacy beyond their home waters.

One objective of this campaign was to seek the help of the legendary Prester John of the East to fight the Muslims and liberate the Holy Land, but the paramount objective was to profit from the spice trade. In a poor country with a population of less than one million in 1500, trade was the only method for the crown to achieve profit and status. 'The benefits of trade, which was tightly monopolised by the crown, were substantial: In 1518, the king obtained more revenue from spices than from the whole of metropolitan Portugal'.[10]

Portuguese merchant ships engaged in long-distance trade were capable of waging naval warfare from the very beginning. The control of maritime commerce in India and the Indies was acquired by the establishment of fortified warehouses (factories) and secure bases around a capacious harbour with a garrison of European soldiers and a flotilla of armed ships. Once they secured a sufficient number of ports, they then began to control the coastal trade of the natives by introducing a system of licensing called *cartazes* to be bought from the *Estado da India* (all Portuguese colonies east of Cape of Good Hope). This offered safe passage and the right to trade for all ships in the Indian Ocean, without which they were liable to be plundered, captured, or sunk. Thus, the Portuguese created a fresh threat of violence to Asian shipping and then sold protection from the threat, at the same time not providing any service in return.[11] This licencing and taxing of indigenous merchants helped to pay the expenses for governing and defending the empire. But the vastness of the region and the shortage of Portuguese ships and personnel made this protection racket only partially effective.

The Portuguese established a commercial empire in the Indian Ocean between 1500 and 1535 by taking possession of the principal coastal cities that were the home ports of Arab, Gujarati, and Malay merchants. The term *Estado da India* referred to all the official possessions of the Portuguese Crown, such as ports, fortresses, and lands in East Africa, India, and South-East Asia. These domains were governed from Goa by a viceroy nominated by the king. Goa, which had a large harbour that was protected by an inshore island, was captured in 1510 by Alfonso de Albuquerque by defeating the Bijapur Sultanate. This gave the Portuguese a strong base to place a strong fleet in the Indian Ocean, which helped them to secure many small ports on the east coast of Africa and the Malabar coast of India. Ormuz, at the mouth of the Persian Gulf, was occupied next, thus gaining control of the spice trade to Persia and the Levant. A fort was established in Ceylon in 1518, followed by another in the harbour of Muscat in Oman. The control of the Indian Ocean trade was wrapped up by establishing a fortified enclave in Diu.

The capture of Goa was followed by the capture of Malacca in 1511, giving access to the spice trade in the far-east. Spices produced in the Sultanate of Banda, Ternate, and Tidore were gathered there, and Portuguese merchants carried them across the Indian Ocean to India or to the north to China and Japan. In 1557, the Portuguese merchants could secure a permanent enclave off mainland China that became Macau. Thus, within a few years, a very complex pattern of international commerce evolved.[12] The *Estado da India*, in the first century of its existence, did not face much competition from other European nations. The dynastic union of the Kingdom of Spain and the Kingdom of Portugal under the Spanish Crown in 1580 brought the entire Iberian Peninsula and Portuguese overseas possessions under the Spanish Habsburg kings.

The discovery of the Americas by Christopher Columbus in 1492 was followed by Spanish settlements on Cuba, Hispaniola, and other large Caribbean islands. These were the bases used to explore the mainland, resulting in conquests like that of the Aztecs in Mexico and the Incas in Peru, which procured huge amounts of precious metals for Spain. The Spanish Crown centralised the control of this enormous wealth, rapaciously looted from the hapless natives of America, through the exploitative and brutal feudal arrangement called *encomienda* (grant by the Spanish Crown to an officials specified number of Native Americans living in a particular area) and *repartimiento* (formal grant of forced labour imposed on indigenous inhabitants to Spanish colonists) by establishing the *Casa de Contratacion* (House of the Indies - central trading house and procurement agency for Spain's New World) in Seville. The paramount concern of the Spanish monarchs and aristocracy was to expel Muslims from Europe, stop Muslim expansion elsewhere in the world, extend the Spanish empire in order to expand the boundaries of Christendom, and re-establish the true Catholic faith as the religion of western Europe. Reversing the Reformation remained the monarch's primary objective, which could not be done without conquering the Netherlands and England. Both attempts failed, especially the catastrophe of the Armada against England in 1588, after which Spanish power in Europe steadily declined.

Thus, the Catholic powers, Spain and Portugal, who had divided the world between themselves in the sixteenth century, were to be eclipsed in the seventeenth century by the rising Protestant states of the North, England, and the United Netherlands.[13] The Spanish monarch preferentially used money minted from American bullion to pay for European wars rather than encouraging industries, agriculture, commercial food production. They paid scant attention to the improvement of interior transportation, the promotion of artisan manufacturing, or by incentivising Spanish merchants to conduct more of the nation's European trade.

This emboldened the Dutch merchants to increase their involvement in European maritime commerce, and by 1540 they swiftly superseded the Spanish and Portuguese merchants in the substantial and valuable commerce between northern and southern Europe. They also replaced the Hanseatic merchants who had long dominated the trade between the Baltic sea and the cities of the Rhine Delta. The Dutch merchants became the leading carriers of bulk commodities like ship timbers, bar iron, naval stores, food grains, salt, and wool to Amsterdam and from there to Spain and

Portugal. At the same time, the needs of the American colonists were also supplied by the Dutch, the English, and the Germans as controls and sanctions obstructed free trade and restricted self-sufficiency in artisan-manufactured products by Spain. This was how Amsterdam became the entrepôt of northern Europe during the first half of the sixteenth century. The immense profit earned by the Dutch merchants and the credit skills they learned from Genoese and Florentine bankers helped them to accumulate the capital that made it possible for them to challenge Iberian control of long-distance commerce to America and the Indies.[14] The Dutch then invested their wealth in intellectual pursuits such as medicine, optics and mathematics, as well as in improving skills in banking, insurance, navigation, shipbuilding, and engineering technology needed to drain land.[15] These developments were the result of the dynamic changes in the social structure of Dutch society as a consequence of the Lutheran Reformation. The oppressive and tyrannical intellectual authority of the medieval church was abolished. There were few institutional restraints, and academics and scholars could promote and publish new ideas and disciplines. By the middle of the seventeenth century, Dutch commerce and learning surpassed that of the Spanish, Portuguese, Genoese, and Venetians.

'The basis for the Dutch global outreach and the opening up of the Indian Ocean world for the European geographical imagination, especially regarding spice markets and non-Christian cultures, was heavily influenced by a geography book published in Amsterdam just before Dutch world hegemony: *Itinerario, voyageofte schipvaert near Oost ofte Portugaels Indien (Discours of Voyages into Ye East & West Indies)* by Jan Huygen van Linschoten in 1596'.[16] Born in Holland, he left for Spain and later moved over to Portugal doing business. Subsequently he went to India as the secretary of the Archbishop of Goa, Joao Vicente da Fonseca, where he had access to privileged information about the Portuguese navigation and commerce in South-East Asia. Using his cartographic and drawing skills, he copied a substantial number of nautical charts that had been meticulously kept secret by the Portuguese for more than a century. The first Dutch expedition to the East Indies left in 1595, with Comelis de Houtman commanding a flotilla of four ships. Further voyages followed, and on the basis of Houtman's information, Admiral Jacob Corneliszoon van Neck sailed to the Java Sea. Between 1599 and 1601, eight syndicates of Dutch merchants sent out 14 fleets composed of at least 65 ships.

The Chartered Company

From the beginning of the seventeenth century, the entry of a new type of public private competitor—*the Chartered Company*—changed this environment. The English East India Company (EIC) received its Royal Charter in 1600 followed by the Dutch East India Company (VOC: Verenidge Oost-Indische Compagnie) in 1602. The Chartered Companies epitomize European hybrid actors designed for maritime profit through violence.[17] Thus, to its activities as a merchant, these companies were forced to add those of a soldier and an administrator. "One can't trade without war or wage war without trade," wrote Jan Pieterszoon Coen, the founder of Dutch supremacy in the Indies.[18] According to Phillips and Sharman several innovative policies helped the company-states to succeed against their chief institutional rivals, namely, unarmed merchant trading diaspora, unincorporated adventurers, and rival European sovereign states. First, by maintaining their own armies and navies, company-states virtually absorbed their protection costs, which conferred a cheaper and reliable form of protection. Second, in addition to employing violence to protect their own trade, the company-states adopted an aggressive attitude to enforce monopolies and attack commercial competitors. With their massive naval and military power, they could instil terror, pressurise weaker local polities, or act as useful allies to more powerful ones. Third, the modern innovation of creating the company as a legally separate entity from its owners, pooling capital in the body corporate, and appointing professional managers protected the company-states where individual missions failed. Thanks to this stock of pooled, patient capital (long term capital), they were able to stay stronger in the investment time horizon, and they could overcome price swings in key commodities such as spices. Finally, the company-states were able to overcome, to an extent, the governance challenges between the European principals (the company-state management) and extra-European agents (those conducting trade, war, and diplomacy in Africa, Asia, and the Americas) involved in long-distance trade and rules. By enabling the principals and agents to buy into the success of the company by means of holding shares, and, at the same time, permitting company employees to engage in private trading, the East India Company was able to gain their cooperation.[19] Thus, though they were not able to eliminate corruption among the agents, the company-states were comparatively more efficient in administering long-distance colonisation in the early modern period.

The vast cultural differences between the regional regimes and the Europeans resulted in significant expenses in negotiation and transaction. As newcomers, the Europeans were unfamiliar with local languages, customs, laws, and institutions. To maintain profitable commercial operations, they had to gain access to native dealers, traders, creditors, translators, negotiators, and middlemen, and, on many occasions, they found that they could not depend on these pre-existing trust networks. It was here that the hybrid nature of the company-states equipped them with unique capacities to ease these challenges. As corporations endowed with institutional permanency, company-states could accumulate knowledge and forge long-term alliances with local partners and patrons. As they did not directly represent European rulers, they were free to adjust their diplomacy to local circumstances without compromising the dignity of their distant European sponsors. This helped them to position themselves alternatively as suzerains, supplicants, or partners to indigenous rulers as the circumstances demanded.[20] The authority to utilise sovereign powers empowered company-states with coercive power necessary to establish and enforce their monopolies to edge into foreign markets at the expense of European and local rivals.

The arrival of the Dutch and the English at the end of the sixteenth century marks a turning point. The organisational cohesion of the Dutch and English East India Companies far surpassed that of the Portuguese. The Dutch government gave the VOC a monopoly on trade with the East and gave it the authority to engage in war and diplomacy, as well as a wide range of other governing, judicial, administrative, and even religious powers. But profit being the prime motive, it initiated some of the most important features of the modern corporation, including joint-stock ownership, corporate personality, limited legal liability, and the separation of ownership from management. Thus, the VOC is considered as a particular political institution in its own terms, one that challenged its critics to think about it as a body politic that was neither a corporation nor an empire but rather a company-state.[21]

The VOC waged a highly successful campaign against the Portuguese possessions in the Indian Ocean in the first half of the seventeenth century, demonstrating the outstanding institutional excellence of the company-state over the sovereign state. During this period, the Portuguese lost their key strongholds such as Malacca, Ceylon, the Spice Islands, and several ports in western and eastern India, while their headquarters in Goa was regularly blockaded, and the Portuguese trading ships were ravaged throughout the region.[22]

The Dutch were fully aware that the only way to protect revenue from long-distance commerce was with adequate expenditures in naval construction, building fortification, and having garrisons of soldiers to defend them. The Dutch presence in the Indies was enhanced in 1616 by sailing directly across the Indian Ocean and entering the Java Sea through the Sunda straits instead of hugging the east coast of Africa and frequently stopping at fortified warehouses. To monopolise production and distribution, they needed secure garrisons with a territorial hinterland, as the Portuguese had in Goa, which they found in the island of Java, and a fort was completed in 1618. A colony at Cape Town was established in 1652, which supplied the Dutch ships with fresh water, meat, fruit, and vegetables.

In India, the Dutch established their first factory in Masulipatam in 1605, followed by Pulicat in 1610, Surat in 1616, Bimilipatam in 1641, and Chinsura in 1653. The Dutch used their superior naval and military power to conquer centres in Ceylon: Colombo in

1656 and Jaffna in 1658, which gave them control of the principal commodities of Ceylon—cinnamon and rice. From their base in Colombo, the Dutch conquered many small Portuguese warehouses along the Coromandel coast, and a Dutch factory was established in Cochin in Malabar in 1663. From 1640 to 1700, the Dutch East India Company was immensely profitable because of its dominant position in Indian commerce and commercial hegemony in the Indies. The First (1652–1654) and the Second (1665–1667) Anglo-Dutch Wars were fought in Europe and the Americas and did not have any major impact in India and the Indies. 'But by the beginning of the eighteenth century, refrainment from armed intervention in India became a self-defeating policy because the Dutch did not adequately protect their trade during the slow disintegration of the Mughal Empire that preceded the death of Emperor Aurangzeb in 1707'.[23] Prof. Poonen comments, 'The years 1729–58 witnessed the discomfiture of the Dutch and the emergence of Marthanda Varma of Travancore as a powerful ruler who dealt a decisive blow to Dutch pretensions. He gained a signal victory over the Dutch at Colachel (1741). The Treaty of Mavelikara facilitated the expansion of Travancore and made it impossible for the Dutch any longer "to play Emperor of Travancore".'[24]

The English EIC established their trading in Surat, which was the principal maritime city of the Mughal Empire. The English and the Dutch East India Companies joined forces to neutralise the Portuguese commerce in India and the Indies but between them were intense competitors for Indian commerce. The English captured Hormuz in the Persian Gulf from the Portuguese in 1622, which reduced the amount of Portuguese and Dutch spices that were carried overland from the Persian Gulf to the Levant. Spices were then delivered to the Mediterranean cities from London, where they had been carried by ships from India, and this reorientation of trade caused great losses to Venetian traders. Emperor Jahangir, in 1624, granted the English merchants the freedom of movement throughout the empire and the licence to engage in coastal trade. This greatly curtailed the business of the Portuguese, who fought back, but they were defeated by a combined Dutch and English fleet. As these conflicts and encounters were stretching the resources of the English EIC, they slowly withdrew from the East Indies and concentrated on India. With the aim of prevailing over the Dutch competition in the 1640s and 1650s, the English negotiated a private truce with the Portuguese in Goa. The successful revolution of the Portuguese in 1640 liberated them from Spain and enabled them to sign a treaty with the English, which ended hostilities between them.

The English East India Company barely survived the 1640s and, in the 1650s was on the edge of bankruptcy, the primary reason being its financial difficulties due to the English Civil War (1642–1646). Another reason for the distraction was the assured returns from the colonisation of Virginia, Massachusetts Bay, and the sugar colonies of the Caribbean islands.[25] To acquire funds that parliament refused to set aside, King Charles in 1635 granted a trading licence to Sir William Courteen under the name of the Courteen Association to trade in India, thereby bypassing the monopoly of the EIC of making all the voyages between England and India. By 1636, the badly managed Courteen Company collapsed, but during the English Civil War, the Crown gave its support to the Courteen Association much to the disadvantage of the EIC. In 1649, the Courteen Association changed its name to Assada Company, the name derived from their plantations in the Assada isles in Madagascar.[26] After the execution of King Charles, the Council of State carried out civil administration. The three applicants for the Eastern Trade—the Company, founding its monopoly from the Royal Charter, the Courteen's Association, claiming its legitimacy also on a royal grant, and the great merchants of London and Bristol - all made every attempt to lobby them demanding open trade in their and the nation's interest. But the Council of State firmly directed the Company to come to terms with the Courteen's Association, as during this time, both the rivals had reached the brink of ruin. Finally, in 1649, the two companies agreed that they should work together with regards to general Indian trade. This coalition of rival bodies under a parliamentary sanction found the basis on which trade with India continued until Cromwell's charter towards the close of the Commonwealth. Cromwell viewed the India trade from a national standpoint, and throughout his life, he had the interest not of the Company but of the nation in mind. Cromwell laid the groundwork for the modern constitution of the EIC. He was the first ruler of England who realised that the India trade was no private preserve of the sovereign and his nominees, but a concern of the nation, to be maintained by national diplomacy and defended by national arms. Under regulations based on his Charter, it cast its medieval skin, shook off the traditions of the regulated system, and grew into one united, continuous, and permanent joint-stock corporation in the full sense of the word.[27]

The Dutch continued to control a substantial volume of Indian trade for several decades after the 1660s, but progressively, the English began to increase their share, and their commerce was mainly concentrated in Bombay and Madras. The number of English regional merchants increased progressively, and they were able to expand their network of trade among other European and indigenous merchants on land and sea. This steadily increased their profits from Indian commerce, which enabled them to increase the number of enclaves they directly governed.[28] But the gradual disintegration of the Mughal Empire slowly led them to the assumption of governance.

The crumbling influence and power of the Mughal Empire resulted in escalating conflicts among the feudal aristocrats who governed provinces. This forced the Company factors to protect the frontiers of their enclaves to save their business. Gerald Aungier, the factor at Surat established in 1619, wrote to the Company directors in 1677: "The times now require you manage your general commerce with your sword in your hands".[29] In 1669, he moved the Company's base to Bombay, the underutilised harbour acquired from the Portuguese as part of the dowry for King Charles II. Here he established the warehouses on an inshore island, which were heavily fortified. To deal with emergencies for the Company, the first professional infantry, cavalry, and artillery units were organised by him. A heavily armed cruiser supported by smaller armed ships was stationed in Bombay, which later progressed to the Bombay Marine. They supported the English and indigenous merchant ships, suppressed piracy, and helped to carry troops. A divergent community of merchants shifted their operations within 10 years of the completion of the fort in Bombay because of the protection it offered and the fair taxation to maintain the army and naval units. After Bombay and Madras, the third fortified warehouse was established in Calcutta in 1692, which became a major business centre. Simultaneously, with the increasing Indian commerce, the trade with China also increased, predominantly in tea. By 1785, the tea trade accounted for about half of the profits of the English East India Company, even though there was a much larger volume of commodities coming from India than there had been in 1700.[30]

The Glorious Revolution of 1688, in which the Catholic King James II was replaced by his Protestant daughter Mary and her Dutch husband William of Orange, was a benchmark event in English commercial policy because it confirmed the previous 50 years of economic development. Thus, during the eighteenth century, the domestic and foreign policies of the English were to be governed by the consideration of mercantile advantages, such as the political economy of the Dutch during the previous 100 years. Though there were attempts to cancel the monopoly charter of the EIC and legitimise independent traders, it soon became obvious that profitable trade in the Indies could not be maintained without coordinated political, military, and commercial policies in England and India.

Increased maritime commerce during the seventeenth century was extremely advantageous to the English merchants, bankers, ships owners, and, particularly, to the government treasury as the augmented revenue from taxing helped England to become a first-rank military power in the eighteenth century. The Anglo-Dutch wars succeeded in replacing the Dutch ships as the primary carriers of European maritime commerce, which diverted trans-oceanic trade away from Amsterdam. Successive conflicts—the War of the League of Augsburg and the War of Spanish Succession—weakened the ability of Dutch commerce to compete with the English for carrying on trade in Europe and in long-distance commerce. The competitive edge of the English EIC steadily increased over the Dutch EIC, and by 1715, they became minor partners to the English in European, American, and Indian commerce.[31] Thus, by 1720, London replaced Amsterdam as the paramount entrepôtand banking centre of Europe, which, in turn, brought about increased trade, especially re-exports of American and Indian commodities. It was these profits that helped to build and maintain the mighty Royal Navy that assisted in defending English maritime commerce.

The French EIC was founded in 1664 by Jean-Baptiste Colbert, but unlike the English or Dutch East India Companies, this was a government enterprise. The French and British interests and efforts in Asia ran along similar lines. Both companies maintained various trading posts throughout India; both came to encourage the pursuit of so-called Intra-Asian or County Trade as a means of raising funds in Asia itself.[32] Unlike the VOC, and very much like the EIC, the French company persistently pursued to consolidate its base in India, generally in a direct rivalry with the British. Both companies began to interfere directly and militarily in Indian affairs from the 1720s onwards. These Franco-British conflicts reached their zenith in the Carnatic Wars of the 1740s and 1750s, which merged into the Seven Years War, ultimately ending in the defeat of the French in India.

The English EIC came to focus on the Indian subcontinent and gained their greatest successes more by diplomacy with local regimes than through war, though the armed forces were an integral part of their business models. The Mughal emperors ruled over 100 million people and commanded hundreds of thousands of cavalrymen, and the English were in no position to directly challenge this rich and mighty kingdom. However, they achieved a series of mutually beneficial deals with the Mughals. The declining power and prestige of the Great Mughals resulted in a growing scale and frequency of war in India. This caused the emergence of influential and powerful regional states, which presented ample opportunities for French and British adventurers to gain a fortune in treasure and revenue rights by training and leading the armies of Indian princes. Following the success in the Battle of Plassey in 1757, the English became the supreme power in Bengal. In 1765, the Mughal Emperor and the nawab were forced to recognise the right of the Company to collect all state revenue in the provinces of Bengal, Bihar, and Orissa. According to Parker:

> It was wealth beyond the dreams of avarice: the net amount of territorial revenue and customs received officially by the Company leapt from nothing before 1757 to almost 2 million pounds in 1761–64, and to almost 7.5 million pounds in 1766–69. With the aid of these funds, it proved possible to build impregnable fortifications, and to raise armies large enough to intervene effectively in the Deccan, in Mysore—indeed anywhere in the subcontinent. By 1782, the British were able to maintain 115,000 men in India, 90 percent of sepoys, and reduce the odds against them in battle from the 10 to 1 of Plassey to only 2 to 1 against states like Mysore. The prospect of the European domination of India, to match the American domination of America, now became a real possibility.[33]

It is estimated that more than 40 percent of the Indian tax revenue was routed to military expenditure between 1761 and 1804.[34]

The Emergence of Organised Resistance

Then, at the eleventh hour, some native rulers adopted Western military techniques with such success that the British were stopped in their tracks. In the Battle of Pollilur in September 1780, as part of the Second Mysore War, the British contingent led by Colonel William Bailey were comprehensively defeated by the Mysore army. The London Chronicle wrote,

> 'Before you receive this, you must have heard of Hyder Aly's Invasion of the Carnatic with a most numerous and formidable Army and of his great Success against our Troops; the Flower of which, in a Detachment under the Command of Lieutenant Colonel Baillie and Fletcher, were defeated, and almost entirely cut off on the 10 September last, at Perambancum, a place within

> a few Miles of Canjeevaram, where our main Army, under the Command of Sir Hector Munro, was then encamped. But he unfortunately did not move to support them, until it was too late; so they were left, for several Hours, to fight the main Body of the Enemy's Army, which was supported by a numerous and well-served Artillery. Thus, has Hyder, in three Months' Time beat us in the Field, driven our Army to the Gates of Madras, taken Arcot, the Capital of the Carnatic, and several other Places; in consequence of which he is completely Master of the open Country.[35] Such a total defeat, taken along with the Battle of Wadgaon in January 1779, was a grim reminder to the English that the native armies of the Indians were no longer easy prey. Besides, by 1780 the mighty British imperial power was further weakened by their war against American independence.[36]

British historians tended to play down the significance of such a total defeat. But Warren Hastings fully recognised the reality that his enemies were coming of age and that there is an inspiring, creative future leader and visionary in Tipu: "He had tried in to rope in the Nizam and the Marathas into a political confederacy to prevent the establishment of British hegemony and tried to catch up with the technological superiority of the British through the help of their arch enemy the French".[37] The isolation and destruction of Tipu became the prime concern of Lord Cornwallis who succeeded Warren Hastings, and he had almost two centuries of contact, observation, knowledge, and experience of the Company behind him in their dealings with India and Indians. (A glimpse into the vastness of the documentation by the EIC can be seen in the Hathi Trust digital library).

In this context, the perception of Indians by the English over the various periods in history is interesting. In William Shakespeare's *A Midsummer Night's Dream*, it is "the Indian boy or changeling" who causes the principal conflict between Titania and Oberon and figures as one of the chief mysteries of the play. In this play, published in 1600, India is imagined as an exotic, mysterious, wealthy, and commercial place.[38]

In a span of 100 years, the impression changed. This is what Sir William Norris, the English Ambassador to Aurangzeb, had to say:

> These poore Gentoos are miserably harassed by ye Moorish Government ever Scince ye Mogull conquerd Golcunda & tooke their Kinge prisoner who was one of their cast (e) & used ym kindly, but ye Mogull, who is a great bigott in his own religion & an Abhorror of their superstition & Idolatry, has already destroyed most of their pagodas only for quicknesse sake permits Jugrenautwch is ye Chiefe& most gainful & will in time bringeym over to his own Religion though I believe ye Gentoos are 50 for one of ye moores, but an Effeminate people.[39]

By the middle of the 18th century, Captain Robert Clive wrote to the chairman of the East India Company Laurence Sulivan in December 1758:

> 'The opportunities afforded me by the last revolution has given me a just knowledge of the subject I am writing upon, experience not conjuncture, or the report of others, has made me well acquainted with the genius of the people and the nature of the country, and I can assert with some degree of confidence, that the rich and flourishing kingdom may be totally subdued by so small a force as 2000 Europeans, ... The Moors, as well as Gentoos, are indolent, luxurious, ignorant and cowardly beyond all conception'.[40]

The loss of the American empire in 1784 prompted the English to create their new empire in India. William Pitt and Henry Dundas felt that the time was ripe to start the process to 'secure India and convert it into the Second British Empire.' The very first thing they did was to remove the "commoner" Warren Hastings and replace him with the "aristocrat" Earl Cornwallis who had returned to

England after his surrender at Yorktown in America in October 1781. For Cornwallis, the lessons of the American experience were as much political as they were military. The war had been caused by bad policy, and bad policy made it extremely difficult to fight effectively. They were operating in a hostile environment and the loyalist militias, their local allies, were incompetent and unmotivated. According to Bew:

> Defeat in 1781 was not met with despair and capitulation. He began to develop a more refined and thoughtful vision of what forms of British power would work effectively overseas in other portions of the empire and how to avoid the stretching of military capabilities on the fringes of the empire in a way that played into the hands of more serious rivals closer to home.[41]

After declining two previous offers, Lord Cornwallis was appointed the new colonial Governor-General in Bengal in 1786. From his defeat in the American Revolutionary War, Lord Cornwallis had learned the necessity for unity of purpose between the military and political elements. His one precondition for taking up the post of Governor-General was that he should also be appointed as the Commander-in-Chief. William Pitt was obliged to pass an Act of Parliament to change the rules specifically for this purpose. Lord Cornwallis continued with vigour the measures initiated by Warren Hastings against Mysore, and the moment he took office as the Governor-General, he began to harmonize and integrate the economic, political, and military preparations for war. He liaised with the governor of Madras, Archibald Campbell, throughout the late 1780s. The pretext for Lord Cornwallis to move against Mysore arrived when Tipu attacked Travancore in December 1789. At this time in 1790, William Medows, Governor of Bombay, was transferred as Governor of Madras and Commander-in-Chief of the Madras army. Unluckily for the English under his command, the war with Tipu did not go well. As the "Commissary of Supplies", the Earl forwarded from Calcutta a stream of reinforcements, money, gunpowder, and ordnance, but major flaws in the strategy and logistical dispositions of Medows resulted in a stalemate. As the war progressed, the Earl's misgivings, arising in part from the thoughts about similar mistakes made in America, increased: "I must own that this amazing proviant puts me in mind of the unfortunate and ruinous system which we pursued in America when we thought it necessary to carry as much provisions with us through the fertile plains of Pennsylvania [*sic*], as if we had been to march from Aleppo to Bussorah".[42]

Such blunders committed by Medows gave Tipu Sultan every opportunity to seize the initiative, and though repulsed at the Travancore Lines, he was able to ravage the Carnatic and outpace and harass Medow's army, which suffered continuous reverses without any appreciable gains. 'Cornwallis followed these events with increasing apprehension. He perceived a number of errors in Medow's conduct of operations remarkably similar to those the earl had himself committed in America. Medows did not keep enough men under his own command, did not procure adequate intelligence, and did not use his allies effectively'.[43] The above-mentioned circumstances forced Lord Cornwallis to take operational command of the British forces—*the first time ever and the only time a Governor-General in India took to the fields.* He left Calcutta on 6 December 1790, reaching Madras nine days later. He immediately launched himself into war with Mysore, and instead of flanking manoeuvres and splitting the forces, he decided to drive straight to the enemy's capital by the passes from the centre of the Carnatic. He directed the Madras army under Medows to join with the Calcutta column under Col. Maxwell to form the Grand Army, which formed the 'Eastern Front'. The 'Western Front' commanded by the forces of General Abercrombie, another American general, who had led Lord Cornwallis's last desperate sortie in the trenches at Yorktown, was reinforced by the 73rd(Perthshire) Regiment of the British Regulars. They were directed to occupy the coastal town of Cannanore and then proceed eastward into Mysore by way of the Coorg pass.

Lord Cornwallis then turned his attention to the most demanding and challenging of his tasks: that of forwarding reinforcements and accumulating supplies of food, clothes, and arm the vast number of personnel that he was planning to send to Tipu's heartland. With the army, he had to move a complete battering train with heavy ordnance for which he employed elephants. Lord Cornwallis was the first British commander to do so, and by July 1791, several hundred elephants were shipped from Bengal. The army assembled to fight Tipu was huge: 27,000 draft and carriage cattle, tens of thousands of camels, and forage for the animals and food for the soldiers and camp-followers. The army had over 100,000 muscats, flints, pistols, 2,000 barrels of powder, different tents, drums, swords, 18-, 24-, and 32-pound siege cannons and much more. Many of these provisions were procured from Calcutta, which also supplied him with money, horses, draft bullocks, reinforcements, and other necessities. Assembling the army personnel in India had its unique difficulties. The sepoys who came by ships from Calcutta required separate accommodation from the Hindus, who were again kept apart according to their caste. He also had to keep in constant communication with his Hyderabad and Poona allies.

The Action: First Stage

Lord Cornwallis joined the southern army of Medows at Vellore, took personal command on 29 January 1791, and decided to march straight to Bangalore. He commanded directly six regiments of regular British infantry, one regular cavalry, seven regiments of Bengal sepoys, one battalion of British artillery, six battalions of Madras sepoys, two battalions of Madras artillery, and five battalions of Madras native cavalry, along with engineers and pioneers. The army totalled around fifteen thousand men with sixty thousand camp followers.[44] Lord Cornwallis left Vellore on 11 February and began his ascent up the Ghats. Tipu tried to stop the British on the way, but Lord Cornwallis created a diversion by pretending an attack on Amboor. Then, instead of using the expected passes of Amboor and Baramahal, he turned north and west, and ascended the Mugli pass (near Nangli village) to reach the tableland of Mysore. Bangalore was stormed and carried on 21 March.

By this time, Lord Cornwallis's supplies and fodder for the animals had deteriorated critically. Hoping to bring about a union with the Maratha armies and the cavalry of the Nizam, Lord

Cornwallis marched towards Seringapatam, joining them on 13 April. However, being badly armed and under no sort of discipline, the Nizam's army was not much of an assistance. Lord Cornwallis pushed upon to Arakerry, about nine miles from Seringapatam, but, by this time, nearly all the bullocks and horses were of no use and the provisions for the troops were running very low. Lord Cornwallis was forced to destroy his siege train and retire disgracefully to Bangalore. General Abercromby, leading the Western Army advancing over the Ghats from Malabar, was instructed to return. To the utter chagrin and disappointment of Lord Cornwallis, later, on the same day, the long-awaited Maratha army, together with two battalions of the Bombay army, were found within 30 miles of his base. Prior information of the impending arrival of the reinforcements would have helped him to change the entire trend of the events, but, by this time, the effective utilisation of the forces was impracticable. Thus, Lord Cornwallis continued his retreat and reached Bangalore on 11 July.

The Action: Second Stage

Bangalore became the headquarters for the next campaign, and this time Lord Cornwallis resolved to prepare himself carefully before advancing towards Seringapatam. He particularly improved his intelligence operation to help him to better familiarise himself with the terrain of Mysore, the size and strength of Tipu's army, and his military movements. He made every effort to gain the cooperation of the Marathas and the Nizam. Enormous energy and pains were invested in assembling sufficient supplies so as to avoid a humiliating retreat of the previous operation. To pay for these and other provisions he would need, he appropriated enough bullion from the China ship to coin 12 lakh rupees. For the Company, army supplies mainly came from Calcutta to Madras. In a country with little forage for the animals or food for the men, the supply needs of an army of 80,000 men (20,000 soldiers and 60,000 followers) for a month was massive and in this mission he was amply supported by Colonel John Murray, the military auditor general at Calcutta. The army needed nearly 80,000 bullocks to transport the rice, ordnance, and forage for 3,000 cavalry and 300 elephants, and the loose shot, musket balls, spirits, and camp equipment. To carry the battering train, ammunition and tools for siege operations would require 1,361 draft bullocks and 1,186 carriage bullocks plus their drivers. Elephants, being a more efficient means of transport than bullocks, were shipped on an average of 100 elephants per month from Bengal. The staple diet of Hindu sepoys and Mahratta armies was rice. Lord Cornwallis told his brother, "It is no easy task to feed between two and three hundred thousand men, one hundred thousand horses, and twice the number of bullocks besides elephants and camels, in a country which nature intended for desert, and which Tippoo has, with the assistance of our friends the Mahrattas, rendered a complete one".[45] He sought the help of the *binjarries*(grain merchants who carry their traffic on bullocks), up to 50,000 men, to carry every species of provisions for his forces and the vast multitude of followers. Since he paid them well and promptly, they were faithful in their duties, and Lord Cornwallis got a satisfactory service. In this manner, Lord Cornwallis utilised the vast resources of India on a huge scale for the final drive on Seringapatam.

The Action: Third Stage

Lord Cornwallis started his second campaign in July 1791 by seizing the important hill forts that lay between Bangalore and Seringapatam to keep open the supply lines. In October, he captured the extremely strong fort of Nanydroog(Nandydurg). Then he moved against Sevendroog(Savandurga) with several regiments of regulars, sepoy battalions, and artillery and occupied it by 22 December, following which most of the other hill forts surrendered. In an official report of Chevalier de Fresne, the Governor of Pondicherry comments on the capture of one of the strongest forts of Mysore, Sevendroog, by a few companies of grenadiers and light-armed troops: "Such strange success can be attributed only to treachery on the part of the officers in command of the fort or to terrifying panic among the garrison and I would much rather believe the success of Lord Cornwallis to be due to the first mentioned cause"

(Mitra, R.C. 1951, 237).[46] By the early weeks of January 1792, Lord Cornwallis began surrounding Seringapatam. In tandem with his military expeditions, Lord Cornwallis made every effort to cox and cajole his reluctant allies, the Marathas and the Nizam. Trying to capitalise on the desperate situation of the British and threatening to withdraw their vital cavalry units, the Maratha generals Hurry Punt and Perseram Bhow (Parshuram Bhau Patwardhan) squeezed out "loans" from Lord Cornwallis. The Maratha's help, especially that of their cavalry, was of crucial support to the British to protect their supply chain. Likewise raids of Parshuram Bhau drew off some of Tipu's forces, thus weakening the defence of the capital. But the assistance from the Nizam was minimal.

With the cooperation of the allies, Lord Cornwallis marched towards Seringapatam from Sevendroog on 25 January 1792. Abercromby moved in the same direction from the west coast through Coorg. By 5 February, the advance reached the plains about seven miles from Seringapatam. Lord Cornwallis also completed a chain of posts around 12 miles apart to protect the supplies all the way back to Bangalore. 'He planned for a three-pronged attack on Tipu's fortifications and started his operations the next day. General Medows would take one division of the army—two Europeans and five native battalions—on the right against the enemy near the Edgah (Eid Gah). Lord Cornwallis would lead the centre division—three European and five native battalions - and he would lead the attack in person and fight like a private soldier. Colonel Maxwell, with one European and three native battalions would take the left to strike near the Karigaut Pagoda. Lord Cornwallis did not reveal his plans until an hour before the attack.'[47]

Fierce fighting went on for days, and Tipu was finally forced to surrender. The battle ended on 24 February, and the Treaty of Seringapatam was signed on 18 March 1782. According to the terms of the treaty, the Peshwa obtained territory up to the Tungabhadra River. The Nizam was awarded land from the Krishna to the Pennar River. The EIC was the main beneficiary, acquiring a majority of the Malabar Coast territories of Mysore and the Baramahal and Dindigul districts. Coorg was also given independence, but it became a Company dependency. Lord Cornwallis also insisted on two of Tipu's sons as hostages to ensure their father's compliance with the treaty.

The war is said to have cost the English Rs 125 million, of which only a part could be worked off by the 13 million that was their indemnity to be paid by Tipu. The territories ceded to the English assured them an income of 4 million (40 lakhs). Tipu's revenue, which was previously estimated at 90 million rupees (9 crores), was reduced by the cessions to 65 million (6 ½ crores) only.[48] The war resulted in an enormous strain on the finances of the EIC and it was perceived that if the war had continued for another year then all the commercial firms, particularly in Bengal, would have been faced with insolvency. But this was compensated to a large extent by the extension of British trade on both coasts of the peninsula, notably the manufacture of coarse cloth in Pondicherry and Cuddalore, and an absolute monopoly of the trade in pepper, cardamon, sandalwood and other produce of Malabar.

The letter of Major George Maule, dated MADRAS, 15 July 1791, an engineer in the Mysore War of 1791–92, to the first Viscount Sydney, in a way, is a pointer for the authentic background and philosophy of the Third Mysore War:

'Your Lordship may assure yourself and your friends that the commencement of a war with Tippoo at this period is a most fortunate event for Britain. I have been eye-witness to his good government, arrangement, vigour, discipline, and attachment of his subject, and in no part of his extended empire does there exist a trace of relaxation. His ambition has been unbounded. Newly built or thoroughly repaired forts, improvements of every description in all parts of his dominion [*gap in manuscript*], the passage only of a very few years would have rendered him infinitely more formidable than ever … and the proof of the attachment of his people exists in the certainty of none of them having deserted his cause … having intercepted all the letters sent by the Mahrattas who were written within a small distance of our army at the period of destroying the cannon, &c., and of the many that the Mahratta chiefs wrote to Lord Cornwallis not one arrived'.[49]

NOTES

1. Sharman, J. C. (2019). Power and Profit at sea- the rise of the West in the making of the International system. *Internal Security,* 43(4): 163-196. doi.org/10.1162/isec_a_00346.
2. Diffie, Winius. (1977). *Foundations of the Portuguese Empire. 1415-1580*, University of Minnesota Press. Minneapolis. p. 229.
3. Parker, Geoffrey. (1996.) *The Military Revolution- Military innovation and the rise of the West 1500-1800*. Cambridge University Press. Cambridge. p. 146.
4. Chancey, M. K. (2006). The making of the Anglo- Hyderabad Alliance, 1788-1823, South Asia: Journal of South Asian Studies, 29:2, 181-214, doi:10.1080/00856400600809963
5. Ellis Jr. John, F. (1993). *Maritime Asia. 1500-1800.The Interactive Emergence of European Domination*. The American Historical Review. 98 (1). Oxford University Press. www/jstor.org/stable/2166383. p. 86.
6. Guilmartin, Jr, John F. (2002). *Galleons and Galleys*. Cassell & Co. London, p. 37.
7. Sharman, J. C. (2019). p. 170, *op.cit.*
8. Sharman, J. C. (2019). p. 167, *op.cit.*
9. *Ibid.* p. 183.
10. Pearson, M. N. (1991). *Merchants and States, in The Political Economy of Merchants Empire.* Cambridge University Press. p. 77.
11. Sharman, J. C. (2019). 176. *op.cit.*
12. Seavoy, R. E. (2003). *Origins and Growth of the Global Economy: From the Fifteenth Century Onwards.* Westport, CT: p. rager. p. 19.
13. McGinty, A. B. (1946). *Anglo-Dutch Rivalry in India. Current History,* 11(63), 383-388.http: www.jstor.org/stable/45306980. p. 383).
14. Seavoy, R E. p. 30. *op.cit.*
15. *Ibid.* p. 27.
16. Saldanha, A. (2011). The Itineraries of Geography: Jan Huygen van Linschoten's "Itinerario and Dutch Expeditions to the Indian Ocean, 1594-1602. *Annals of the Association of American geographers,* 101(1). 149-177. www/jstor.org/stable/27980165.
17. Sharman, 177, *op.cit.*.
18. Kroef, Justus M van der. (1948). "*The decline and fall of the Dutch East India Company*." The Historian. 10.(2). p. 119. https://www.jstor.org/stable/24436034.

19. Philips, Andrew; Sharman, J. C. (2020): *Company-states and the creation of the global international system*. European Journal of international Relations. 26 (4) 1249-1272. DOI: 10.1177/1354066120928127 SAGE p. 1256.
20. Phillips & Sharman p. 1260. *op.cit.*
21. Arthur Weststeijn - The VOC as a Company-State: Debating Seventeenth Century Dutch Colonial Expansion quoted Sharman 177. *op.cit.*
22. Phillips & Sharman. p. 1257. *op.cit.*
23. Seavoy, R. E. p. .43. *op.cit.*
24. Poonen, T. I. (1958). A Chapter in the History of Kerala. Proceedings of the Indian History Congress, 21, p628. www.jstor.org/stable/44145270
25. Buckwalter, J. The Transatlantic Slave Trade and the Creation of the English *Weltanschauung*. 1685-1710. www.eiu.edu> historia. PDF: 'Most of the officials of the Royal African Company, who shipped more African slaves to the Americas than any other company in the history of the Atlantic slave trade, established interests in the English East India Company'. p. 4.
26. Hunter, Sir William Wilson. (1900). *A History of British India.* Vol II. Lon 1900. Archives.org.in.ernet.dil.2015.502092, p. 114.
27. *Ibid,* 135
28. Seavoy p. 48. *op.cit.*
29. Seavoy p. 48, quoting Holden Furber, (1976) Rival empires of Trade in the Orient, 1600-1800.Minneapolis, University of Minnesota p. ress p. 33.
30. Seavoy p. .50, quoting Kristof Glamann, *Dutch-Asiatic Trade, 1620-1740,* Copenhagen, Danish Science Press 1958.
31. The English were also profoundly helped in increasing their commerce by the Navigation Act of 1651 daringly introduced by the Council of Trade, a committee established by the first parliament of the Commonwealth under Oliver Cromwell. Subsequent amendments strengthened and regularised the earlier acts. Imports from Asia, Africa and America had to come directly to England only in English or colonial owned ships.
32. Gottmann, F. (2013). French-Asian Connections: The Compagnies des Indes, Frances Eastern Trade, and new directions in historical scholarship. *The Historical Journal.* 56(2) p. 542. www.jstor.org/stable, 24528847)
33. Parker, G. p. 135.op.cit. Parker further quotes(p. 230) P J Marshall ('Eighteenth-century Calcutta' in Ross and Telkamp, Colonial cities,

p. 90): The massive new Fort William at Calcutta, built between 1765 and 1771 at a cost of 1 million an example of how the Bengal settlement allowed the Europeans to change the art of defensive warfare in India.

34. Seavoy, Ronald. (2003) *Origins and Growth of the Global Economy: From the Fifteenth century onwards.* Praeger. p. 108.
35. The London Chronicle, Vol XLIX, NO: 3805-From Thursday April 19 to Saturday April 21. 178- published the following Extract of a Letter from Madras, which was received by the last Dispatches from that Place, dated Fort St. George, Nov 25,1780- British Library London. Newspaper Collection
36. Edmunds, A. J. (1913). A Forgotten Victory of the American Revolution. *The Pennsylvania Magazine of History and Biography.* 37(1). 89-93. http://www.jstor.org/stable/20085628: 'During the last few years of the War of American Revolution, Great Britain was opposed by half the world. After December 1780, she was fighting five nations in arms: the Americans, the French, the Spaniards, the Dutch and the Hindu Muhammadans. Besides these, Russia, Sweden and Denmark, as the "Armed Neutrality," were ready to declare war at any moment, to resist the "right of search"; while Prussia and Austria joined them in 1781; Portugal and Turkey in 1782; and Naples in 1783. When the English attacked the French settlements in India in 1778, the battle there fought were just as much a part of the American Revolution as those of Mammoth and Yorktown. Like the French and Indian struggle, the Revolution was a world war.'
37. Yadav, Bhupendra. (1990). Tipu Sultan: Giving 'the Devil' his Due. *Economic and Political weekly.* 25(52). P2837 www. jstor.org/stable/4397149.
38. Fetters, Bronwen. (2016). *Pivotal and Puzzling: The Indian Boy in A Midsummer Night's Dream.* . The Alpha Chi Journal of Undergraduate Scholarship. Huntington University. Indiana Beta Chapter. Vol. 1, Issue1, p. 8.
39. Das, H. (1959).*The Norris Embassy to Aurangazib.(*1699-1702). Firma K L Mukhopadhyay, Calcutta. Archives. org> 2015.507639. The Norris_djvu.txt, p. 157.
40. I.O.R. Home Miscellaneous Series, Vol. 809, f364 et seq. British Library. London.
41. Bew, J. (2014). The Case for Cornwallis. *The National Interest,* No.134 (2014): www.jstor.org/stable/44151228, p. 61.
42. Wickwire, Franklin and Mary (1980). *Cornwallis, the Imperial Years.* The University of North Carolina Press. Archive.org>details>cornwallisimperi0000wick.p134

43. *Ibid.* p. 135.
44. *Ibid.* p. 141.
45. *Ibid.* p. 156-157.
46. Mitra, R. C.(1951). Some light on the Third Anglo-Mysore War from French sources. *Proceedings of the Indian History Congress,* 14, p. 237.www.jstor.org/stable/44303974)-quoting Pondicherry Archives Ms 1594.
47. Wickwire, Franklin and Mary. (1980). Cornwallis op.cit. p. 166.
48. Mitra, R. C. (1951). Some light on the Third Anglo-Mysore War from French sources. *Proceedings of the Indian History Congress, 14*, p. 232-238. www.jstor.org/stable/44303974-quoting Pondicherry Archives Ms 1594.
49. Martin, E. J. (1944). AN ENGINEER IN THE MYSORE OF1791-1792. *Journal of the Society for Army Historical Research, 22(92). 324-338. www.jstor.org/stablr/44228373.*

2

The Naval Battle of Calicut 1503

Calicut is now a crowded, prosperous, ordinary city in Kerala State, built on the ruins of a historic harbour town, which was the capital of the medieval kingdom of Kozhikode. Even in the beginning of the 12th century, it was just a no man's land, with saltpans and marshes. During the 14th and 15th centuries, the end of which Vasco da Gama visited the Zamorin Raja of Calicut in 1498 AD, it had been transformed into one of the most prominent centres of international trade. The meeting point of East and West, in the streets of which merchants from China and Southeast Asia brushed shoulders with those from Abyssinia and Europe.[1]

The heritage of Calicut as an important entrepôt of Asian Commerce—the "Emporium of the East" is well known. However, a military past of Calicut as a "Theatre of War", in relation to a pan-Indian background, during the Age of Discovery and the Age of Modern Colonialism is seldom explored. There are only a few references to two important military conflicts that took place in Calicut: first a sea-battle in 1503 and the other a land battle in 1790. What these battles were about, what was the background in which these were fought, who were the protagonists, what was the significance in local, Indian, and world history and politics and, finally, "why Calicut" are some questions that require exploration. Here is an attempt to analyse these extremely fascinating battles!

A Brief Historical Background

During the major part of the five millennia that separated pharaonic Egypt from the Age of Discovery, maritime warfare in European waters was dominated by rowing ships known as "galleys". Viking long ships, Aegean polyremes, Roman pentaconters, Byzantine dromonds, Norman snakes, and the English barges all belonged to this class. These ships had long, shallow, and light-weighted hulls and a low freeboard that was pierced by one or more banks of oars. The galleys were also fitted with a single mast and a square-rigged sail to provide relief to the rowers during long voyages. The ships carried a variety of weapons such as bow rams, "Greek Fire", ballistae, and the like, while their standard armament consisted of the personal weapons of the men on board. However, strategically the decisive move in a clash of the galleys was the combat between the armed fighters of the respective ship's companies, which took place in roughly the same manner as when they fought on land. Thus, since time immemorial, soldiers were at the centre of a sea battle that was fought at close quarters, using what is designated as the "Ram, Board, and Fight" technique.

Rowing Ships

Viking Longship

Aegean polyremes

Norman snakes

Roman pentaconters

Byzantine dromonds

Open Resource

Weapons

Bow rams

Greek fire

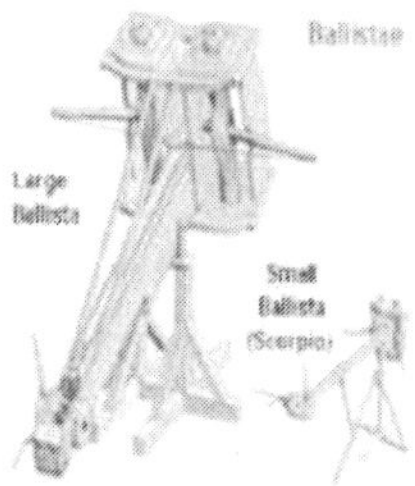

The naval battle in early 1503, fought between the Portuguese and a combined Indo-Arab fleet of the Zamorin of Calicut, is a matter of great historical significance. It is one of the first recorded naval combats where a new tactic that later came to be known as "Sailing in Line and Using Broad-side Gunnery" was deployed.[2]However, by using this new tactic, the Portuguese could sink or disable enemy ships that were at a distance. Though less glamorous and less publicized, historically, these victories of the Portuguese are of immense significance when compared to similar naval encounters in the Mediterranean. The induction of gunpowder-based heavy artillery, on purpose-built ships, using novel tactics, ushered in a new era in sea warfare around the turn of the 16th century. It is against this backdrop that the Portuguese victories over the rulers in the Indian Ocean during the first half of the 16th century are to be viewed.

Between 1800 and 1914, the Western states expanded their global empires to about 84 per cent of the world's land surface. Nonetheless, it is more pertinent to note that during the earlier period, that is, between 1500 and 1750, 35 per cent of the land surface was acquired by the West.[3] The key to success in creating the first truly global empires depended on the upgradation of technology to wage war. This has been termed "the military revolution" by Michael Roberts.[4]He observed that by maintaining control of gunpowder-based weapons, the monarchies of Europe were finally able to establish their military supremacy over their feudal nobles and this led to the creation of a national standing army. The gunpowder weapons also transformed the manner in which battles were fought and led to a change in both battlefield tactics and campaign strategy. This gave the European armies an edge over their enemies who had not gone through a similar process and were, therefore, technologically on an inferior plane.

A similar transformation was taking place at sea also. The 'Man of War'—a powerful sailing ship—by combining the striking power of massed artillery with sea-keeping qualities and the logistical capacity of cargo ships, was ahead of the antique methods that had been in vogue for a long time. It also became the means by which European overseas empires were created. These empires lived off trans-oceanic trade, which alone provided the financial and material base for a strong naval force. The working of this superior loop was the core of what Naval Historian and theorist Rear Admiral Alfred Thayer Mahan called "Sea Power"[5]. In military terms, the essential requirement was a fleet capable of maintaining access to the sea for one's own commerce while at the same time denying entry to adversaries.

Sardar K. M. Panikkar wrote,

> ... the 450 years which began with the arrival of Vasco da Gama in Calicut (in 1498) and ended with the withdrawal of British forces from India in 1947 and of the European navies from China in 1949 presents a singular unity in its fundamental aspects. These may be briefly stated as the

> dominance of maritime power over the land masses of Asia and the domination of the peoples of Europe who held the masterly of the seas.[6]

Professor Carlo M. Cipolla, brilliantly explored the fascinating historical problems related to the unsurpassed dominance of the West over the oceans of the world. He raised several important questions: Why did Renaissance Europe succeed when Europe of the thirteenth and fourteenth centuries failed? Why, at the end of the fifteenth century, Europeans could not only force their way through to the distant Spice Islands, but also gain control of all the major sea routes and establish overseas empires? What enabled the Europeans to bring about the dramatic and sudden transition from a state of insecure defence to a position of bold and aggressive expansion? How did the "Vasco da Gama era" come into being?.[7]

For his second voyage to India in March 1502, Da Gama sailed with ten ships of burden and five caravels rigged with square sails[8] for the passage. All these vessels were heavily armed, and, in the main fleet, under Da Gama, there were about 800 soldiers. The fleet followed Cabral's route, exacting tribute, and submission under their guns from Mozambique, Kilwa, and Mombasa. From Malindi, they crossed the Indian Ocean, reaching the Indian coast of Dhabul, some 350 miles north of Calicut. Here the caravels were re-rigged lateen style—the heavy artillery was hoisted to position from their holds, and all was prepared for a campaign of extortion and terror down the Malabar coast.[9]

Vasco da Gama unhesitatingly conveyed the spirit and purpose of his campaign to the ambassador of the Vijayanagaram empire at Bhatkal, a vassal state of the Vijayanagaram empire, who came to meet him. He said:

> This is the fleet of the King of Portugal, my sovereign, who is Lord of the Sea, of all the world, and also of this coast, for which all the rivers and ports which have shipping must obey him and pay tribute to their people who sail in their fleets, and this only as a sign of obedience in order that thereby the ports may be free and

> that they may carry on in them their trade and profit in security, neither trading in pepper, nor bringing in Turks, nor going to the port of Calicut for because any of these three things the ships that shall be found to have done them shall be burned with as many as may be captured in them.[10]

Terror was an integral part of the campaign of the Portuguese. After reaching Cannanore (present Kannur in Kerala) on 29 October 1502, Da Gama sailed down, plundered, blockaded, and bombarded the port of Calicut. In one instance, he captured a fleet of small vessels carrying rice to Calicut. He ordered the hands, ears, and noses of the prisoners to be hacked, their legs bound together, and teeth pushed down their throats lest they bite through the cords. He then bundled them into one of the captured vessels, spread mats and dry leaves over them, the sails were trimmed, the craft set afloat, and the leaves set on fire. Another vessel loaded with butchered members was sent, unlit, towards the shore. The Miri incident is well known. On 3 October 1502, the ship that was returning to Calicut from Mecca with 240 men, women, and children aboard was fired upon, and all burnt without pity.[11]

Factors That Helped Europe to Emerge as the Pioneer in Oceanic Voyages

At the beginning of the Age of Renaissance, in the last half of the fifteenth century, Europe was relatively less developed in political and economic terms than the other areas of the world, particularly India and China, in size, wealth, and antiquity. European expansion into the eastern Mediterranean was challenged by the military and political power of the Ottoman Empire. It was under such circumstances that the Europeans were forced to find direct routes to the Spice Islands and the Coast of West Africa.

Origins of Atlantic Navigation

European navigation in the fifteenth century in the Atlantic opened up a new and virtually unprecedented chapter in human history. The experience of the Europeans with waterborne travel was probably the most significant factor that enabled them finally conquer the Atlantic. The Africans seemed to have focused their boat building talents on coastal and riverine sailing and not on oceanic navigation because of the difficulties they encountered in their voyages in the South Atlantic. Meanwhile, the people of the Americas were known to have undertaken long sea voyages, but they lagged in technology in comparison to Europe.

Map of the Mediterranean, the North Sea and the Baltic Sea. Source: Open Resource

The Europeans had two large inland seas: the Mediterranean in the south and the Baltic and North Sea in the north. The commencing of regular commercial operations between the Mediterranean Sea and the Northern Seas in the late thirteenth century led to Europeans navigating the Atlantic. Sailors who were familiar with these two great water bodies and the adjacent riverine areas were the players in the larger oceanic economy of the Atlantic. This maritime trade also involved bulk shipping that resulted in the diffusion of shipbuilding techniques between the Mediterranean and the North Atlantic. Thus, the sturdy round ships of the North Sea and the Baltic were blended with the long and manoeuvrable galleys of the Mediterranean.[12] "A right combination was to be found in the square sail and stern rudder of the north with the fore and aft sail and carvel construction of the south……Of the various main traditional types of fore and after sail, the lateen was probably the oldest…enabling vessels to sail into the wind and keep off rocks".[13] This diffusion of ship-building techniques, eventually, resulted in the creation of vessels sailing under a variety of conditions.

In many ways, during the days of the wooden sailing ships, the ocean was as much channelled as were the rivers by the direction of flow that is clearly defined. This was crucial for the development of Atlantic navigation, for the winds and currents had created barriers for traffic for thousands of years. This resulted in limited contact between the Mediterranean and Africa for a very long time and prevented whatever the Africans could have potentially contributed towards effective navigation in the Atlantic and beyond the coastal waters. The constant north to south flow of the Canary current along the Saharan coast made it possible for ships from the Mediterranean to sail southward as far as West Africa, but prevented the return voyage. For the Mediterranean sailors, Cape Bojador, just south of the Canary Islands, represented a point of no return. As the winds and currents off the Saharan Coast checked the Mediterranean sailors from entering the African portion of the Atlantic, a similar hazard hampered African navigation. The current that prevented return trips to the Mediterranean also frustrated African efforts to sail to the Mediterranean.

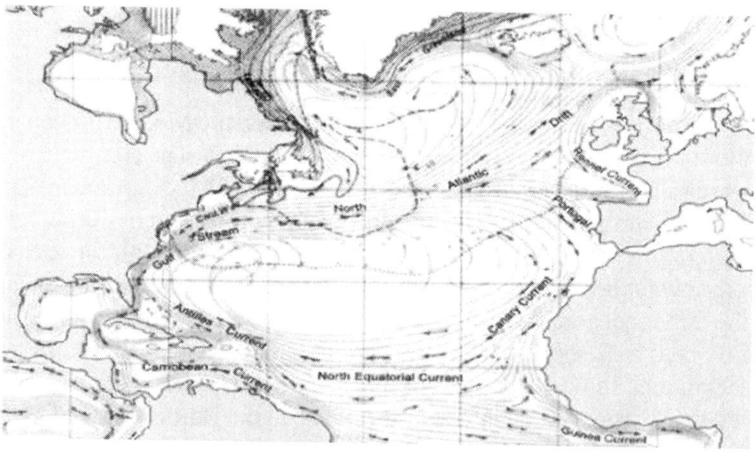

Source: Image: Ocean currents 1943 (borderless).png

'The North Atlantic Gyre', a clockwise-swirling vortex of ocean currents in the Northern Atlantic Ocean

European Expansion to the Atlantic

It is against this background that the European expansion to the Atlantic Ocean is to be viewed and categorised into two directions: the African wing and the Atlantic wing. The discovery of the Canary Islands by Genoese Lanzarotta Malocello in 1312 (or rediscovery, as they were known in classical times) provided the common starting point for both.

African Wing

The raiding and commerce of the Canaries provided the base and the motive for European voyages further down the Atlantic coast of Africa. Following the Castilian conquest in 1402, the aboriginal population of the island (the Guanches) were taken captives by the Europeans. The slaves were forced to labour in the construction of *levadas* (irrigation ditches) in Madeira. Repeated attacks on the Canaries and the Saharan shores resulted in the ability to navigate beyond Cape Bojador.

Atlantic Wing

Madeira (400 miles from the Iberian coast) was colonised by 1425 and the Azores (750–1000 miles) in 1440. Thus, the European navigation in the South Atlantic was neither the result of a long-range visionary scheme nor an explosion of pent-up commercial energy or even a response to new technology. On the reverse, it was the cautious advance to a new frontier, using or slightly modifying existing technology and relying on small sums of private capital. To quote Thornton:

'Thus, by the late fifteenth century the pioneers had fully tested the regime of wind and currents that dominated the Atlantic navigation. By discovering this key, the Europeans were able to unlock the commerce of the Atlantic, and since they had single-handedly developed the routes, their dominance of the Atlantic high waters was ensured in a way that was not possible in any other extra-European area of navigation.[14]

Factors that Facilitated the Emergence of Portugal as a Pioneer Sea-Faring Nation

There are several reasons why the Portuguese, along with Castile, turned out to be the first Europeans to embark on voyages to the Atlantic in the fifteenth century.

1. Portugal developed into a major sea power from the time of King Henry the Navigator (1394–1460) mainly because of its geographical location in the southwest extreme of Europe. Contact with bordering countries involved travel through the hostile kingdoms of Aragon and Castile. Moreover, the Pyrenees Mountains on the border of France posed an obstacle. Sailing through the rough and unpredictable Atlantic Ocean required great courage and skills. Sea travel meant braving the stormy, wild, and difficult Atlantic in comparison with the placid waters of the Mediterranean.
2. There existed in Portugal a seagoing merchant class skilled in overseas commerce. During the development of medieval maritime trade, Portugal's status was that of a 'wharf between two seas'[15]—the Channel Ports and the Mediterranean. Meanwhile, the Jewish and Genoese visitors had created in the Portuguese merchants and captains a sense of value for maps and the magnetic compass.
3. The Portuguese were also good shipbuilders. An array of ship types was used during the European Age of Expansion. However, historical records depicted one vessel as the harbinger of discovery—the *caravel.* By the middle of the fifteenth century, the caravel with its lateen sales, fine lines, shallow draught, and axial rudder eventually emerged as a very efficient sailing ship. It could sail closer to the wind than any other vessel. However, the caravels were of relatively small tonnage and the Portugal shipbuilders and owners turned to *naus (nao)* to transport trade goods. The *naus* was a modification of the northern European cog that was adopted by the Mediterranean shipwrights. It combined the driving power of the square sail with the manoeuvrability of the lateen rig found on Genoese and Venetian galleys.[16]

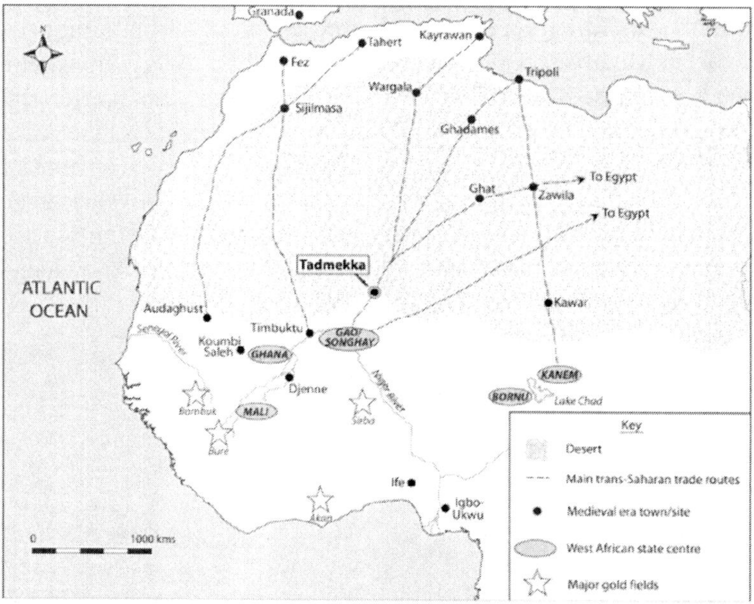

Source: Rehren, Thilo & Nixon, S.(2014). Refining gold with glass – an early Islamic technology at Tadmekka, Mali. *Journal of Archaeological Science.* 49. 10.1016/j.jas.2014.04.013.

Map showing major early Islamic Saharan trade routes, the principal West African gold fields, and sites mentioned

The turning point for European journeys to West Africa came in 1415 when the Portuguese, under King John I (Dom Joao I), mounted a military expedition and occupied Ceuta on 21 August 1415. Ceuta was, then, one of the most renowned commercial entrepôts on the south coast of the Mediterranean. It was also the northern terminus of several caravan routes. The products of the trans-Saharan trade also included gold, believed to have originated from a wealthy nation called Guinea spread across the Sahara Desert. The possibility of discovering gold in this new land was too tempting for the Portuguese to resist. To profit from the occupation of Ceuta, the Europeans had to find a way to expand their power in North Africa or circumvent the sphere of influence of the Ottomans, which was east of the Mediterranean. A feasible option was to explore the uncharted coast of Africa along the western Mediterranean into the Atlantic. The limited knowledge the Portuguese had of West Africa was of mainly the interior and not the coast. The map of Africa drawn to date (1375), "the Atlas of Abraham and Jafuda Cresques of Mayorca", revealed an interior with prime places such as Timbuktu, Mali, and Gao, but was vague about the coast of the south of the Canary Islands. As the Portuguese advanced in their journey along the coast of Africa, their knowledge of the geography of the uncharted Atlantic increased.

Source: Unknown. Retrieved on 14.07.2016

Map of Europe and the Mediterranean from the XIX century of Catalan Atlas of 1375

On the direction of Henry the Navigator, Cape Bojador was daringly crossed by Gil Eanes in 1434. For many generations, it had been considered as the point of no return for wise seamen. Legend had it that beyond this point, "the white sailors would turn black, the sun would pour down sheets of liquid flame, and the currents and reefs considered non navigable".[17] Crossing Cape Bojador removed a psychological barrier that provided an impetus for further explorations along the African Coast. The first slaves were captured at Rio de Oro in 1441. Once it became evident that such voyages could be revenue-generating, the rate of exploration accelerated and the activities took an aggressive commercial and political dimension. The caravels reached Senegal and Cape Verde by 1445 and Sierra Leone by 1460. The exploration of the Gulf of Guinea and its islands (San Tome and Principe) started in the 1470s. The Portuguese crossed the equator in 1474. Diego Cao reached the Congo and as far south as Walvis Bay in Namibia during 1482–1484. Finally, in 1488, Bartolomeu Dias went round the Cape of Good Hope and the seaway was opened to the Indian Ocean.

Author with a replica of Diogo Cao's padrao at Cape Cross, Namibia (2022)

Following the return of Bartolomeu Dias in 1488 after the discovery of the Cape route to the Indian Ocean, more than eight years elapsed before the next known expedition of Da Gama to India in 1497. In the interval between the voyages of Bartolomeu and Vasco da Gama, Portugal and the world were struck by the news that, as Rui de Pina wrote, "Columbus came from the discovery of the islands of Cipango (Japan) and the Antilles, where he went by order of the kings of Castile, from which land he brought the first examples of the people, and gold and some other things".[18] Thus, the Portuguese knew the whole Atlantic Coast of Africa before 1492. As Sauer argues:

> They had developed a highly profitable trade in sugar, slaves, and also in gold. They had also introduced a variety of ships, especially the light and speedy caravels with lateen sails and three masts, and well equipped to withstand the prevailing weather conditions. The Portuguese had wide experience of the wind systems of the Atlantic, and could lay their course across, against, or with them.[19]

Portuguese Voyages to India

It is evident that even before Vasco da Gama rounded the Cape on his way to Calicut, he was in effect the advance agent of a powerful royal corporation, the operating and marketing system of which was already well established and ready to expand. The basic resolution to persevere in the establishment of contact with India was made more than a year before Da Gama's departure and not, as one would expect, after his return.

The First Expedition: Vasco da Gama

Da Gama embarked on his voyage on 8 July 1497 with a fleet of four vessels and returned to Portugal in July 1499. He sighted India on May 18, 1498. When he sailed, his objectives were clear. He was ordered to find the way to India, tap the spice market of Asia, and make contact and possibly enter into treaties of peace and alliance with Christian rulers who supposedly lived there. His mission was essentially exploratory and not of a commercial nature. He carried a few trade goods with him.[20] His fleet consisted of two *naus* of approximately 100 to 120 tonnes, a caravel of 50 tonnes, and a small store-ship.[21] His ships showcased the expertise of the experience of almost a century of high-sea sailing and explorations that the Portuguese shipwrights and mariners possessed.

The Second Expedition: Cabral

Cabral's fleet with 13 ships, caravels, *naus*, and 1200–1500 men was strong enough to show off Portugal's naval power, to establish commerce with the East, and open diplomatic relations with the Zamorin and other rulers. He set sail on 9 March 1500, and after embarking at Brazil on 2 May, he reached India on 13 September.

The Zamorin of Calicut was conducive to adding the Portuguese to his list of customers. However, his older and numerous Arab clientele did everything they could to prevent the sale of pepper to Portugal. When Cabral attempted retaliation, the Muslims stirred up a riot against the Portuguese who had gone ashore. They raised a mob that stormed the factory at Calicut and slaughtered as many as 40 to 50 Portuguese. Cabral then bombarded Calicut. This forced the Zamorin to enter into an alliance with the Egyptian Mamelukes, the Gujaratis of Cambay, and, less visibly, the Venetians—all of whom were opposed to Portuguese hegemony in the region.

The Third Expedition: Vasco da Gama

Cabral's report signalled a change in Portugal's objectives from one of peaceful trade to aggressive domination of trade. The Portuguese realised that in order to trade, they must first conquer.[22] This was the ground reality when Da Gama, now Dom Vasco, was put in charge of the next expedition. He wanted to avenge the humiliation from the Zamorin and his merchants. However, the main objective was quite different. It was:

> To place Portuguese power in the Indian Ocean on a permanent basis by journeying with sufficient forces so that a squadron would be left behind when the main fleet sailed back home with the cargo. This Indian squadron was to be based in one or the other of the friendly Hindu ports of Cochin, Cannanore, or Quilon and to direct the entire trade of the Indian West Coast away from Calicut to these ports by means of patrols, blockades, and a systems of licenses; any ships bound to or from any other port or without a license (*cartaz*) was

> to be seized, plundered and destroyed. Considering the distance involved and the scale of losses of the first two expeditions, this must surely rank as the most audacious plan of conquest ever conceived.[23]

Da Gama felt confident about achieving his objectives due to two reasons:

(i) The overwhelming superiority of the gunned ships.

(ii) The realisation that petty rivalries and jealousies among local rulers would help the Portuguese to forge alliances with some of them.

As Diffie noted: "the political disunity the Portuguese found in India.... Absence of a feeling of nationality and that they comprised a special geographic entity of any kind".[24] Obviously, there was a total lack of geopolitical sense prevailing among the local rulers.

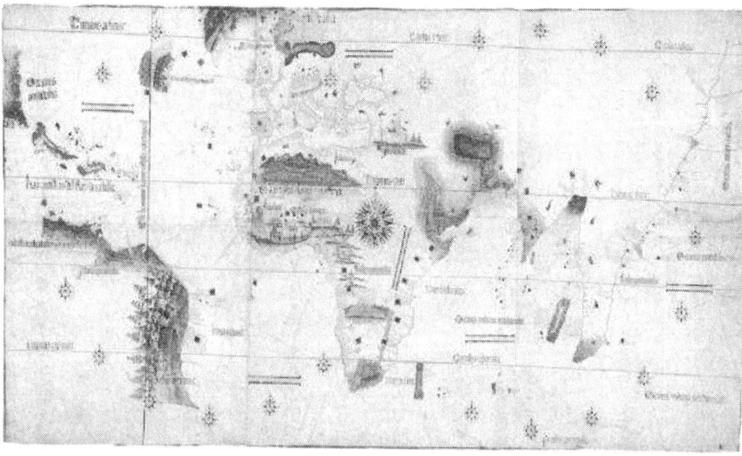

Source: Cantino Planisphere (1502), "Bibliotheca Estense".

Portuguese map of the world

Da Gama was confident he could defeat the Indo-Arab fleet. His orders to his captains were not to go aboard, but to fight with their artillery. These orders were identical to those of his predecessor, Cabral. As Padfield noted, "It is therefore certain that by this time a technique has been evolved on the Atlantic seaboard which enabled a numerically inferior fleet like Gama's to counter traditional methods of attack such as boarding and entering…".[25] The instructions given by King Manuel of Portugal to Pedro Alvaris Cabral in 1500 for his voyage to India specified that if he met any Moorish ships, "you are not to come to close quarters with them if you can avoid it, but you are to compel them with your artillery alone to strike sail so that this war may be waged with greater safety, and … less loss may result to the people of your ships".[26]

Da Gama sailed from Portugal in March 1502 with 10 ships of burden (carracks and *naus*) and five caravels rigged with square sails and all the vessels were heavily armed. Correia's *Lendas da India* cite da Gama's in 1502 as 'each one carries 30 men, and four heavy pieces (bombards) below, and six *falcoes* (11 cm bore 4-pdr stone throwing gun) above, and set on the half-deck and timberheads ten *bercos* (5 cm bore 1-pdr iron) and two of the falcoes fire from the stern; the ships carry six pieces below the upper deck, and two smaller ones astern, and eight *falcoes* above and many bercos, and in the *porpao (deck over stern)* two smaller pieces that fire forward; the cargo vessels go very well armed'.[27] Arriving on the Indian coast at Dhabul, near Goa, about 350 miles north of Calicut, the caravels were re-rigged lateen style. All was prepared for a campaign of terror and extortion down the Malabar Coast.

The Zamorin was forced into hectic war-like preparations and started the construction and assembly of vessels of all types, from rowing craft to *proas*[28] and large ocean-going dhows all along the rivers of the province. At Cochin, Da Gama was given the disturbing news by the local raja that the Zamorin had hired the services of a warrior emissary from the Sultan of Egypt named Cojambar (Khoja Ambar). Several large ships had slipped past the Portuguese blockade and were now in Calicut and had joined the fighting fleet under the command of the Calicut admiral, Khoja Kassim. The assembled Calicut fleet was estimated to possess 20 large ships, 40 gun-mounted sambuks (large dhows), and innumerable smaller oar-powered *proas* and carried several thousands of armed men. Kassim knew that his fleet stood no chance against the Portuguese artillery in a manoeuvring battle at sea and he planned to attack

Da Gama while loading for the homeward passage in Cannanore. The Rajah of Cochin, who got prior information, advised Da Gama to return to Portugal without going to Cannanore. Da Gama replied that he had specifically come to avenge the wrong done to Cabral by the people of Calicut. 'I brought these caravels which are here, and which are so good at fighting, that they are sufficient for whatever fleet Calicut may possess…the King my sovereign was much vexed at the Moors of Calicut having said that Pedralvarez did not dare to fight with his fleet. Therefore Sire, I hope in God that if I fall in with this fleet, I shall take upon it a part of the vengeance which my heart longs for; for nothing in this world would I desist from returning Cananore (Kannur) to take the ginger which is purchased there; for if I did not go thither, and thus wanting to the King of Cananore, I should be committing so great an error that the reputation borne by the Portuguese would be lost forever; and I would sooner die a hundred deaths that that anything should be wanting through me, to that befits the state of the King, my Sovereign'(Stanley).[29]

The caravels deployed by Da Gama had several disadvantages. They were lightly armed when compared with the ships of burden; they were smaller and lower and hence entering them was easier; they had fewer men to repel boarders and had no armed castles at bow and stern that served as citadels for *naos*. However, the remarkable advantage these ships had was that of great speed and significantly better performance in the wind.

However, these were advantages only if the intention was to force a stand-off artillery action. The new naval tactics could have been learned, apparently unrecorded, in the combat with the Moors of North Africa. The tactics would not have been used during the exploration of Africa, against other Europeans (since they remained unknown), or in the Indian Ocean before the first devastating use there.[30]

Da Gama's confidence and his subsequent actions are clear indicators of the evolution of new tactics. It clearly points to the development of stand-off artillery battle in the Atlantic waters before the Portuguese entry into the Indian Ocean. Moreover, he had them re-rigged as lateen caravels at the same time as their heavier guns were brought up from below and mounted. John II's lateen caravels had been famed for the bombards mounted so low and horizontally that they could send their shots "skimming over water".

The Naval Battle of Calicut—Strategy and Tactics

Da Gama sailed from Cochin on 18 January 1503, and divided his fleet into two squadrons—one of caravels and the other of carracks. He sent Vincent Sodre ahead with five caravels and three small ships (*naus*) to move along the shore. Da Gama himself followed with the main body of laden ships sailing in the outer sea. With this strategy planned, the Portuguese sighted the Indo-Arab fleet of Pandarane (Pandalayini) The ships were arranged in a long line stretching over the horizon. Captain Cojambar was in the forefront with the large ships, which were as many as 20, with many *fustas* and large *sambuks*,[31] which together totalled about 70 sailing ships.

The wind was off the land on the starboard hand of the northbound Portuguese, and, as Sodre saw the approaching fleet, he hauled up as close to the wind as he could. Peter Padfield observed that this was a highly significant move in any study of tactical development. Da Gama ordered the caravels to edge in close to shore, one astern of the other in line, and to run under all the sail, firing as many guns as they could. One or more shots hit Cojamber's mast and brought it down and other shots hit three other vessels, which sank. In the ensuing confusion, the dhows and smaller rowing crafts got entangled and the Portuguese "fired into the thick with their heavy guns, so that they shattered many in pieces, killing many people, on account of which there were shrieks and cries amongst the Moors."[32]The wind drove the vessels further towards the sea as Da Gama's heavy ships, again sailing in line, reached the scene and joined in the work of destruction with their heavy guns.

The second wave of the Indo-Arab fleet, under Coja Kassim, consisting of more than a hundred sails, held onwards the Portuguese with an intention to close and board. But the Portuguese were able to keep their distance. They went straight for the flagship of Kassim and poured in a destructive fire from bombards and swivels. The Portuguese ships kept their steerage way, maintaining a distance from the Moorish ships, passing among them all firing bombards from both sides into the enemy hulls between "wind and water", and swivels at the mass of men on the deck. In this process, they brought down masts and yards, destroying the outward rope and beam steering gear. In return, they received small shots and showers of arrows that damaged their own sails but could not penetrate the wooden scaffolds behind which most of the men lay hidden. Sodre's squadron wrought such destruction on the flimsy craft of Kassim that he was forced to retreat towards the shore, leaving behind a trail of disabled hulls and drowning men clawing at the debris. The remaining of Cojamber's dhows also moved away in whichever direction they could. Admiral George Alexander Ballard in his book, *Rulers of the Indian Ocean*, elucidates in detail the strategies and tactics used both by the Portuguese and the Indo-Arab forces of the Samorin.[33]

Da Gama sent his ship's boats armed with falconets and swivels and 20 cross-bow men in each to join the chase. Thus, the battle ended in isolated boarding actions over a wide area. Sodre, not content to let the victory pass without a celebration, had the caravels take a number of enemy vessels in tow and sailed with them to Calicut, where they were tied to each other and set alight on the sea breeze so that they were driven ashore. There is no clear estimate of the damage done to the fleet of Calicut or the casualties suffered by them. The Portuguese did not lose a single ship or even a boat and their casualties were light. As Padfield notes: "Thus ended the first serious challenge to the Portuguese in the Indian Ocean. It was a massacre rather than a battle, but it ought to stand out in naval history as the first recorded sea battle fought in a prearranged pattern as a stand-off artillery action by squadrons sailing in close-hauled line ahead".[34]

NOTES

1. Narayanan, M.G.S. (2006). *Calicut: City of Truth revisited.* Publication Division, University of Calicut, 2006, p. 17.
2. Konstam, Angus. (2008). Sovereigns *of the seas- the quest to build the perfect Renaissance battleship.* New Jersey: John Wiley & Sons Inc. p. 305: A combat tactic in which a naval fleet of ships forms a line end to end and makes the best use of its full fire power without getting in each other's way. It was Robert Blake, General-at-Sea of the Commonwealth of England under Oliver Cromwell, who first advocated this tactic in his book 'Sailing and Fighting Instructions' published in 1653.
3. Parker, G. (1996). *The military revolution, military innovation and the rise of the West 1500-1800.* Second Edition. Cambridge: Cambridge University Press. This observation was made by Geoffrey Parker quoting Daniel R. Headrick in '*The tools of empire: technology and European imperialism in the 19th century*' (Oxford 1981) p. 5.
4. *Ibid.* p. 1. Michael Roberts first examined the concept of 'Military Revolution' in his lecture given at Queens University of Belfast in January 1955.
5. Manship. H. K. (1964). Mahan's Concept of Sea Power: A lecture delivered at the Naval War College on 23 September 1923. *Naval War College Review.* Vol. 16, No. 5, p. 17. www.jstor.org/stable/45236517. Captain Kaminer Manship of United States Navy comments: In the course of his studies, Albert Mahan, the author of the monumental work, The Influence of Sea Power upon History, 1660-1783, discovered that "control of the sea was an historic factor which had never been systematically appreciated and expounded". His own analysis of the factors relating to sea power impressed upon him the role it played as an instrument of national power.
6. Panikkar, K. M. (1953). *Asia and Western Dominance, A survey of the Vasco da Gama epoch of Asian History.* George Allen & Unwin Ltd. London p11
7. Cipolla, Carlo M. (1965). *Guns, Sails and Empires: Technological Innovation and the Early Phases of European Expansion 1400-1700.* Minerva Press, p. 19.
8. Square-rigging is the aerodynamically most efficient 'running rig'. The triangular lateen rig rises better towards the wind and is far more manageable allowing tacking and beating to the wind.
9. Stanley, H.E.J. (1869). *The three voyages of Vasco da Gama and his viceroyalty, from the Lendas Da India of Gasper Correa.* Hakluyt Society, London (Nebu Public Domain Reprints). pp. 277-284.

10. Stanley, H. E. J. *op.cit.* p. 311.
11. Sanjay Subramanyam describes in detail this inhuman episode. (See: - Subramanyam, Sanjay. (1997). *The Career and Legend of Vasco da Gama*. Cambridge: Cambridge University Press.1997, pp. 205-210).
12. Thorton, J. (2000). *The birth of the Atlantic world* in *Carribean slavery in the Atlantic world.* Ed: Shepherd and Beckles. Ian Randle Publishers Limited, Jamaica, (pp. 55-68) —For a full discussion on this topic.
13. Goodenough Simon. *Sailing ships.* London: Albany Books. (1981). p. 49.
14. Thorton, J. The *birth of Atlantic world in Caribbean slavery in the Atlantic world.* Ed: Shepherd and Beckles. Ian Randle Publishers Limited, Jamaica, 2000, p. 60.
15. Diffie, W Bailey. (1960). *Prelude to Empire: Portugal Overseas Before Henry the Navigator.* Nebraska University Press. p. 20.
16. Schwarz, George Robert. (2008). The history and development of Caravels. Master's thesis, Texas A&M University. Available electronically from https://hdl.handle.net/1969.1/ETD-TAMU-2647.
17. Thomas, H. (1997). *The slave trade-the history of Atlantic slave trade 1440-1870.* London: Picador. p. 15.
18. Diffie, Bailey, W. and Winius, George, D. (1977). *Foundations of the Portuguese Empire 1415-1580. Europe and the World in the Age of Expansion.* Vol.1, Minnesota: University of Minnesota, p. 166.
19. Sauer, Carl (1966). Ortwin. *The early Spanish Main.* University of California Press, p. 10.
20. Diffie, *op. cit,* p. 177.
21. Schwarz, George Robert. (2008). The History and Development of Caravels. Master's thesis. Texas A&M University. Available electronically from https://hdl.handle.net/1969.1/ETD-TAMU-2647
22. Diffie, *op.cit.* p. 177.
23. Padfield, P. (1979). *Tide of empires- decisive naval campaign in the rise of the West Vol 1,1481-1654.* Rutlege & Kegan Paul Ltd, p. 46.
24. Diffie, *op.cit.* p. 361.
25. Padfield, P. (1979). *Tide of empires- decisive naval campaign in the rise of the West Vol. 1,1481-1654,* Rutlege & Kegan Paul Ltd. p. 25.
26. Parker, G. (1988). *The military revolution-military innovation and the rise of the West 1500-1800.* Cambridge: Cambridge University Press, p. 93-94.
27. Barker, Richard. (1996). *A Gun-List from Portuguese India*. Journal of the Ordnance Society, 8. p. 56 quoting Gasper Correia, Lendas *da India.*

28. A small warship also used to carry merchandise. The *proas* was widely used in the Indian Ocean.
29. Stanley, H. E. J. *op.cit.* p. 356.
30. Barker, Richard. (1996). A *Gun list from Portuguese India, 1525. Journal of the Ordnance Society* 8, 1996, p. 55.
31. *Fusta*: a light and fast ship with shallow draft, powered both oars and sail, found mainly in North Africa and the Barbary Coast. *Sambuk:* is a type of dhow, a traditional wooden sailing vessel.
32. Stanley, H. E. J. *op.cit.* p. 369.
33. Ballard, G.A. (2021). *Rulers of the Indian Ocean.* Life Span Publishers and Distributors. New Delhi, pp. 45-48.
34. Padfield, Peter. (1979). *Tide of empires-decisive naval campaigns in the rise of the West Vol. I. 1481-1654.* London: Routledge & Kegan Paul Ltd. p. 52.

3

The Battle of Tarvananghurry

Almost another 300 years separate the next important battle in Calicut—a land war, a key episode of the late eighteenth century. The East India Military Calendar, containing the services of General and Field Officers of the India Army, describes a minor battle in an obscure part of India, fought on 10 December 1790, between the forces of the East India Company and the occupying forces of Tipu of Mysore.[1] Charles Mallet, in his letter to Lord Cornwallis, mentions this battle: "I have received by a private letter from Bombay the very pleasing and important intelligence of Colonel Hartley's having gained a complete victory over Tippo's army on the Coast of Malabar commanded by Hussam Ally Khan and reduced the forts of Tricalore and Furruckabad".[2] Tarvananghurry is now known as Tirurangadi and is located 30 kilometres south of Calicut in Kerala.

State of Affairs in India after the Battle of Plassey 1757: A Historical Overview

The Honourable East India Company was an English and later British joint-stock company, which was formed in 1600 in England to trade in the Indian Ocean region. By 1753, it became clearly evident that the British in India were interested in more than just friendly trade. The Battle of Plassey (1757) made them the de facto masters of Bengal, and in 1765, the Mughal Emperor Shah Alam formally conferred on the Company the rights of *diwani* (right to collect revenue).The relative ease with which they acquired the massive wealth of Bengal encouraged further attempts to increase landholdings in South Asia through a combination of conquest, intrigue, and subterfuge, often with the active collaboration of Indian merchants, the landed gentry, and others who saw advantages for themselves in helping the British expand in India.

By 1784, the East India Company had won a substantial part of the Indian empire. Bengal was virtually an English province, and Oudh was garrisoned by their troops. When the Company gained Bengal, its rich reserves of wealth and manpower changed the balance of power on the subcontinent. In 1767, Hyder Ali of Mysore faced an army of 800 Europeans and 5000 sepoys. By 1782, the East India Company maintained an army of 1,15,000 men, 90 percent of them sepoys, mostly from Bengal.[3] The Carnatic Nawab had large parts of his revenue mortgaged to the East India Company or to private Englishmen. Bombay, though small and cut off from the hinterland by the Western Ghats and the Marathas, became a naval fortress and a ship-building centre. Interestingly, these three Presidencies, Calcutta, Bombay, and Madras, remained distant from each other and were not connected by land.

The English were now enjoying their opportunity of shaking the proverbial pagoda tree of the East. Mir Jafar was made the first Nawab after the Battle of Plassey in 1757, and within a span of eight years, the English received gifts, bonuses, and presents worth £3,770,833 (Current value about 8,000 million pounds: 75,000 crores rupees) from Bengal alone.[4] The taxes raised from 30 million people were sent to England as profits of the Company. An annual remittance of over 1.5 million sterling (about 30,000 crore rupees) was to be made from a subject country to the shareholders in England. A stream of gold was to flow perennially from the revenues of a poor nation to add to the wealth of the richest nation on the face of the earth.[5] "Enormous fortunes, says Macaulay, were rapidly accumulated at Calcutta, while thirty millions of human beings were reduced to the extremity of wretchedness. They had been accustomed to live under tyranny, but never under tyranny like this".[6]

However, something else changed the English attitude. The paramount slave-trading nation in the history of mankind,[7] which was jubilantly pillaging Bengal, started viewing India from an entirely new perspective. According to Fry, "since the loss of America, she [India] had been, even amid a spreading network of tropical outposts, the axis of a British world-wide trading system, far and away the chief source of raw materials both for Britain, and in lieu of exchanges with third countries".[8]

The end of the American war turned England towards India as a substitute for the empire they had lost. This vision was implemented mainly by two individuals, William Pitt, the prime minister, and Henry Dundas, a Scottish lawyer and politician and member of the Board of Control of India, who had played a major part in shaping the policy of England towards India.

A war would further promote these processes, but this was inconsistent with the Indian Policy of the Europeans since 1784 (Pitt's India Act), which advocated the maintenance of peace. Under this policy, the British authorities in the East could neither take up arms against nor enter into a treaty with any native ruler. The only exception was when a European power joined one side; then the English could take the side of the other. France happened to be that power. By the end of the Seven Years' War, France had been reduced to a minor power in the subcontinent, but the country maintained its friendship with Britain's greatest foe there, Tipu Sultan. He and his father, Hyder Ali, were the most formidable adversaries whom the British had ever encountered in the East: "Tipu was undoubtedly far removed from the class of other Indian potentates both in global views and his geo-political sense".[9] Edward Thompson, in his classic work *The Making of the Indian Princes*, writes that "Haider and Tipu brought the East India Company nearer to ruin than any other India foes, and nearer than any subsequent foe".[10]

The American War of Independence of 1775–1783 signalled significant changes in the activity of the English in the East. According to Marla Karen Chancey:

> In the Deccan and Carnatic the two formidable players during this period were the Marathas headed by the Peshwa controlling the central regions of the sub-continent, and Mysore ruled by the indomitable Hyder Ali and later by his son Tipu Sultan. The Nizam of Hyderabad ruled a large area of South India and the Nawab of Arcot with his ally the East India Company controlled a major share. All four were evenly matched in strength—with armies of between 80,000 to 1,00,000—and in training, with the India states having acquired Western methods and instruments of war.[11]

In theory, the nominal sovereignty over the whole region continued to reside with the Mughal Emperor in Delhi. However, in the power vacuum that appeared in India during the mid-century owing to the weakening of Mughal control, the four great powers began fighting each other in a series of wars over boundaries and territories. At some point, they were both allies and enemies of the others. But two factors would finally determine the allegiances of the great states for this decisive period of British expansion. They were, (i) the growing strength of Mysore which threatened to upset the balance of power, and (ii) the seemingly small *Circar* dispute.[12]

Politics in the Deccan and Carnatic in 1788

Henry Dundas and William Pitt, the Younger, wanted the right man for the office of the Governor-General, one who could be rated as an improvement over Warren Hastings (1774–1785) and other rapacious nabobs. Dundas believed he would find the proper degree of *noblesse oblige* in Lord Cornwallis (1786–1793). Heaping flatter on Lord Cornwallis, he wrote: "Here there is no broken fortune to be mended! Here is no avarice to be gratified! Here are no beggarly, mushroom kindred to be provided for! No crew of hungry followers, gaping to be gorged".[13] What Dundas sought to achieve first and foremost was to make a fresh start to introduce a new philosophy that would turn the Indian Government irrevocably from a policy of mercantilist pillage to responsible imperial administration. To Archibald Campbell in Madras, appointed at the same time and on the similar grounds of his probity, Dundas wrote: "Lord Cornwallis and you have gone to India, not like former Governors for the purpose of enriching themselves, or providing for needy connections, but you have undertaken the much nobler task of redeeming a lost empire and upon that foundation establishing a monument to your fame in the gratitude and affection of our country".[14]

The East India Company was the strongest power, there being a long history of a relatively small number of disciplined, well-armed and well-led Company forces defeating much larger armies. But the Company's superiority over Tipu Sultan was not overwhelming. By the 1780s, Mysore was growing in strength and was "arguably the strongest antagonist of the British".[15] The potential threat from Tipu also periodically enhanced the fear that he would receive assistance from the French, though by the 1780s, the latter were militarily weak in India. By this time, the English had identified Tipu as the main obstacle in their plan for hegemony in India.

Dundas commented, "I own I never look with very sanguine expectations to the continuance of peace in India while Tipu lives".[16] During the Second Mysore War in 1784, the English had set out confidently against Tipu, hoping to conquer his lands, but it ended with the Presidency of Bombay ceding territory to him. Neither Dundas nor Lord Cornwallis could believe this settled the score. Though externally, the Governor-General adopted a mask of impartiality towards the native states, he, in fact, did what he could to undermine Mysore and abet her enemies.

The Guntur Circar was, by the treaties of 1766 and 1768, to be ceded to the East India Company by the Nizam of Hyderabad after the death of his brother Bazalet Jung. Bazalet died in 1782, but a fit opportunity did not arise for making this claim.[17] The Nizam had, under various pretexts, evaded this obligation. The Circars, the Maritime Provinces on the eastern coast of the subcontinent, were of great strategic value. The two Mysore Wars had shown that Hyder and Tipu would not hesitate to attack the Company during the monsoon when it was virtually impossible to reinforce the southern presidency by sea, and Guntur formed an important link in the land route from Calcutta to Madras. The directors of the East India Company were anxious to acquire the Circar: "Despite Guntur's history as a potential powder keg, Lord Cornwallis was sent to India with instructions to obtain it".[18] Lord Cornwallis believed that the British had never had a better opportunity for pressing their claim to Guntur than in 1788 because they were in the unusual position of being at peace in both Europe and India.

A diplomatic mission under Captain John Kennaway, aide-de-camp to Marquis Cornwallis, was sent to Hyderabad to demand the full execution of the treaty. At the same time, Lord Cornwallis also believed Kennaway's mission to be virtually impossible through diplomacy alone. According to him, the Nizam's known character for duplicity and intrigue would probably lead him to ally with Tipu or the Marathas to prevent the British from taking the area. So even before Kennaway began his journey, the Governor-General had decided to take possession of the Circars with a body of troops from the Carnatic after giving the Nizam a short prior notice. He did not intend to give the Nizam Ali time to plan or execute defensive measures in the area. Lord Cornwallis was also aware that three new regiments of European soldiers were expected to arrive in Bombay.[19] about the same time that Kennaway's mission reached Hyderabad, a fact that the Governor-General believed would "set our power in a point of view in which it is equally to be courted or feared".[20]

The Company's own perception was that if it attacked Mysore, it would probably win, but it could do so with some help. In the build-up to the decisive conflict with Tipu, the Third Mysore War, Lord Cornwallis wrote to Charles Malet, his emissary to the Marathas court in Poona, on 27 January 1790, emphasizing the importance of their support: "It is unnecessary to explain to you that the cooperation of the Marathas in this contest would be of the greatest importance to our interests".[21] On 26 April, he wrote to

Capt. Kennaway: "I need hardly state to you that though it would be desirable to obtain terms of precise equality in our treaty with the Marrattas, yet as their hearty and early cooperation with us is of utmost importance to our interests, I would even designedly give them some advantage rather than retard the commencement of operation of their forces".[22] In a letter to Pitt in 1790, another company official wrote:

> The sufficiency of our military force in that part of the world, for such an undertaking is, I conclude, unquestionable; but the resources for the inevitable expenses, and for supplies and stores and provisions necessary for so important an undertaking must be less certain. It will be fortunate if the politics of the two courts, of the Marathas and the Nizam are found sufficiently steady to be counted upon, in the pursuit of a great political plan (Oak and Swamy, 2010, p. 8).[23]

The "great political plan came to be: the central component of the Maratha confederacy, the Peshwa in Poona formed an alliance with the Company and the Nizam of Hyderabad and played an important role in defeating Tipu in the Third Mysore War".[24] It was this agreement that was finally entered into that permanently changed the face of South Indian politics. The Tripartite Treaty was ratified by Lord Cornwallis on 5 July 1790.

The transformation in the Indian balance of power as the British took control over the larger part of the subcontinent was effected through a variety of means; but in literature, it is the wars of the period that generally hold centre stage—often to the exclusion of diplomacy, espionage, and political intrigue. As Chancey states: "Bringing the wealthy and powerful State of Hyderabad under British domination was the greatest political victory of the age."[25] From Fort William, in his letter dated 7 June 1790, to Capt. John Kennaway, Lord Cornwallis wrote: "I felt a very serious concern at receiving Mr Malet's letters of the 7th and 10th ultimo for without the cooperation of the Marathas I could not flatter myself with a certain prospect of the speedy conclusion as well as the decided success of the war, two events which are absolutely necessary to save this Government and indeed the English Company's affairs from the greatest possible distress."[26] From the very outset, Lord Cornwallis was fixed on the idea of isolating Tipu by drawing the Nizam and the Peshwa into an alliance of mutual benefit against him; but almost ineradicable jealousies and irreconcilable interests separated these two powers: "The task of coordinating and reconciling the clashing interests of Lord Cornwallis's coveted allies were placed in the hands of two of the ablest British diplomats, Charles Warre Malet and John Kennaway, the Residents at Poona and Hyderabad."[27]

Military Operations in the Third Mysore War

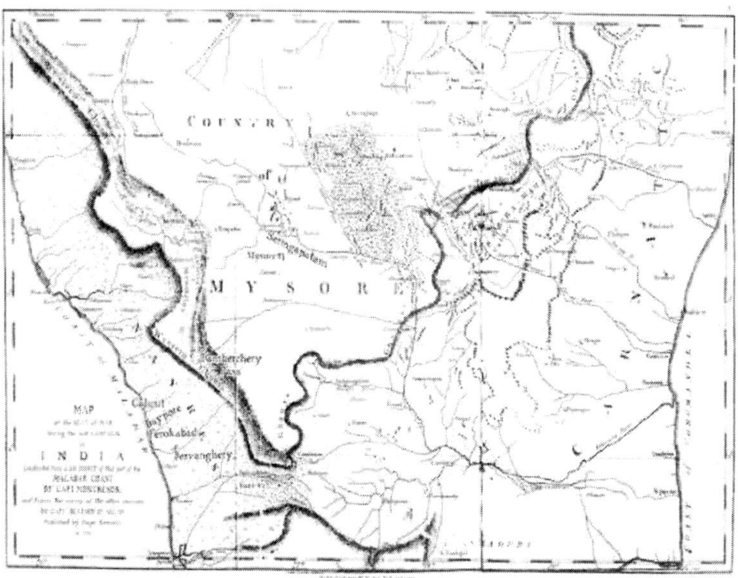

Source: Dirom, 1793, London.

Map of South India during the Third Anglo-Mysore War

By early 1790, the war with Tipu Sultan was becoming more probable and it was declared on 12 April 1790. The *casus belli* was Tipu's attack on Travancore in January 1790. Military operations against Tipu in Seringapatam, a locale situated between the Western and Eastern Ghats, and far away from the coast, were a logistical nightmare. Lord Cornwallis, Governor-General and Commander-in-Chief, planned his assault by a pincer movement, first by clearing the coasts and then ascending the Ghauts.[28]

The Eastern Front

The Madras Army

The English military strength on the Eastern front rested on the Madras Army, commanded by Major General Medows, comprising a force of 15,000 men, "the finest and best English army which had ever been assembled in India", in the opinion of Lord Cornwallis. However, owing to the corrupt practices of the Madras governors, the Holland brothers John and Edward, General Medows was unable to march from Trichinopoly before 26 May 1790. The army arrived in Coimbatore on 23 July after taking possession of the fort at Caroor (Karur) on 15 June. Colonel Stuart captured Dindigul (Dindigul) and later seized the fort at Palagcaducherry (Palghat) on 22 September 1790. But here, the success of the campaign ended. Medows quite unwisely separated his force into three divisions and placed them at a great distance from each other, thereby blocking mutual support. Tipu took advantage of this error in strategy and, by a masterly movement, descended the Gujelhutty Pass, and attacked and defeated the foremost division under Colonel Floyd. He also captured several forts, but the subsequent union of the three divisions restored the power of the English forces. Lord Cornwallis lamented, "We lost time and Tipu gained reputation."[29] General Medows returned to Coimbatore on 23 September and was joined by Col. Stewart from Palagcaducherry.

Bengal Army and Operations of the Centre Army

In the meantime, Lord Cornwallis sent a Bengal Column by land to Madras. This battalion of Bengal sepoys under Lt. Col Cockerell left Berhampore on 27 February 1790, and arrived in Conjeevaram (Kanchipuram) on 1 August.[30] About the end of the month, the whole force came under Col. Kelly, and this was denominated as the Centre Army. Col. Kelly died on 24 September and was succeeded by Lt. Col. Maxwell, who marched to Baramahal at about the end of the month. He entered Vaniyambaddy (Vaniyambadi) on 24 October and on 3 November arrived at Caveripattam (Kaveripattinam) where he camped for about a fortnight. On 17 November, Col. Maxwell joined General Medows at Poolanhally, about 12 miles south of Caveripattam. On 20 November, the army was re-brigaded as the Grand Army. Tipu then attacked Trichinopoly and the chain of English posts and depots in that quarter, and General Medows closely followed his track. In these aimless movements, the troops were subjected to pointless exhaustion and began to lose confidence in their commander, who was evidently unequal to the direction of operations on a large scale. The character of the campaign was, however, redeemed by the brilliant exploit of Colonel Hartley.

The Western Front

General Sir Robert Abercrombie, Governor and Commander-in-Chief at Bombay, selected Lt. Col. James Hartley[31] to command a strong detachment to support the Company's ally, the King of Travancore, whose state had been invaded by Tipu. This armed force consisted of his own regiment, the 75th Highland Regiment of Foot [32] and two battalions of Bombay sepoys (The 1st Grenadiers and 7th Battalions). They sailed from Bombay on 10 April 1790 and landed at Rayacotta, an island near Cochin on 24 April.[33] While in Travancore, he received instructions to correspond with General Medows, then commanding the Grand Army in the Carnatic. Medows advanced from Trichinopoly towards Coimbatore and wrote to Hartley to attack the fortress of Palagcaducherry. When Hartley arrived within 40 miles of that place, he received information of its surrender to Col. Stuart. Then, Hartley proceeded to Palghat and was entrusted with the special duty of watching the movements of Hussein Ali, the Mysore general based in the Fort of Ferokia.

The Battle of Tarvananghurry – Course of the Battle

The details of the battle are given by Lieutenant Colonel Hartley in his letter to Lord Cornwallis sent from Ferokia (Feroke) dated 12 December 1790.[34] Hartley had learned that Mehtab Khan, one of Tipu's leaders, had advanced as far as Chougats (Chavakkad) Fort. This threatened the Trishore (Trichur) district and interrupted the communication with Cochin. Hartley marched on 17 November from Palagcaducherry and reached Tertalla (Thrithala) when he realised that the enemy had withdrawn to Paniany (Ponnani). He proceeded there on 26 November but on his arrival found that Mehtab Khan had rapidly retreated to Ferokia.

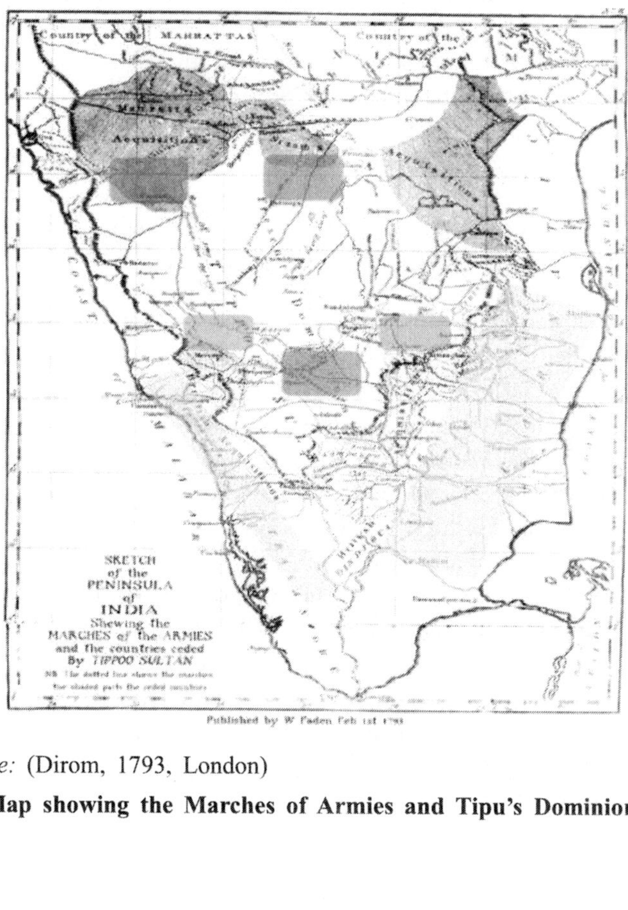

Source: (Dirom, 1793, London)

Map showing the Marches of Armies and Tipu's Dominions

Hartley decided to return to Palghat on 6 December as it was difficult to attack an entrenched army without artillery for siege operations. But when he realised that the enemy had advanced to Vincticottah (Kottakkal), he decided to move there. From reliable sources[35] he got information that Hussein Ali Khan, Tipu's chief commander in Calicut had joined his forces with Mehtab Khan, forming an army of 9,000 disciplined men and 4,000 Moplahs (Mappila-Local Muslims), and that he was encamped at Tarvananghurry, 10 miles away with a determination to risk an action. Hartley resolved to attack him and marched from Vincticottah at sunrise, on December 10.

The English advance party fought with Tipu's forces that were strongly posted in thick jungle and elevated banks. From there, they were driven to the village from where they resisted the English battalions for some time, but were forced to fall back to the Fort of Tricatore. Hartley ordered the 75th Highland Regiment and the 1st Battalion of Native Infantry (Grenadier) to push to the right of the battlefield. The artillery focused on their centre and the fort. The 7th Battalion of Native Infantry charged to their left. This move proved to be a resounding success for the English.

> Mehtab Khan, with the horse, and most of the Infantry fled across the river to Ferokia. Hussein Ali Khan, with the regular troops being hard pressed, and his retreat cut off by the Highlanders and Grenadiers, ran to the fort, but the 7th Battalion overtaking him in the covered way, cut off about four hundred of his men from entering the place with him. All the troupes now poured in a heavy fire of musquetry on all sides of the fort, and having completely surrounded it, Hussein Ali and his men loudly and incessantly called out for Quarter which was granted. One of their Principal Sirdars, or Head of a Cassoom, and one hundred men were found dead in the ditch, and at the gateway their wounded were numerous. Hussain Ally Khan, two Sirdars and about nine hundred men are taken—their loss, upwards of one thousand men.[36]

Mehtab Khan retreated with his cavalry and infantry across the Kadalundi River to the Fort of Ferokia. Hartley pursued him there on 11 December but found that he had fled the night before with 200 men and all the treasure loaded on elephants towards Tembercherry (Tamarasseri) Pass. 1500 men who remained laid down their arms. The new fort of Ferokia was found evacuated. Baypore (Beypore) and all the vessels in the harbour surrendered as did six thousand inhabitants.

Lord Cornwallis wrote to Hartley

I had the pleasure of receiving your letters giving me an account of the great and important advantages you have gained, and which do so much honour to yourself and to the officers and soldiers under your command[37] ... The battle of Tarvananghurry and the surrender of Farrukhabad (Feroke) were the first successful engagements of this war (Third Mysore War). They claim admiration, no less for the signal bravery displayed by the British troops and their commanders, than on account of the important consequences which resulted from them, as they not only defeated Tipu's views on the western side of India, but opened to the main army an abundant source of grain and provisions.[38]

War against Tipu, 1790–1792 (The Third Mysore War) and Its Significance

The war against Tipu from 1790–1792 (The Third Mysore War) can be divided into three major campaigns according to the periods of achievements or failures of the several plans of attacks carried out against him.[39]

The First Campaign commenced in the middle of June 1790. This was directed towards the southern part of the peninsula with a view to assist the Rajah of Travancore whose country had been attacked by Tipu Sultan. The conquering of the rich southern provinces below the Eastern Ghats was entrusted to the Main Army commanded by General Medows. The Bombay Army commanded by General Abercromby was in charge of attacking the country below the Western Ghats as far as the Baliapatam (Valapattanam) River in the north. Colonel Hartley started the campaign against the occupying forces of Tipu in Malabar. This campaign was terminated in 1790 when the main army retreated to Trichinopoly, and was ordered from there to Madras.

The Second Campaign carried the war into the heart of Tipu's dominions by Earl Cornwallis. Alarmed by the ineffectual campaign of General Medows, Lord Cornwallis resolved to take command of the war personally on 12 December 1790, and made every effort to resume operations in the field.It is highly significant that for the first time the British armies in India had been personally led in the field by a Governor-General in person, who enjoyed the undivided exercise of all the civil and military powers of the state and commandeered the resources of all the Presidencies.[40] The British army under Lord Cornwallis concentrated in Vellore, ascended the Ghats through the Amboor and Mooglee passes and reached the plateau of Mysore on 17 February 1791. The important fortress of Bangalore surrendered on 21 March, which shifted the seat of the war into Tipu's domain. The armies met at the battle of Arikara (Arakere) on 15 May, where Tipu fought heroically but was not successful. However, this offensive of Lord Cornwallis against the citadel of Tipu, Srirangapatnam, had to be terminated half-way through the campaign. Tipu's horse cavalry had cut-off all the supply of provisions or forage and had created a desert around it.[41] The English camp was falling prey to hunger and disease. Realising that rescue and salvage of the army depended on an immediate retreat, instructions were given to General Abercromby fighting from the western front to return to the Malabar Coast. Lord Cornwallis issued a general order explaining to the soldiers the true motive of the measure, destroyed his own battering train and heavy equipment, and drew back to Madras on 26 May 1791.

This debacle was the outcome of the half-hearted and indifferent response of the Nizam and the Marathas to the conditions of the Tripartite Alliance. The armed forces of the Nizam consisting of about 10,000 cavalry had assembled in Hyderabad in May 1790, but did not move out to aid the English till September to avoid engagements with Tipu. Once they entered Mysore territory, instead of marching to join the English, they remained there for six months and plundered the country. Only when they heard about the capture of Bangalore did they move forward and join the army of Lord Cornwallis in April 1791. However, they were reluctant to take up arms and remained behind the English soldiers.

The Maratha cabinet of Nana Fadnavis in Poona had agreed to furnish a body of horse cavalry in support of the war with Tipu as per the coalition treaty. The Governor-General agreed to supplement their army with a British detachment and accordingly Captain Little embarked at Bombay with two battalions of sepoys and one company of European and two of native artillery. He reached the rendezvous at Coopta (Kumta), 40 miles south of Karwar, and an open roadstead[42], but found only a few Maratha mounted soldiers. Although a treaty, both offensive and defensive was signed by Nana on 1 June, the envoys of Tipu were endeavouring to purchase the neutrality of the Marathas through a concession of territory. Only when this clandestine operation failed did Pureshram Bhao, the Maratha general, join the English army on 5 August 1790. However, his primary intention was to recover the fortresses and territories lost to Tipu rather than to annihilate Tipu. From September 1790 to March 1791, he concentrated his attention on blockading the Fort of Dharwad and moved from there only after the fall of Bangalore.

A second Maratha army, consisting of 25,000 cavalry and 5,000 foot soldiers marched to Mysore from Poona under Hurry Pant in January 1791. These two outfits united on 24 May 1791 and marched towards Milgota (Melukote) to assist the English. But two days later, when they came up with the English army, they were surprised to know that the British were retreating from the battlefield. This miscalculation resulted from the failure of the intelligence services of the English and the resourcefulness of Tipu's spies who intercepted all their communication, thus keeping the allies mutually ignorant of each other's movements. If this information had been available a week earlier, the campaign would have presented a very different picture.

The Marathas, who had supplies and provisions with them, sold these at an exorbitant price to the famished English soldiers. Taking advantage of the distress of the English, the Maratha sirdars set up a plea of poverty and demanded a loan of 14 lac rupees. Lord Cornwallis was fully aware of the consequence of the refusal of this blatant extortion—the Marathas would transfer their alliance to Tipu, who was ready to purchase it at any price. A special messenger was sent to Madras to take the necessary specie out of the hold of the ships that was to be sent to China for the annual investment.[43]

After his withdrawal from the capital in May 1791, Lord Cornwallis spent the rest of the year in the conquest of Baramahal and the subjugation of the fortresses and fortifications with which the country was studded. The ease and rapidity with which many of these secure and impenetrable fortifications were captured had caused alarm and amazement in the minds of the princes of the country: "While the Marathas had taken six months and half besieging Dharwar, and the Nizam's army had been detained five months before Copaul, such fortresses as Kistnagherry, Nundidroog, Severndroog and others, which seemed to defy all human approach on their inaccessible peaks were captured in a few weeks".[44] But the Maratha generals, Hurry Pant and Pureshram Bhao, who moved with the English were mainly interested in recovering the territories that the Marathas had lost. Bhao left Lord Cornwallis in July 1791 promising to return to the army whenever required; but did not join the English camp till a fortnight after the termination of war.

The Third Campaign commenced almost immediately after the failure of the earlier campaign. Lord Cornwallis began his move against Tipu on 25 January 1792. His force consisted of 22,000 men, 44 field-pieces, and 42 siege guns. His allies were the Nizam's army consisting of about 8,000 men and a small body of Marathas under Hurry Punt. On 16 February, General Abercromby joined the camp with a reinforcement of 6,000 men from the Malabar Coast. Tipu was forced into submission and the confederates left John Kennaway, the British plenipotentiary, to settle the conditions of the treaty. The severe terms dictated by Lord Cornwallis were that Tipu should cede half his territories, pay three crore rupees toward the expense of the war and surrender two of his sons as hostages. The Tripartite treaty had provided that the territories conquered by the joint exertions of the allies should be equally divided among them. According to Marshman,

> ... though the Marathas had given no assistance in the war, and the Nizam's forces had done nothing but consume provisions and forage, Cornwallis was determined to adhere to the original compact with the most scrupulous fidelity and made a third of the indemnity, as well as of the territory, to each of the confederates, annexing another third, to the dominions of the Company. It comprised the district of Dindigul and a large strip of fertile territory with great commercial resources on the western coast (including Malabar) which was annexed to Bombay, and formed the first real domain of the Presidency.[45]

This was the first acquisition of territory since it had been resolved to control the growth of the British Empire in India by Acts of Parliament.

Lord Cornwallis could have dismembered Tipu's realm completely but he wanted to retain him as a counterweight against the Peshwa and the Nizam.[46] He avoided imposing overtly punitive terms and eschewed interest in setting up "some miserable pageant of our own, to be supported by the Company's troops and treasures, and to be plundered by its servants." [47]

NOTES

1. The East India Military Calendar containing the services of General and Field Officers of the India Army. By the Editor of the Royal Military Calendar. Vol. II. The Naval and Military Press. England. 2007. Reprint in facsimile from Original 1824.

   "Lieut. Col. Hartley, on leaving Palicaudcherry, executed Gen. Medows orders, by keeping open the communication with Cochin and the Paniany River; and lastly by the Battle of Tervananghurry on December 10, and the capture of Furruckabad, on the December 12,

1790 which compelled Tippoo's troops to retire from the countries of Zamorin and King of Cochin. These objectives were accomplished against an army of Tippoo's, commanded by Hussein Ali Khan consisting of 9,000 disciplined men, and 4, 000 Moplas: Leiut. Col Hartley's little army amounted only to 1,000 King's and Company's troops, with 500 auxiliaries, belonging to the King of Travancore." pp. 113-114.

2. Ray, N.B. (Ed.). (1937). *Poona residency correspondence, Vol. III, The Allies' war with Tipu Sultan 1790–1793.* Section 4. No.193. Letter from C.W. Mallet to Cornwallis, G.G. Bombay. The Government Central Press. pp. 256-258.
3. Parker, G. (1995). Ed. *Cambridge History of Warfare*, p. 179.
4. Dutt, Romesh. (1969). *The Economic History of India under Early British Rule*, Vol. 1, Delhi, p. 33 (As quoted in the House of Commons Committee's Third Report).
5. *Ibid,* p. 39.
6. Durant, W. (1954). *Our Oriental Heritage*. Simon and Schuster. New York, p. 614.
7. Tibbles, Anthony. (2005) Ed: *Transatlantic Slavery against Human Dignity*, Liverpool, 'The evidence suggests that almost 11,000 ships were fitted out in England for the slave trade between 1698 and 1807 and may have been responsible for transporting about three million Africans into slavery. This was equivalent to just under half of the estimated 6.7 million slaves shipped from Africa to America in the eighteenth century.' p. 667.
8. Fry, M. (2004). *The Dundas Despotism*, Edinburgh, p. 218.
9. Habib, Irfan. 2001. Ed: *State and Diplomacy under Tipu Sultan, Documents and Essays*, New Delhi. For a detailed discussion on this topic see pp. 26-27.
10. Thompson, Edward. (1943). *The Making of the Indian Princes*. London Oxford University Press, p. 4.
11. Chancey, Marla Karen. (2003). *In the Company's Secret Service: Neil Benjamin Edmonstone and the First Indian Imperialists, 1780-1820.* Unpublished PhD dissertation submitted to the Florida State University, Florida, p. 37.
12. *Ibid,* p. 39. (The Circars, namely Cudappa, Kurnool, Bellary, and Anantapur are commonly referred as Ceded Districts).
13. Fry, Michael. *op.cit.,* p. 119.
14. Chancey, Marla Karen. *op.cit.* p. 124.

15. Ramusack, B. N. (2004). *The Cambridge History of India. III. 6. The Indian Princes and their States*. Cambridge, p. 66.
16. *Ibid,* p. 219.
17. Dirom, Major. (1793). *A Narrative of the Campaign in India which terminated the war with Tipu Sultan in 1792,* , W. Faden, London, p. 254.
18. Chancey, Marla Karen. (2003) *op.cit.,* p. 40.
19. Mileham, Patrick. (1988) *The Scottish Regiments (1633-1996).* Spellmount Ltd. Kent. The three new regiments were : 1st Battalion of 73rd (Highland) Foot (p. 105), 74th Highland Regiment (p. 109), 75th Stirlingshire Regiment (p. 244).
20. *Ibid,* 41.
21. Ray, N.B. (1937). Poona Residency Correspondence, Vol. III. Section I. No. 60. pp. 54 to 56.
22. *Ibid,* Section 3. No. 116, p. 146 to 147.
23. Mandar Oak & Anand Swamy, 2010. "Commitment and Conquest: The case of British rule in India", Department of Economics working papers 2010-08. Department of Economics Williams College. Massachusetts, p. 8.
24. *Ibid,* p. 8.
25. Chancey, Marla. '*The Making of the Anglo-Hyderabad Alliance, 1788-1823' in South Asia: Journal of South Asian Studies*, n.s.Vol. XXIX, no. 2, August 2006, p. 181.
26. Ray, N.B. (1937), *op.cit.* Section 3, No. 121, pp. 156-157.
27. *Ibid,* pp. v-vi. Introduction.
28. Wilson, W. J. *(1882). History of the Madras Army,* Vol. II, Madras, p. 190.
29. Marshman, J. C. (1869). *The History of India from the earliest period to the close of Lord Dalhousie's administration.* Vol II. London, Archives. p. 14.
30. Wilson, W. J. (1882). *History of the Madras Army,* Vol. II, Madras, p. 199.
31. Hartley earned the highest distinction in 1778-79 in the war with the Marathas. *The East India Military Calendar.* Vol. II. The Naval and Military Press England, 2007, pp. 102-117.
32. As part of strengthening their forces in India the British government decided to send four regiments to the East in 1787, and the Board of Control united with the Court of Directors in recommending to His Majesty to appoint Hartley as Lieut. Col in the 75th regiment. (*op.cit:* East India Military Calendar, p. 111).

33. East India Military Calendar, *op.cit.*, p. 112.
34. Askari, Syed Hasan. Ed. (1976). *Fort William-India House Correspondence and Other Contemporary Papers relating thereto - Foreign, Secret, and Political*, Vol. XVI:1787-1791, Delhi, pp. 359-360.
35. Bayly, C. A. (1996). *Empire and Information-Intelligence gathering and social communication in India, 1780-1870.* Cambridge University Press. UK. Professor Bayly describes the evolution of the British intelligence gathering in India and its dramatic change towards the end of the Second Mysore War. The pioneering role of Colonel William Fullarton of Madras Infantry is detailed, pp. 66-69.
36. Askari, Syed Hasan. ed.(1976). *Fort William-India House Correspondence.* pp. 359-360.
37. The East India Military Calendar, p. 114.
38. *Ibid,* p. 114.
39. Dirom, Major. (1793). *A Narrative of the Campaign in India which terminated the War with Tipu Sultan in 1792*, W.Faden, London. p. vii.
40. Marshman, J. C. (1867). *The History of India- from the Earliest Period to the close of Lord Dalhousie's Administration.* Vol. II. Longman Green. London. Archives. Org. p. 16. How much the English were apprehensive of the capabilities of Tipu is evident in this unique event.
41. Barua, P.(1994).Military Developments in India 1750-1850. *The Journal of Military History. 58*(4) pp. 599- 616.www.jstor.org/stable/2944270.
42. A partially sheltered offshore anchorage area for ships with relatively little protection from sea or wind.
43. Another example of how far the English were prepared to go to annihilate Tipu and the methodology they used for it!! Cornwallis, as the Governor General and the Commander-in-Chief is using his colossal civil and military power.
44. Marshman, J. C. *The History of India,* Vol. II, *op.cit.* p. 22.
45. Marshman, J. C. *The History of India,* Vol. II, *op.cit.* p. 25.
46. Kulke, H & Rothermund D (2004), *A History of India.* Fourth Edition. Routledge. London, p. 240.
47. Bew, J. (2014). The Case of Cornwallis. *The National Interest,* p. 134. www// jstor.org/stable/44151228

4

How the English Managed to Subdue and Dominate the Nizam and the Marathas

The Nizam based in Hyderabad ruled a "successor state"—a province that had broken away from the Mughal Empire. By the time of the Third Mysore War, though large in terms of territory, militarily it had declined in significance. Edward Thompson quotes G. W. Forrest: "Another nominal officer of the Emperor, the Nizam of Hyderabad, he sees in the position of a star destined to become a satellite but now the object of contention between rival heavenly bodies: His dominions are of small extent and scanty revenue; his military strength is represented to be most contemptible; nor was he at any period of his life distinguished for personal courage or the spirit of enterprise. On the contrary, it seems to have been his constant and ruling maxim to ferment the incentives of war among his neighbours, to profit by their weaknesses and embarrassments, but to avoid being a party himself in any of their contests, and to submit even to humiliating sacrifices rather than subject himself to the chances of war."[1]

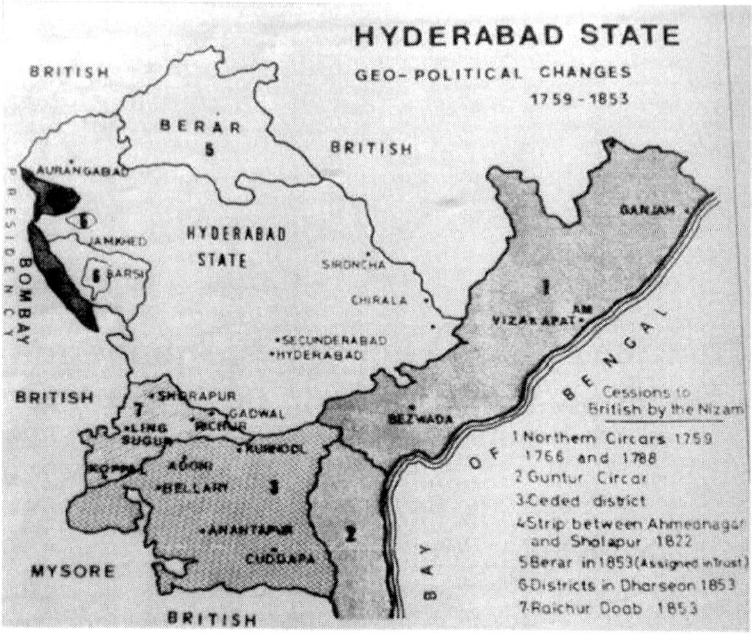

Source: Pinterest.

Map of Hyderabad state: Geo-political Changes-1759-1853

A Brief History of the Origin of the Arcot Nawabs

Gunpowder Empires

The disssolutioon of the Mongol Empire encouraged and inspired indigenous rebellions against the foreign rulers resulting in their expulsion. Korea, Russia, and China returned to the hands of native dynasties and the local elites took over the reins of the government. But the Muslim territories experienced a more complex transition from their Mongol rule. "Instead of returning to the control of Arabs who had been the traders, the intermediaries, the bankers, the shippers, and the caraven drivers who connected Asia and Europe, a new cultural hybrid emerged that combined a Turco- Mongol military system with the legal institution of Islam and the ancient cultural transitions of Persia. The eastern part of

Muslim world had found a new cultural freedom in which they could still be Muslims but without the domination of Arabs whom they never allowed to regain power." This was the origin of the so called Gunpowedr Empires- the Ottoman of Turkey, the Safavids of Persia, and the Mughal of India.[2]

The three "gunpowder empires" that had sprung up almost at the same time in the first quarter of the sixteenth century were gradually destroyed in the "crisis of the eighteenth Century".[3] (The phrase 'gun powder empires' or 'Islamic gunpowder empires' was coined by Marshall G.S. Hodgson and his colleague William H. McNeill at the University of Chicago, referring to the three Muslim Empires: the Ottoman, Safavid and Mughal Empire that flourished from the sixteenth to eighteenth century. Hodgson used the phrase in the title of Book 5 - *The Second Flowering: The Empires of Gunpowder Times* - of his highly influential three-volume work, *The Venture of Islam*, 1974. The multinational, multilingual Ottoman Empire was conquered by the armies of the Habsburg dynasty and later the Czar of Russia. The Safavids lost their empire completely to the Afghan tribesmen. The Mughal Empire carried on, although the sacking of Delhi by Nadir Shah showed that their power had evaporated. The main reason for the predicament of these mighty empires was "Imperial outreach" when monarchical control decayed, and regional powers became powerful: "In India the rise of such regional powers was rather spectacular. The unified employment agency of the Mughal empire had vanished, but the huge reservoir of military manpower did not disappear, only men-at-arms and cavalrymen were now available to regional or even local rulers if they managed to raise enough funds."[4]

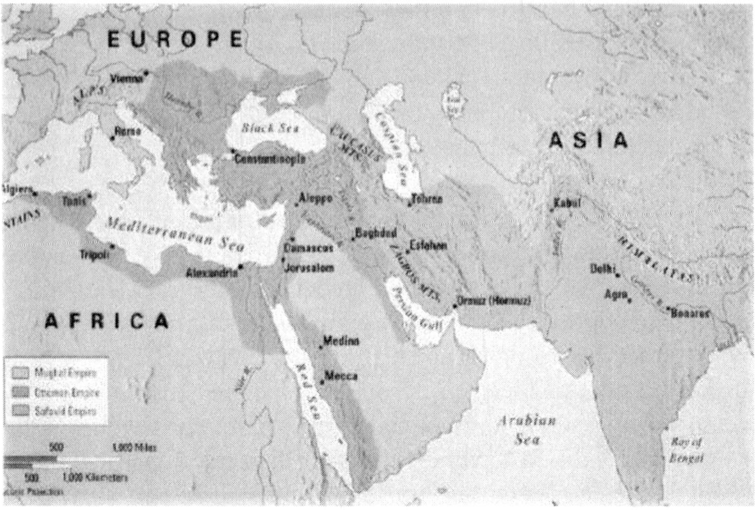

Source: Wikipedia Commons

Map: Muslim Mughals, Safavids, Ottoman Empire. Author: Pinupbettu. Own Work

Events in India after the Death of Aurangzeb

The death of Aurangzeb in 1707 started the decline of political stability of the Mughal Empire. The Mughal Emperor Farrukhsiyar made Nizam-ul-Mulk Feteh Jung the Viceroy of the Deccan in the South in 1713. Uniting with another powerful Mughal noble, Sa'adat Khan, Nizam-ul-Mulk overthrew the Sayyid brothers who had deposed and killed Farrukhsiyar in 1719. Sa'adat went on to found the Awadh dynasty. After two years as the Vizier of the new Emperor Muhammad Shaw, Nizam-ul-Mulk left for the Deccan with an aim to set up a virtually self-governing kingdom. He defeated Mubariz Khan, Subedar of the Deccan in the Battle of Shakar Kheda in 1724. The Emperor conferred the title of Asaf Jha to Nizam-ul-Mulk and reappointed him as the Subedar of the Deccan province on 25 June 1725. The hereditary dynasty he founded in Hyderabad was thereafter known as the Asafia dynasty.

Nizam-ul-Mulk (1671–1748) was the most remarkable personage in the history of the later Mughals. He was a clever strategist and a far-sighted statesman. He clearly envisaged and truly estimated the magnitude and the extent of the difficulties that arose for the Mughal government during the inefficient reigns of Aurangzeb's successors, lacking both in military genius and administrative capacity. With rare tact and courage, he undertook the stupendous task of restoring the Mughal conquests and re-establishing the imperial authority in the Deccan. Then came the invasion of Nadir Shah of Persia who attacked, plundered, and ravaged Delhi in March 1739. 'The effect of his expedition proved disastrous for the country, which was sucked dry of its treasures. Industry and trade were so completely paralyzed that it was never again restored to its former prosperity.'[5] It became clear that any real Mughal central authority had collapsed. Europeans in South Asia soon realised that the regional Mughal officials with whom they had been dealing now lacked support from the centre and that this weakness could be manipulated and exploited.[6]

Regional Powers as They Emerged in the Eighteenth Century

The Afghans, who earlier had been subjugated by Nadir Shah, once more rose to power in the north of the Indian subcontinent. The Nawab of Awadh, who was a Mughal governor earlier but had now become an independent ruler, controlled the plains to the east of Delhi. Bengal was dominated by an equally powerful nawab. The central highlands were claimed by the Nizam of Hyderabad. Western India was ruled by the Marathas under the overall control of the Peshwa, with his headquarters in Pune. In the south, various successor states of the erstwhile Vijayanagaram Empire were ruled by the Nayaks, who were the governors of their respective territories but had now emerged as independent as the nawabs of the north. Wedged in between the Nayaks and the Nizam was the Nawab of Arcot, and the Nizam claimed a kind of suzerainty over Arcot. The Mughal Empire, though defunct, had not ceased to exist. However, Mughal supremacy was no longer a force to be reckoned with, and ambitious rulers had already started gnawing into the heart and soul of the empire. It is important to realise that until the middle of the eighteenth century, the European presence was marginal in the Indian political scene; their military interventions were modest and mainly restricted to their maritime bridgeheads.

The Origin of Arcot Nawabs and Their Succession

The period between the war of Austrian succession and the termination of the Seven Years' War (1740 to 1763, which includes the three Carnatic wars) was a decisive period in the slow but steady establishment of European hegemony in India. The role of the nawabs of the Carnatic and the Nizam of Deccan is momentous and critical.Pimmanus Wibulslip rightly says: "Despite its seemingly interesting and important political power in the eighteenth century, the history of Arcot is akin to a black hole in Indian history."[7]

India experienced the rule of various Muslim powers for a long time. North India came under their sway since the eleventh century, and central India and the Deccan since the thirteenth century. However, until the late seventeenth century, most of the southern-most parts of the subcontinent were still ruled by various Hindu rajas. The establishment of the Vijayanagara Empire by the southern powers in the Deccan by the 1340s was with a view to ward off the Islamic invasion. By the 1370s, this dynasty expanded southwards, conquered and controlled for almost two centuries the entire Tamil world. In the late fifteenth century, structural changes were brought about to this direct administration. Various Telugu warlords from the Deccan, the so-called Nayaks, were granted certain territories to exercise their control in various localities of the Tamil country. Under the Nayaks, there were numerous smaller warrior chieftains, the Palaiyakkras or Poligars, appointed by them to govern the localities under their indirect control. The entire southern peninsula was under the Vijayanagara rulers until 1565 when they faced a major military defeat in the Battle of Talikotta by the united army of the Deccan sultanates.

The Vijayanagaram Empire gradually disintegrated into various successor Nayaka-Poligar states—the major ones, for example, were the Nayak kingdoms of Madurai, Ginjee, and Tanjore and the Poligar chiefdoms of Pudukkottai, Ramanathapuram, and Maravar Setiipati. By the early 1650s, the Deccan Sultanates of Golkonda and Bijapur started to expand their power southwards and gained control over some port cities on the Coromandel Coast. In the late 1680s, Aurangzeb annexed these regions and expanded his military campaigns into the south. In 1692, the eastern Tamil country (the Payenghat or the land below the Ghats from Nellore to Kanyakumari) was annexed and declared a province of the Mughal Empire, known as the "Carnatic-Payenghat or Arcot Subadari". An imperial governor was appointed under the title "Nawab", the subahdar or chief military and revenue officer. This was the origin of the nawabs of Arcot. In theory, under the Mughal administrative line, the Nawab of Arcot was third in rank, subject to the Mughal Emperor in Delhi and the Nizam of Hyderabad, the Mughal southern head-governor stationed in the Deccan.

S. No.	Name of Nawab	Beginning of reign	End of reign	Notes
1.	Zulfiqar Ali Khan Nusrat Jung	1692	1703	Appointed by the Mughal Emperor Aurangzeb as the first Nawab of the Carnatic in 1692. Recalled to Delhi in 1703 and continued as the commander of Mughal forces in the eastern Deccan against the Marathas.
2.	Daud Khan Panni	1703	1710	Appointed by Emperor Aurangzeb as successor to Zulfiqar Ali Khan. Recalled to Delhi in 1710.
3.	Muhammad Sa'adatullah Khan I	1710	1732	Appointed by Emperor Bahadur Shah, successor to Emperor Aurangzeb. Moved the capital from Ginjee to Arcot. Picked his nephew Dost Ali Khan as successor. Rejected the authority of Bahadur Shah's successor, Emperor Jahandar Shah.
4.	Dost Ali Khan	1732	1740	Nephew and successor to Muhammad Sa'adatullah Khan. Killed by the Marathas when they invaded the Carnatic in 1740.

S. No.	Name of Nawab	Beginning of reign	End of reign	Notes
5.	Safdar Ali Khan	1740	1742	Son of Dost Ali Khan. Recognized as the Nawab of the Carnatic by the British. Assassinated by his brother-in-law Murtaza Ali in 1742.
6.	Muhammad Sa'adatullah Khan II	1742	1744	Minor son of Safdar Ali Khan, proclaimed as Nawab of Arcot by the British, supported by Nizam-ul-Mulk Asaf Jah I of Hyderabad. Anwaruddin Muhammad Khan was appointed as regent to the minor Nawab. Like his father, assassinated in 1744. End of the first dynasty of the Nawabs of Arcot.
7.	Anwaruddin Muhammad Khan Wallajah	1744	1749	Regent to the previous nawab. Confirmed as nawab by the British and Nizam-ul-Mulk. Founder of the second dynasty of the Nawabs of Arcot. Helped to restore Madras and Cuddalore to the British after these towns were captured by the French in 1746. Killed in battle in August 1749, at the age of 77, fighting with the British against the French and Chanda Sahib.
8.	Chanda Sahib	1749	1752	Chanda Sahib installed as the nawab by the French in 1749.
9.	Muhammad Ali Khan Wallajah	1752	1795	Son of Anwaruddin Muhammad Khan, restored as the nawab by the British after defeating Chanda Sahib's forces, a campaign in which Clive Robert played a crucial role. A staunch ally of the British in the Carnatic.

Emperor Aurangzeb chose Zulfiqar Ali Khan Nusrat Jung as the first nawab of the Carnatic in 1692. He was succeeded by Daud Khan Panṇi in 1703. His deputy, Sa'adatullah Khan, was selected as the nawab by the new emperor, Bahadur Shah, in 1710. Sa'adatullah Khan is regarded as the first true nawab of the Carnatic. He rejected the authority of Emperor Jahandar Shah, successor to Emperor Bahadur Shah, and transformed the Mughal Carnatic domain into the first permanent and independent sovereign state amongst the various Nayak-Poligar kingdoms in the Carnatic.[8] He was a Navayat, and this was to be of considerable importance in later years. He ruled for two decades and before he died in 1732, he chose Dost Ali Khan, his nephew, as his successor. With the aid of his son, Safdar Ali, and son-in-law, Chanda Sahib (Hussain Dost Khan), Dost Ali subjugated many southern Nayaka-Poligar principalities that included Trichinopoly, Madurai, and Tanjore. However, by this time, Dost Ali had already lost most of his authority to his son and son-in-law and had become a titular ruler. Chanda Sahib declared himself as the nawab after dispossessing Queen Minakshi of Tiruchi and this victory created great apprehension in Arcot. The heir apparent, Safdar Ali, and the diwan, Mir Asad, tried to influence Dost Ali to recall the self-styled "nawab of Trichinopoly". However, as Dost Ali was too weak to take action, Safdar Ali decided to act for himself and attacked Tanjore. He imprisoned the Maratha Rajah Sayaji. Chanda Sahib continued his expansion by seizing Tirunelveli palayakkars and Pudukkottai.

The Nizam and the Marathas, the two other stakeholders outside the Carnatic, were furious at the success of Chanda Sahib. Nizam-ul-Mulk had not forgotten the fact that Dost Ali had become the nawab of the Carnatic without his consent and he persuaded the Marathas to attack the Carnatic. The Marathas themselves were angered by the subversion of the Hindu kingdoms of Madurai and Tanjore and King Sahu resolved to invade the Carnatic. Dost Ali encountered the Marathas in the Dhamalacheruvu Pass, about 19 miles north of Chittoor. He was defeated and killed. Safdar Ali (1740 to 1742) was recognized as the Nawab of Arcot by the Marathas, but Chanda Sahib refused to accept his suzerainty and established his regime in Trichy. The Marathas besieged the Tiruchi Fort, defeated Chanda Sahib, and sent him as a prisoner to Satara, the Maratha capital. Murari Rao Ghorpade was made governor of Tiruchi. However, the Marathas did not keep their promise to maintain the Hindu rule, which meant the Madurai Nayak ruled in the Carnatic, but handed over Tiruchi to Nizam-ul-Mulk in return for a payment. Thus, the

Maratha invasion failed to achieve what the Hindu powers in the Carnatic had hoped for.

Safdar Ali Khan found it difficult to restore peace and order to his distracted viceroyalty and was murdered by his cousin and brother-in-law, the Governor of Vellore, Murtaza Ali on 2nd October 1742. However, his triumph was short-lived. Faced with stiff opposition from the chiefs, the Marathas, and a group of Navayats, he gave up his claim and retired to the impregnable fort of Vellore. The *masnud* (throne in Urdu) fell vacant and an infant son of Safdar Ali, Mohammed Saeed (Sadatullah Khan II, 1742–1744) was proclaimed as the new nawab by Mir Azad, the diwan.[9] In 1743, Nizam-ul-Mulk marched to Arcot with a massive army. The Nizam, who had resented the fact that Dost Ali and Safdar Ali had made themselves nawabs without any reference to him, settled the claim in favour of Mohammed Saeed. As he was a minor at that time, Anwaruddin Khan Wallajah, the right-hand man of the Nizam from his days in Delhi, was made the regent and the boy was placed under his care. However, in June 1744, Mohammed Saeed was murdered. It was rumoured that Murtaza Ali organised the assassination of the boy and that Anwaruddin himself was involved in the conspiracy.[10] This was the end of the first dynasty of the Navayats as the nawabs of Arcot.

Anwaruddin Khan Muhammad Wallajah became the Nawab of Arcot in 1744 and the second dynasty of Arcot, the Wallajah, was founded. His accession to the throne of the Carnatic coincided with the War of Austrian Succession of 1740–1748.[11] The first potential for military intervention in the subcontinent by European powers opened up, particularly between the English and the French East India Companies, during the reign of Anwaruddin.

European Involvement in Local Politics: The First Carnatic War, 1746–1748

> 'The study of the dynamics of European overseas expansion necessitates a study of the changing military balance between the West and the rest of the players in the field. But here a major paradox appears. By 1650

> the West had already achieved military mastery in four separate areas: in Central and South America; Siberia; coastal areas of sub-Saharan Africa and Indonesian and Philippine archipelagos. Yet in India, until the mid-eighteenth century, the European presence had virtually no impact on even the minor states of the subcontinent. Indeed, the sudden progress of Western military methods in the region after the 1740s was so rapid that it left many Europeans bewildered.'[12]

The Europeans originally came to Asia to trade, not to conquer. They resorted to military tactics either to pressure reluctant buyers or in order to safeguard themselves against attack from their European rivals. The cost of defence would otherwise have devoured all profit that was amassed from trading. The Europeans enjoyed precious little by way of technological superiority once they left their ships. Parker believes: "For them, to control areas of India beyond the range of their broad-side firing vessels, they had to develop and exploit the potential of Asian populations in the use Western military practices. Many Indian armies were huge."[13] However, essentially, they remained aggregations of individual heroic warriors. Native princes had long employed muskets and cannons, but the drill, tactics, and disciplined volley fire available to the Europeans was absent. In 1749, John Grant, a British officer serving in India, reported that the armies of Indian rulers were hardly armies at all, "having no regularity or discipline among them".[14] Geography limited the manpower and the resources at the command of the Europeans in India, since transporting large bodies of troops from Europe was practically unsustainable. Hiring local bands or contracting local alliances could enhance numbers, but the core of European forces could not equal the princely armies in size. The initiation of the Indian soldier sepoy is attributed to Benoit Dumas, who was the governor of Pondicherry from 1735 to 1741. He recruited about 500 Indians and trained them strictly in Western ways such as discipline and drill. However, it was Dupleix, his successor, who made effective use of these trained soldiers. To defeat the Nawab of Arcot in 1746, he joined 700 sepoys to his existing force of 300 Europeans. The British followed the French example.

The Battle of Adayar: The Beginning of the Turn of Events in Favour of Europeans

The Nawab Anwaruddin became aware of the outbreak of war between the English and the French in Europe and their preparations to commit hostilities against each other in all their settlements on the Indian coast in 1745. This included their headquarters in Madras and Pondicherry that were under the jurisdiction of the Carnatic. In earlier European wars, hostilities had never extended to any part of the Mughal emperor's dominions. As the representative of the Mughal emperor and the Nizam of Hyderabad, he wrote letters to the English and French Companies directing the two nations to live at peace and forbidding their squadrons to engage off the Indian coast.[15]

Initially, the directors of both the French and English trading companies were eager to avoid a potentially disruptive and destructive conflict in South Asia. However, once the English realised that the British government was willing to commit naval forces to protect their investments, the directors of the English East India Company were ready to rid themselves of their French competition in South Asia.[16] A royal squadron under Commodore Curtis Barnett brought French commercial shipping to a standstill.[17] Francois Dupleix, the governor of Pondicherry, sought the help of Admiral La Bourdonnais, the governor of Ile de France and Ile de Bourbon, to come to his assistance.[18] Their plans involved the destruction of the English squadron and the capture of Madras. Commodore Edward Peyton, who took over the command of the English squadron after the death of Commodore Curtis Barnett, attacked La Bourdonnais off the coast of Nagapatanam. The clash was inconclusive, and the English were forced to break off the action. Payton refused to continue fighting and withdrew to Trincomalee. This left La Bourdonnais unopposed on the Coromandel Coast and helped him to lay siege to Madras, which was captured on 21 September 1746.

The English complained to Nizam Asaf Jah of Hyderabad and got a favourable response from Prince Nasir Jang, the son of the Nizam. He asked Anwaruddin, the Nawab of Arcot, to ensure that "the lawful proprietors are Righted, and dispossess the Usurpers".[19] The Nawab sent an army commanded by his son, Mahfuz Khan, and (the future Nawab) Muhammad Ali to drive the French out of Madras, thus triggering the First Carnatic War. However, the French under Captain Louis Paradis de la Roche went on to defeat this superior army on 24 October 1746 (Battle of St. Thome/ Battle of Adayar) with the classic European technique of the musketry salvo: 300 Europeans and 700 native troops, drawn up in three ranks, moved forward against their 10,000 adversaries firing successive volleys of shot. Almost immediately they were the masters of the field.

The Battle of Adayar River was a turning point in Indian history.[20] The conflict announced emphatically the value of the development of arms and tactics introduced in the preceding 80 years.[21] The use of a combination of a core of European soldiers along with a larger number of European trained Indian troops was not new. All the Western powers in the Orient including the Portuguese from the sixteenth century onwards had tried to compensate for their numerical weakness by recruiting members of the "martial races" of Asia. However, these various recruits served as auxiliaries, not regulars: they fought in their traditional fashion with their traditional weapons and in their traditional formations. The French, however, trained native troops to fight in the European fashion with European weapons and European uniforms, and, after 1751, they supplied them with European officers and non-commissioned officers also.[22] The English were well aware of the threat, and by the 1740s, they started raising their own companies, battalions, and eventually regiments of sepoys. There were two sepoy battalions in the company's service by 1758 and five by 1759. This numerical strength was enhanced by more reliable flintlock muskets and the quick-firing field artillery.

It is important to appreciate the fact that during this period, neither the French nor the English dreamt of acquiring territorial possessions. India was a minor theatre of war, where the combatants aimed at injuring trade and not making conquests, though, in fact, the conflict was to generate conditions that rendered conquests at once possible and desirable.[23] According to Dodwell:

> Quite independently Floyer and Dupleix had taken sides in local quarrels at almost the same moment and in common defiance of the policy laid down with similar emphasis alike at Paris and at London. Peace had left both with unemployed bodies of troops expensive to maintain, but who could not be sent back to Europe because the shipping season had not arrived. Neither governor therefore was sorry to relieve himself of heavy charges by temporarily placing these troops at the disposal of princes who would contribute to their maintenance.[24]

The War of Austrian Succession ended with the Treaty of Aix-la-Chapelle in 1748. In India, France secured the agreement by promising to evacuate the great trading post of Madras, which had been captured from the British. In return, France regained the fortress of Louisbourg on Isle Royale (Cape Breton Island, Canada).[25]

By the Treaty of Aix-la-Chapelle signed in mid-April 1748, the first phase of the Anglo-French rivalry in India came to an end. However, this treaty, at best, brought about only a truce and not a lasting peace between the two rival companies:

> At Fort St. David as well as at Pondicherry, it was seen that a new order had come into being and that henceforth they could no longer maintain themselves as simple traders but must play their part in the great game before them or lose their place in India altogether. Added to this were, at both places, considerable bodies of troops, as they had never had before.[26]

The Second Carnatic War, 1748–1754 and the Peaceful Interlude in Europe

The Nizam-ul-Mulk Asaf Jah I of Hyderabad died on 21 May 1748. In the Carnatic, his death "at once released the disruptive forces which had still now been held in check by the terror of his name".[27] It marked the signal for the outbreak of the war of succession in the Deccan and Carnatic and plunged the Deccan Peninsula into civil war and turmoil.[28] This struggle intimately developed into a scramble for power in the Deccan between the Nizam, the Marathas, the English, and the French.

Nasir Jung, the second son of Nizam-ul-Mulk, succeeded him as the subedar of the Deccan. His eldest son, Ghazi-ud-Din, was at the court in Delhi as the prime minister. However, very soon, Nasir Jung realised that Muzaffar Jung, a favourite grandson of Nizam-ul-Mulk from his daughter, had also put forward his claims for the Deccan Subedari. Thus, a civil war for succession broke out between the two contestants. This opened a window of opportunity for Navayat Chanda Sahib (Hussain Dost Khan) who wanted to become the Nawab of the Carnatic. When the Navayats were the nawabs of Arcot, the French were in a favourable position compared to the other Europeans, but by the time of the Wallajahs, their relationship had become very unpleasant and unfriendly. The French realised that if the power over the Deccan and the Carnatic fell into the hands of Nasir Jung and Anwaruddin Wallajah, it would be very disadvantageous to them.

This was the opportunity for the French to undermine the power of Nasir Jung and Anwaruddin and they supported Muzaffar Jung in his fight against his uncle, Nasir Jung, to seize the throne of Hyderabad. The French also paid a ransom and secured the release of Chanda Sahib, who had been a prisoner of the Marathas at Satara for almost a decade.[29] Chanda Sahib joined hands with Muzaffar Jung and assisted by the French, returned south with a 40,000 strong army, determined to defeat Anwaruddin Wallajah and restore power back to the former dynasty. The fratricidal wars of succession that followed had the collaboration of rival powers, with each candidate supported by either the French or the British. This period 1748 and 1754 is referred to by historians as the Second Carnatic War.

The Battle of Ambur was the first major battle of the Second Carnatic War. The battle was initiated by Muzaffar Jung, supported by Dupleix, and led by Chanda Sahib, who sought to overthrow

Anwaruddin Wallajah, the Nawab of the Carnatic, for supporting Nasir Jung's claim to be the Nizam of Hyderabad. The French forces, led by Marquis de Bussy, proved decisive in giving the allies a resounding victory. The battle had a special significance. For the first time, it was in Ambur that the European forces stood out as principals in an Indian battle when Indian soldiers remained in the background. Dupleix said: "Our forces were not on the foot of the auxiliaries. They acted as principals and during the whole course of the war we have never looked ourselves in any other light".[30] Anwaruddin Wallajah was killed in the battle on 3 August 1749. Chanda Sahib seized control of the Carnatic and took the city of Arcot. Muzaffar Jung declared himself the subedar of the Deccan and proclaimed Chanda Sahib as the Nawab of the Carnatic.

The eldest son of Anwaruddin, Mahfuz Khan, was taken prisoner, while the second son, Mohammed Ali, escaped to Trichinopoly. There he established his resisting army and declared himself the new nawab of the Carnatic. Thus, there were two men claiming to be the nawabs of the Carnatic: one in Arcot and one in Trichinopoly. The one in Arcot was appointed by Muzaffar Jung and was recognized by the French; the one in Trichinopoly was acknowledged by Nasir Jung and the British. Chanda Sahib conferred on Dupleix, the villages of Villiyanallur, Valudavur, and Bahur, along with 81 villages in the neighbourhood. Muzaffar Jung conferred on the French the seaport of Masulipatam and Divi Island, an area of 22 miles that yielded an annual revenue of eight lakh rupees.[31] Dupleix informed his superiors in Europe that "[a]ll my efforts are directed towards attaining for you vast revenues from this part of India, and consequently placing the nation in apposition to maintain itself here even when it may lack support from Europe".[32]

The English resented the granting of places to the French as it rendered their trade and commerce vulnerable. It was time for them to enter the fray and they offered their help to Mohammed Ali at Trichinopoly on the condition that he should procure for them a *mansab* (Arabic for rank or position) and a jagir (grant of public revenues to a person with power to collect them and to administer the government) from the Nizam Nasir Jung to match the possession that the French had acquired from Muzaffar Jung and Chanda Sahib. At the same time, the English instigated Nasir Jung to attack the Carnatic. He proceeded from his capital, Aurangabad, and reached Hyderabad in June 1749. There he heard about the disastrous battle of Ambur and the death of Anwaruddin. Nasir Jung marched upon the Fort of Ginjee near Pondicherry with an estimated army of three lakh soldiers assisted by the Marathas, Mughal tributaries, and a small force of the English under Major Stringer Lawrence.[33] The huge army, combined with appeals made by his uncle, unnerved the rival Nizam Muzaffar Jung, who gave himself up on the promise of pardon. However, this resulted in his imprisonment, which infuriated the nawabs of Kurnool, Cuddapah, and Savanur, who were instrumental in convincing Muzaffar Jung to surrender. Dupleix took advantage of this discontent, which led to a chain of events that resulted in the death of Nizam Nasir Jung at the hands of Himmat Bahadur Khan, the Nawab of Kurnool.[34]

Muzaffar Jung, a prisoner under sentence to death, then and there became the subedar of the Deccan on 14 December 1750. Nawab Muhammad Ali and Shah Nawaz Khan, on hearing of Nasir Jung's death, fled to Chetpattu, near Ginjee. A grateful Muzaffar Jung heaped riches and awards on Dupleix. He was appointed as his deputy for the territories that lay to the south of the river Krishna and was also made the Nawab of the Carnatic and Mysore. Chanda Sahib was given the title of the Nawab of Arcot. The French were also given Yanam, Masulipatam, and Karikal. The revenue of these territories was estimated at 36,000-pound sterling. Nasir Jung's brothers Salabat Jung, Nizam Ali Khan, and Basalat Jung were elevated to the rank of 7,000 horse[35] while Nasir Jung's sons were imprisoned. However, his collaborators, the Pathan nawabs, remained dissatisfied even after receiving a handsome share of the spoils and plotted against Muzaffar Jung.

Muzaffar Jung decided to proceed to the Deccan, but as he was apprehensive of the intentions of the Pathan nawabs, he requested Dupleix to send along with him a French contingent to Aurangabad. Dupleix knew that he could always influence the Nizam through the French contingent and he agreed to send one under the command of de Bussy. By this subtle diplomacy, Dupleix made Pondicherry the political axis of the Deccan and the Carnatic. French influence in the whole of South India became profound and supreme. The presence of the French detachment with the Nizam ensured that there would not be any change in the Nizam's policy towards the French. Their companionship also acted as a deterrent against anti-French cliques in the Nizam's court and made Dupleix the virtual master of the whole of South India, through the Deccan subedar, who was the representative of the Mughal Emperor.[36]

The growth of French influence and power was a source of apprehension for the English with regard to the security of their trade on the Coromandel Coast. The English decided to defend their interests at the point of the sword.

> Consider that the whole success of the Company's affairs here depends on having "a force to curb the French". It might have been better for trade if the Country powers had been left to decide their own quarrel; but once the French attempted to surround the English settlements so as to cut off their trade and supplies of provisions, it was judged necessary to oppose them, to avoid a situation ill in peace and worse in war.[37]

In view of the grants made by Muzaffar Jung to the French, the only way for the English to save their trading interests was to promote the interests of the rival candidate, Nawab Mohammed Ali, against Chanda Sahib. The English sent to him a detachment consisting of 280 Europeans and 300 sepoys under Captain Rudolf de Gingens. They also garrisoned the Fort of Trichinopoly under Captain Cope. At the same time, they appealed to the Mughal Emperor and the Dalwai of Mysore (commander in military in South Indian dynasty) against the encroachment of the French and Chanda Sahib. The Rajah of Tanjore also appealed to the English for help. Thus, the English formed an oppositional conglomerate in the Carnatic consisting of Nawab Mohammed Ali, the Dalwai of Mysore, and the Rajah of Tanjore against the French and their nominee, Chanda Sahib.

Muzaffar Jung left Pondicherry for the Deccan on 7 January 1751, but in spite of the support he received from the French, his position on the throne was far from secure. The Mughal Emperor, on hearing of the death of Nasir Jung, conferred the Deccan Subedari on Ghazi-ud Din Jung, the eldest son of Nizam-ul-Mulk. While informing Nawab Muhammad Ali of the same, he also appointed the latter as the Nawab of the Carnatic Painghat.[38] Muzaffar Jung with his army reached the village of Rayacotta near the Lakkireddipalli Pass, a village 25 miles south of Cuddapah. There, on 13 February 1751, he was mortally injured by the Pathan Nawab of Kurnool. Thus, within six weeks of becoming Nizam, Muzaffar Jung was killed. The news created great panic and confusion amongst the Mughals, who had hardly recovered from the shock of the death of Nasir Jung. This unforeseen calamity greatly affected the French also. The death of Nawab Muzaffar Jung destroyed all chances of their interfering in the affairs of the Deccan. However, the astuteness and courage of de Bussy saved the French interests. He rose to the occasion and made all the Mughal nobles and generals accept Salabat Jung, the third son of Nizam-ul-Mulk, as the subedar of the Deccan.

> The smooth manner in which Salabat Jung was chosen as Subedar reveals the extent to which the French had gained a hold in the mind of the Indian chiefs.... The situation which contained potential germs for internecine warfare, and which would under ordinary circumstances have entitled an appeal to the far-off Mughal Emperor was brought under control by the strong personality of Bussy. The French action in getting Salabat Jung chosen as the Nizam without any reference to the Emperor was a veritable revolution. In fact, it was a challenge to the supremacy of the Emperor.[39]

Salabat Jung confirmed all the grants made by Muzaffar Jung to the French, but also placed the whole country south of the river Krishna, including Madura and Tinnevelly (Tirunelveli) Districts, under French control. He also granted to the French the territories of Nizampatnam, Alamannar in Krishna district, and Kondavid and Narasapur in Godavari district, thus demarcating the French territory around Masulipatam. De Bussy, with the French detachment, accompanied Salabat Jung to Aurangabad and reached there on 29 June 1751.

Salabat Jung issued a firman by which he agreed to pay one lakh rupees for the French detachment, and he also empowered Dupleix to depute anyone he preferred as the Nawab of Carnatic. Referring to this grant, Dupleix wrote to the Directors of the French East India Company, "It is a question of securing the Arcot Government for the Nation with power of regulating the annual payment to the Royal Treasury. This affair is of the highest importance to the Nation, deserves the closest attention. For it will dispense with the need of sending funds to India for your investment".[40] On the request of Salabat Jung, Dupleix agreed to maintain a 2000 strong contingent at Aurangabad.

Map of Deccan, Carnatic and Malabar Coast: Important cities and battle sites

> The time had not arrived when a European power could openly assert supreme dominion, but in January 1751, almost the whole of south-eastern India recognized the moral predominance of Pondicherry. The country between the Vindhayan range and the river Krishna, including the provinces known as the Northern Sirkars was virtually ruled by the French general (de Bussy) whose army occupied the capital of the Subhadar of Dakhan (Salabat Jung). South of the River Krishna the country known as the Karnatak including Nellur, North and South Arkat, Madura, and Tinnevelli was ruled virtually from Pondicherry. The only place not subject to French influence was Madras, restored to England by the Treaty of Aix-la-Chapelle; Fort St. David, within a few miles of Pondicherry held by the English; Tanjur, whose Rajah had not acknowledged the supremacy of the French nominee (Chanda Sahib); and Trichinapalli held by a rival candidate for the Nawabship supported by the English.[41]

French Fortune in the Deccan and the Carnatic

While the French influence was being shored up in the Deccan, in the Carnatic, which was the base of French power, it was crumbling. For, from this period began the decline of the French and the rise of the British, with the fall of Chanda Sahib and the ascent of Mohammad Ali respectively.[42]

Following the Battle of Ambur in 1749, in which his father Anwaruddin Wallajah was slain, Mohammed Ali once again withdrew to the fort of Trichinopoly. Chanda Sahib had planned to besiege him, but the need for funding led him instead to besiege Tanjore first. However, the movements of his Maratha enemies and the prospect of the appearance of Nasir Jung prompted Chanda Sahib to withdraw from Tanjore discreditably. The siege of Trichinopoly began in March 1751. The besieging forces of Chanda Sahib was larger, as he enjoyed the support of the French and the Nizam Salabat Jung. Yet, the hostilities that dragged on with minor battles and the siege of Tiruchi lingered on. Thomas Saunders, who replaced Floyer as the Governor of Madras, was determined to resist Dupleix to the last. In May 1751, an English regiment under Captain Rudolf de Gingens was sent to intercept a large army of Chanda Sahib marching to support the siege of Trichinopoly held by Mohammed Ali. Being steward, Robert Clive accompanied this force as commissary and also fought as a volunteer.[43] However, against sustained cannonade, the English were forced to retire to Trichinopoly. Clive returned to Fort St. David and volunteered for military service and was made a captain. He took a small detachment to Trichinopoly through Tanjore. The expedition was uneventful, but it is of historic importance in that while he was at Trichinopoly, Mohammad Ali won him over to his favourite military plan. This was to make a diversionary attack on Arcot, a town 60 miles inland from Madras. This was the capital of the Carnatic and the seat of Chanda Sahib's government but had been left without a strong enough garrison owing to most of the enemy forces being gathered at Trichinopoly. Ali was convinced that such an attack would draw off some of the enemy forces.[44]

The Capture and Siege of Arcot

Clive was put in charge of the expedition, and he was given all the soldiers they could spare, amounting to 130 Europeans and some sepoys. On 22 August 1751, the party sailed to Madras, where the Deputy Governor Richard Prince provided 80 more Europeans. On 26 August, the expedition began its march to Arcot—a distance of about 64 miles. The expedition was a remarkable piece of cooperation between Clive at Arcot, the Prince at Madras, and Saunders at Fort St. David; each situated at different points of a triangle and separated from the others by 60 to 100 miles of hostile country.

When the English reached Arcot, they were amazed to find that the 11,000 strong garrison had fled during the night, having heard from their spies of how the English had marched unconcernedly through a blustering storm and inclement weather overnight, unmindful of the omens of heaven. This to them denoted superhuman courage and they reckoned it was no good trying to resist such a foe.[45] Clive treated the inhabitants, the merchants, and the bankers with dignity and humanitarianism and thus won their support. Saunders also took care to instill in Clive the importance of legitimacy, of maintaining the pretence that the English were acting as auxiliaries, and that the place had been taken in the name of the Mughal Emperor who in theory was Mohammed Ali's overlord. Clive set to work preparing the fort to stand a siege. He had made two attempts to dislodge the former garrison of Arcot, which was disrupting the supply of provisions. The enemy reorganised and moved close to the city. Clive had already experienced how deadly a night attack on an Indian camp could be. Clive waited until two hours after midnight (on 14 September) then marched silently with most of his force and attacked them while they were asleep. They fled in confusion without even firing a shot. The next morning none of the enemy remained in sight.[46]

According to Malcolm, "Chanda Sahib detached 4000 of his troops, horse and foot, from Trichinopoly who in their route were joined by his son Raza Sahib with 150 Europeans from Pondicherry, and together with the troops already collected in the neighbourhood of Arcot, entered the city on September 23".[47] Clive and his men shut themselves in the fort. Intense fighting ensued with no predictable results. Gradually, the total strength of Raza Sahib's army increased to 10,000 when forces from the nearby garrison of Arcot and the fortress of Vellore joined them. From then on, Clive and his men were closely besieged, and the blockade dragged along its slow length. Knowing that the Marathas had promised assistance and another force was coming from Madras, Raza Sahib offered Clive honourable conditions that he refused. Raza Sahib decided to venture an assault on 14 November, the day of the Mohammadan festival of Muharram, but Clive was alerted by a spy about this. A brisk engagement ensued, but Clive was able to win the battle which lasted for about an hour. Under the cover of fire, Raza Sahib raised the siege and withdrew his army to Vellore. Clive's force had achieved an amazing feat in the face of the overwhelming numerical odds against them. The siege of Arcot marked a sea of change in the British experience in India: "For Arcot was the turning of the tide. It may have been luck, it may have been bungling on the part of the enemy, but it created the legend of English courage and invincibility which was to carry English arms in India from one success to another".[48]

Though the siege of Arcot was over, Clive still had to drive the enemy out of the surrounding country. Raza Sahib with his whole force joined the French reinforcement. They met Clive and the Marathas near the town of Arni on 3 December. After a well-contested action, Raza Sahib and the French were completely routed. Arni was Clive's first victory in the field. Clive next moved against Conjeeveram and for two days bombarded the temple town and took possession of it. These victories of Clive had been psychological rather than productive in terms of any solid territorial gains for Mohammed Ali.

Battle of Kaveripak (22 February 1752)

Just like Clive had reduced pressure on Trichinopoly by his march to Arcot, Raza Sahib collected his scattered army and moved towards Madras trying to prevent the English from relieving the garrison of Mohammed Ali and Gingens by threatening Madras itself. Governor Saunders and his Council sent Clive to Madras to build up a force to command against the enemy. By the middle of February 1752, his army consisted of 400 Europeans and 1,300 sepoys and they moved towards Conjeevaram. They were attacked by Raza Sahib as they approached the village of Kaveripak at dusk: "Keeping his main force in a deep ditch, he sent a detachment round to the enemy's rear by the light of the moon, and their volley on the unsuspecting French caused a panic and scattered the whole force".[49] As Bence-Jones notes, it was "[a] daring move, mutual trust between the Indians and their commander—these were the classic ingredients of Clive's success, and together they made the victory at Kaveripak. But there was also a third and unsavoury ingredient which was treachery in the enemy ranks".[50]

Kaveripak was a decisive victory. It destroyed the army built up by Dupleix and Raza Sahib in the previous autumn, which was finally disbanded. Moreover, it brought territorial gains for Mohammed Ali giving him a potential annual revenue of four lakh pagodas. For the English, psychologically, the victory greatly enhanced their reputation: "Sir John Malcolm attributes to the Battle of Kaveripak the distinction 'of restoring or rather of founding the reputation of the British arms in India'; for before that 'no event had occurred which could lead the natives to believe that the English as soldiers were equal to the French.' That was most undoubtedly its moral effect".[51]

Siege of Trichinopoly

Following the victory in Kaveripak, Clive and his troops marched southwards and reached the fort of St. David. Soon they set out for Trichinopoly where Mohammed Ali was being besieged. It stood close to the banks of the river Cauvery, and at this point was divided from a separate arm known as the river Coleroon by the Island of Srirangam. Trichinopoly itself was fortified, and within the walls of its fortress stood its characteristic feature, a rock that was 273 feet high. By the end of 1751, Mohammed Ali had secured the support of the armies from Tanjore and Mysore as well as Morari Rao and his Marathas.[52]

Clive was entrusted with reinforcement from Bengal and all available troops. At this moment, Major Stringer Lawrence also arrived back from England. On10 April 1752, they were within 10 miles of Trichinopoly. The French officer, Jacques Law, tried to prevent the convoy of Lawrence uniting with the main British force, but he failed in his attempt and was forced to retire to the island of Srirangam. Protracted skirmishes took place and in subsequent tactical manoeuvres that followed, Clive excelled and forced Jacques Law to resort to negotiations. He surrendered on 13 June 1752. Chanda Sahib who had given up to the Maratha general, Murari Rao Ghorpade, on solemn assurance of safety, was betrayed to Mohammed Ali and beheaded the next day.

The surrender of Law left Pondicherry undefended. Dupleix agreed to recognize Muhammad Ali as the Nawab of Carnatic but demanded the release of all prisoners as a preliminary step to discussing terms. Saunders declined to negotiate on such conditions. The war therefore continued. On 6 September 1752, a French force under de Kerjean was defeated by Stringer Lawrence at Bahur and this victory weakened the French military activity for some time.

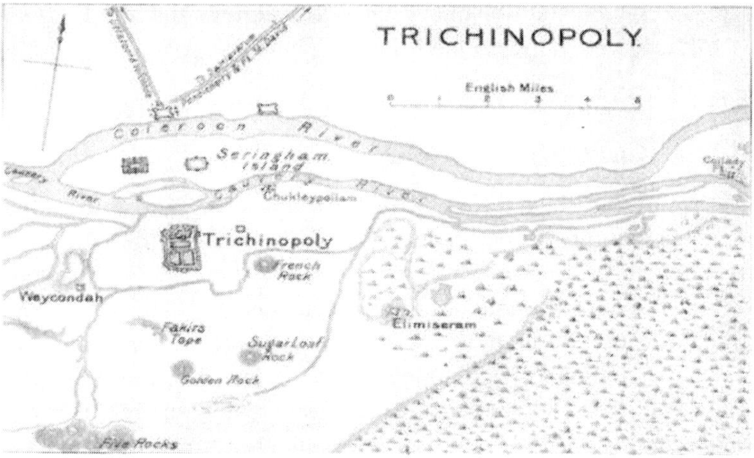

Source: History of the British Army" volume II by J. W. Fortescue. Public domain.

Map of a part of Trichinopoly

In the meantime, Nawab Ghazi-ud-Din Khan arrived at Aurangabad on 28 September 1752 at the head of a large force with his Maratha allies wanting to claim his right as the subedar of Deccan. While the negotiations were going on between the nawab, Dupleix, and de Bussy, Ghazi-ud-Din was poisoned and murdered in October 1752 by his stepmother. Peshwa Balaji Rao conveyed his willingness to open negotiations if Salabat Jung was prepared to give him the same grants as were promised by Ghazi-ud-Din. Salabat Jung agreed to these terms and the Treaty of Bhalki was concluded between Nizam Salabat Jung and the Marathas on 22 November 1752.[53]

The French supremacy in the court of Salabat Jung was bitterly opposed by the nobles of the court. The treasury of the Nizam was almost empty, and his troops had not been paid for some time. Salabat Jung found it still more difficult to pay the French detachment. Dupleix advised de Bussy to ask Salabat Jung for the grant of the four Northern Sarkars—namely Ellore, Kondapalli, Rajahmundry, and Chicacole—towards the maintenance of the French detachment. The Northern Sarkars constituted the most fertile coastal strip of the Nizam's dominions. On 23 November 1753, a grand durbar was held at Aurangabad and the Treaty of Aurangabad was signed between Salabat Jung and the French. By this treaty, the four Northern Sarkars were granted to the French and its acquisition was an important landmark in the history of the French in India.[54] Thus, by 1753, superficially, the French position was firmly established in the Deccan.

Dupleix kept up his intense diplomatic activity and widened the breach between the Mysoreans and Muhammed Ali. He was able to disengage the Marathas under Morari Rao from his enemies. The presence of the French troops in the Deccan and the control exercised by de Bussy over Salabat Jung helped Dupleix to obtain these favourable terms. Nonetheless, several military failures forced the French to show a policy of conciliation towards the English. Negotiations were opened and it was held at the Dutch factory in Sadras from 21 to 25 January 1754.[55] Dupleix, while determined to maintain his position as the Nawab of the Carnatic, authorised his commissioners to make liberal concessions for the English on other points. As for the English, they were prepared to give way on many points, but they were inflexible regarding the rights of Muhammad Ali. After three meetings full of deception, duplicity, and deviousness over the validity of the titles of Muhammed Ali and those of Dupleix, the negotiations were broken off and war was renewed.[56] The real significance of the Sadras conference is that the two foreign companies felt free to try and dispose of the highest officers in the Carnatic and the Deccan as suited their interests.[57]

Concerns in France and England and Recall of Dupleix

The directors of the French Company de Indies and the Ministers of the King were becoming increasingly weary of this distant war who felt this was interfering greatly with commerce without bringing neither glory nor profit. They were of the opinion that the resources of France were being squandered to promote the vanity and the ambition of one individual. Regrettably they could not guess, or they could not comprehend the advantages already acquired – the control of the councils of the Subedar of the Deccan, the most powerful ruler in South India; and the cession to France in absolute gift of the Northern Sarkars comprising Ganjam, Vizagapatam, Godavari, and Krishna, with Rajamahendri and Masulipatam that was the vast influence exercised by the genius of one man:

> They heard, first of Law's disaster, then the loss of De la Touché and his 700 hundred men, then of the defeats in succession of Astruc, of Brennier, of Mainville, and found that these military operations had resulted in a great loss to the French commercial interests. They need be but one scapegoat, and it was finally agreed that this scapegoat must be Dupleix.[58]

Charles Godeheu de Zaimont, former commissioner of the French Army during Dupleix's reign, was sent as acting governor general of Pondicherry to supersede him. Godeheu arrived in India on 2 August 1754 and Dupleix left Pondicherry on 14 October. The objective of Godeheu seemed to be not only to belittle Dupleix, but to bankrupt him financially: "Having thus effectively ruined the man who had all but won an Empire for France, he allowed him to depart, beggared but not dishonoured, blasted in fortune, cheated out of the fruits of his then ripening labours."[59]

Soon after his arrival, Godeheu entered into a truce with the English. According to the treaty, called the Convention of Sadras (11 October 1754 to 11 January 1755), both Companies agreed not to become involved in any alliances with or intervene in the internal disputes of the native powers in India. As regards the Northern Sarkars, the exclusive right granted by the subedar was not recognised. It was resolved that both the Companies should have subordinate factories at Rajahmundry and Chicacole without any claim to the territorial revenues of the country. Muhammed Ali was to be recognised as the Nawab of the Carnatic and Salabat Jung as Subedar. Thus, in this treaty, Godeheu renounced all that Dupleix had fought for. The only thing he did not do was to recall de Bussy and his troops from the court of the subedar. However, this treaty was not to be valid until the two Companies in Europe ratified it. As it happened it never was ratified, for the Seven Years War broke out in the meantime.

This truce arranged by Godeheu, clearly showed that the English were the victors. Till then, the English did not directly interfere in the Deccan, but by making themselves supreme in the Carnatic, they were able to dictate terms to the French in the Deccan. By being a party to this truce, the French violated the trust reposed in them by the Nizam. Not only the truce concluded without the knowledge of Salabat Jung, but even the allies of the French, the Mysoreans, and the Maratha leader Murari Rao Ghorpade were not consulted.[60] Naturally, the news of the agreement was received with a great deal of surprise and agitation in Hyderabad. Dupleix's recall from India was a great shock to Salabat Jung and his nobles and resulted in enormous damage to the prestige of the French in the Deccan.

The arbitrary manner in which the English and the French tried to take possession of territories by the Convention of Sadras in 1754, territories that belonged to the Nizam both legally and technically, made the Nizam and his courtiers extremely dejected. Moreover, they also heard that the French had recognised Muhammad Ali as the Nawab of Arcot. The Nizam had incurred a heavy loss by not recognising Muhammed Ali as the Nawab of Arcot and leaving the affairs of the Carnatic in the hands of Dupleix. He was extremely indignant to hear that an agreement was reached regarding the Carnatic without any reference to its liege-lord, the subedar of the Deccan.[61] Salabat Jung inveighed against de Bussy in the following manner:

> Your Sovereign promised to support me against my enemies, to establish my authority ... yet it is the King of England who specially concerns himself with the affairs

> of India even with those which affect me ... you have allowed to be placed at the head of one of my tributary provinces, a man whom I have never employed, who has always rebelled against my authority ... The state of my affairs necessarily demands the support of a European Power, on this condition I am able to govern, either you remain here or I must enlist the English in my interest. Are you disposed to render me the service which you have rendered hitherto.[62]

Salabat Jung asked de Bussy to accompany him on a campaign against Mysore, but at this time, the French were the allies of the Rajah of Mysore. Moreover, according to the Convention of Sadras, the French and the English had agreed not to assist the Indian princes in their wars. De Bussy sought clarification from Godeheu, but before his letter could reach Pondicherry, Godeheu had already left for France on 16 February 1755. De Bussy was determined to accompany Salabat Jung, but at the same time, in order to protect the interest of the Rajah, he informed the Rajah of the danger and advised him to satisfy the Nizam.

Dual De' Leyrit, the new French governor (March 1755), on his arrival in Pondicherry, became fully aware of the course of events on the Coromandel Coast. He realised that the truce agreed at Sadras would not last long. He wrote to the Dalwai saying that he would write to de Bussy to help the Rajah of Mysore by bringing about an amicable settlement between the Nizam and the Mysoreans. The Mysore campaign had widespread repercussions on the course of the Anglo-French struggle in the Carnatic. The intervention of de Bussy in the Mysore expedition on behalf of the Nizam prompted the English to help Nawab Muhammad Ali to occupy Vellore and the surrounding countries. Thus, in spite of the truce, both the Companies actively helped their Indian allies in local wars and acquired territories in the name of their allies.[63]

The East India Company and the Compagnie des Indes Orientales regarded, above all, their tropical settlements as places of trade. They were willing to accept Muhammed Ali as the Nawab of Carnatic and also Dupleix's claim to the dominion of the countries from Krishna to Cape Comorin. However, they declined absolutely to give up the Sarkars of Masulipatam and Condavir granted in 1753, while the English were resolved not to acknowledge them as a territorial power of such magnitude. On this point no agreement could be reached. The reason for this failure of negotiations marks the beginning of a new order of ideas as regards Indian policy. Political and commercial motives now became interwoven. Up to this end, the French and the English Companies had looked to the extension of their trade by commercial methods. Thanks to Dupleix, they became aware of the possibility of employing political methods as well. They realised that the enjoyment of revenues and the administration of territories would provide decided commercial and financial advantages.

In the meantime, Clive had returned to England with a fortune in October 1753. On the eve of his return, he married Margaret, thus linking his fortunes with the Maskelynes—an English intellectual family of some note. The most famous member was Nevil Maskelyne, Margaret's brother, who became the fifth Astronomer Royale. His patron was the Earl of Sandwich, the First Lord of Admiralty. Clive tried to enter the House of Commons with his Sandwich connection as a seat in the Commons was both a social and business investment. Sandwich-Clive collaboration won narrowly at the polls but lost on petition.[64]

The threat of a new war (The Seven Years War, 1756–1763) was now across the political and diplomatic scene in India and it was inevitable that France and England would be on opposite sides. Besides contesting for the balance of power in Europe, competition for the opening world markets in India, West Indies, and the Far East was dramatically unfolding. The powers of China and Japan were still too strong for their sovereignty to be openly ignored. The sugar colonies of the West Indies were already European controlled. It was in India that the unifying power of the Mughal Empire was fast disintegrating and the previous experiment of fighting over the heads of local princes was repeated with increased vigour. The French had the advantage of de Bussy's presence and the virtual control of the great Mughal splinter state of Hyderabad, which outweighed the British support of Muhammad Ali. De Bussy had received the revenues of the Northern Sarkars for his French force in Hyderabad.[65] If he could draw revenue southward to pay his troops, he could also march north through his own controlled territory. He, thus, became a threat at once to Madras and Calcutta.[66]

The Third Carnatic War: The Indian Counterpart in the Seven Years War (1756–1763)

The granting of the Northern Sarkars caused great anxiety and dismay for the Home Government in England and for the directors of the English East India Company. The ambitious policy of the French especially in the Carnatic, and their vast acquisitions in the Deccan caused substantial interruptions in the trade and created great expense for the English. Moreover, the revenues would enable the French to control Salabat Jung and the whole south. A plan was thus formed for a surprise attack on Salabat Jung and the French by entering into a secret alliance with the Peshwa, supposedly to fight against the Angrias.[67] To justify such an attack, the Secret Committee[68] suggested that the English should first demand from Salabat Jung the restoration of the Divi Island and the English factories at Masulipatam seized by the French.

The Home Ministry had sent a squadron to India under Rear Admiral Watson, with four ships of line and a frigate[69] having a regiment of foot[70] on board, which sailed from England in February 1754. At the same time, Robert Clive also returned to India for a second term with three companies of artillery. This was after signing to serve the East India Company as deputy governor of Fort St. David with succession to the chair at Madras. Clive was to command the proposed expedition. His military commission, Lieutenant Colonel of Foot, "in the East Indies only" was part of a plan for striking a further blow at the French power in India. However, the Bombay government did not approve the plan and the Home Government also agreed to drop the scheme.[71] Instead, when Watson arrived at Bombay in 1755, his first task was to support the East India Company's own navy—the "Bombay Marine"—against the Maratha Sea power on the Malabar Coast. Tulaji Angria, the

Maratha admiral (pirate to the English)[72] was a persistent menace to coastal trade and sometimes even to the big East Indiaman. The Peshwa, Balaji Baji Rao, also had sought the help of the Bombay government to put down the defiant Tulaji. Watson and Lieutenant-Colonel Clive launched an amphibious attack on Angria's main base of Gheria.[73] On 14 February 1756, Gheria or Vijaydurg —the stronghold of the Angrias—surrendered.[74]

Clive returned to Madras in May 1755 as Second in Council. On 10 April 1756, the Nawab of Bengal Alivardi Khan died, and he was succeeded by his grandson Siraj-ud-Daula. He occupied the English subordinate factory at Cossimbazar and later marched to and occupied Calcutta in July 1756. Then followed the tragic incidence of the "Black-Hole".[75] When it was learned that Calcutta had fallen, it was decided to go all out to recover Calcutta. The command went to Clive and the expedition sailed from Madras on 16 October. The Nawab of Bengal, Siraj-ud-Daula, was defeated in the Battle of Plassey on 23 June 1757 and later killed. Plassey was a decisive battle and the consequences, perhaps, the greatest ever gained. However, it can never be considered a great battle: "It was only when treason had done her work, when treason had driven the Nawab from the field, when treason had removed his army from its commanding position, that Clive was able to advance without the certainty of being annihilated".[76]

Clive wrote two letters after the Battle of Plassey, which summarise the attitude of the English of their assessment and experience in India for the one and a half centuries since their arrival in 1600 as a trading company.[77]

Events in Deccan and Carnatic: The Beginning of the End of French Dominance

There were various plots, machinations, and intrigues against the French, both from the Nizam's court and from the Marathas. There were several insurrections and rebellions against the French by various nobles, rajahs, and zamindars. Because of their basic weakness in the Carnatic,. the French were finding their position in the far-off Deccan quite untenable. By his tact, diplomacy, and gallantry, de Bussy was able to outpace the difficult period. In the meanwhile, de Bussy received letters from Siraj-ud-Daula asking him to come to his assistance. Confident that the French authority was sufficiently restored in the Sarkars, he decided to assist the Nawab of Bengal against the English East India Company. He dispatched Jacques Law in advance to Bengal. However, by the time Law reached Rajamahal, de Bussy received the news of the defeat of Siraj-ud-Daula at the hands of the English. As it was futile to go to Bengal, de Bussy tried to retaliate against the English by capturing the English factory at Vizagapatam on 24 June 1757. However, the political atmosphere in the Deccan remained very unstable with intense struggle for power between the Marathas and Salabat Jung with his two brothers—Nizam Ali and Balasat Jung. De Bussy reached Hyderabad on 15 July 1758 and on his arrival, he found a letter from Comte de Lally,[78] dated 13 June, ordering him to come over to Pondicherry along with Moracin so that they might lead an attack against the English at Madras. He left Hyderabad on 18 July 1758. With the departure of de Bussy from the Deccan, the power and glory of the French also departed from the Deccan.

The French ministers realised the enormous mistake they had committed in not efficiently supporting Dupleix. They notified De Leyrit that they were preparing a considerable force to send to India to support the French interest there: "The force was large enough to expel the English from Southern India, to restore by means of their troops the policy of the governor they had recalled and ruined".[79] In September 1757, a French squadron of ten vessels under the command of Captain Bouvet de Lozier arrived at Pondicherry. On board was the first detachment of 1,000 men of the Regiment de Loraine under the command of Major General M. Soupier. In April 1758, Lally and d'Ache reached Pondicherry with the remainder of the expedition. This consisted of the Regiment de Lally,[80] about 1,000 strong with a detachment of artillery. Comte D'Ache had nine ships of line (eight of which were French East India Company ships).

Immediately on his landing, Lally decided to attack Fort St. David at Cuddalore (Gondelour) and the garrison capitulated on 2 June 1758. The fall of the place produced a great effect on the country's powers and upon the English, who now prepared for the inevitable siege of Madras. Lally dispatched an order to de Bussy to move over to Arkat, leaving no French troops at the court of the subedar and only as many in the Northern Sarkars as would suffice to maintain them. The command of these and the general supervision of the province he directed de Bussy to entrust to Marquis de Conflans, who had just arrived from Europe.

Meanwhile, D'Ache fought fierce but indecisive battles on 29 April and 3 August against Vice-Admiral George Pocock.[81] At this crucial juncture, instead of following up his success in capturing Madras, Lally marched south to compel the king of Tanjore to pay the bond, which he had given to Chanda Sahib as a war indemnity. As long as Madras was in British hands, no victory was decisive. However, Lally had two principal difficulties in his way. One was that he was acutely short of money. The other reason was that D'Ache would not cooperate and refused to engage Pocock's fleet which lay unbeaten off the coast between Pondicherry and Madras.[82] His alleged reason was a lack of victuals. Both sailors and soldiers in the French force openly grumbled about the poor quality of the food on offer.[83] Lally marched south, got a little plunder in Nagore, and arrived before Tanjore on 17 July 1758. He attacked Tanjore but could not follow it up owing to lack of ammunition and provisions. Finally, he raised the siege on 8 August on hearing that Pocock had beaten D'Ache off Karaikal and that Pondicherry itself was under threat. With great loss of reputation, Lally withdrew to the coast.

Lally now took up again his scheme for capturing Madras. At the same time, the English had been diligently preparing to defend themselves, laying in supplies of provisions and gunpowder, and improving their works.[84] They had been strengthened by the arrival of His Majesty's 64th (Drapers Regiment), and a detachment of marines landed by Pocock before his departure. In all, the garrison amounted to 1,700 Europeans and Topasses, 2200 sepoys with Lawrence, Draper, and Brereton at their head.

Lally advanced northwards and entered the Black Town in Madras on 14 December 1758. The English had withdrawn before them. Later, Draper and Brereton attempted a sortie that resulted in some confused fighting. The French remained silent for three weeks and on 2 January 1759 started a cannonade, but they could not make a breach because the defence within the place was eminently successful. The English commander of Chinglepet Captain Achilles Preston joined with Major Caillaud and Yousuf Khan from Trichinopoly for a flank attack of the besieging French but could not achieve much. Under frequent alarms and because of the resolute defence of the fort, Lally's hope of success was steadily sinking. The British used frigates and transport ships to supply the garrison by sea. By 15 February 1759, the long-expected reinforcements from Bombay arrived with six Royal Navy vessels with 600 troops. The French were forced to lift the siege of Madras and retreated in two detachments, with Soupiere's battalion going to Conjeeveram and Lally's to Arcot.

April to June 1759 saw a lull in military activity. Lally returned to Pondicherry and sent a request to Mascarine (Mauritius) for the rapid return of D'Ache's squadron. The British, meanwhile, were keen to seize the moment and go on the offensive. Lawrence took Conjeeveram in April. By August 1759, D'Ache reappeared off the coast of India with seven companies and four regular navy ships of the line. His fleet was able to fight off nine British ships of the line in a battle on 10 September. They were also able to bring reinforcements, money, and supplies to Pondicherry, despite extremely heavy casualties.[85] He immediately announced his intention to return to the Mascarine. This declaration was received with extreme dismay by all in Pondicherry. Initially D'Ache was deaf to all their overtures. Later as a compromise, he disembarked 500 of the troops he was supposed to be taking back to France. On 1 October, he set sail again, never to return. Until now, Lally had mainly relied upon his troops and D'Ache's squadron for defeating the enemy. Neither had answered his expectations and he now turned to seek the help from the country's powers. Basalat Jung, a son of Nizam-ul-Mulk, was seeking an independent position for himself in the south. Lally decided to send de Bussy to bring the prince into the Carnatic. Realising how ill-supplied his proposed allies were with money, Basalat Jung decided the alliance was not worth cultivating by an impoverished and disadvantaged prince like himself.[86]

The English received important reinforcement in April 1759. Lieutenant-Colonel Eyre Coote commanding the 84th Regiment of Foot was assigned for service against the French. At the head of the united forces, he took the forts of Wandiwash and Carangoly on 19 November. Lally with the help of a body of Maratha horse sent by Morari Rao resolved to retake the lost forts. On 22 January 1760, the Battle of Wandiwash was fought. In numbers, there was no great disparity between the armies.[87] The English were completely victorious. This led immediately to the reduction of the territory that the French held in the province of Arcot. Pondicherry was now within measurable distance of being closely besieged by land and sea. Lally made a last effort by turning his attention to Hyder Ali of Mysore, but this did not give him any advantage. The blockade dragged on, lasting several months, and on 15 January 1761, Pondicherry surrendered at discretion.

The End of French Dominance: The Battles of Kondur (9 December 1758) and Machilipatnam (7 April 1759)

Marquis de Conflans lacked the talents and experience of de Bussy, and his difficulties began the moment he took over charge. At first, he had to deal with people to whom he was a stranger and who were strange to him. After that he had to meet the combined dangers of insurrection and invasion. Reports reached the Northern Sarkars that the main French army had been compelled to retreat from before the walls of Tanjore. Anandraz Gajapati, successor of Vijiyaram Rajii and rajah of Vijayanagaram, made the first move against the French. He marched upon and took possession of Visakhapatnam, imprisoned the French commandant, and hoisted the English flag. On hearing this, de Conflans marched against the rajah who made an urgent appeal to the chief of Bengal Presidency for assistance.

Robert Clive persuaded the Bengal Council to send an expeditionary force to the Deccan.[88] To most of the members of the Council, these schemes seemed rash and dangerous. Bengal was threatened by an invasion by Shahzadah, eldest son of the Mughal Alamgir II and the sentiment of the Murshidabad durbar under Mir Jafar was hostile. To deny the presidency of a large body of troops to support the revolt of a local chief seemed, in the eyes of the majority, to be a little short of madness. But with his experience in Madras, Clive thought differently. He knew that the weakening of the British force in Bengal would entail some risks, but the support offered by Anandraz was encouraging. Clive realised that the success of the expedition would transfer the valuable districts on the coast from the French to the English and the predominant influence they had at the court of the subedar of the Deccan can be nullified. Moreover, a diversion like this would prevent the French in the northern Sircars from aiding Lally in his designs; he was put in action against Madras.

Clive selected Lieutenant-Colonel Francis Forde (Ford, 1910)[89] to lead the company troops in this venture. Having first carried his point in Council, he handed over to him 470 Europeans, 1,900 native troops, six-pounders, and a small battering train. Forde sailed on the 12 and arrived in Visakhapatnam on 20 October 1758. An agreement was signed with Anandraz on 2 November 1758.[90] With his help, Forde defeated de Conflans in the Battle of Condor (Chandurti) on 9 December 1758.[91] Next, the small garrison fort of Rajahmundry was captured by the English and handed over to Ananda Gajapati. The Battle of Condor was a battle won solely by the genius and resolution of the English leader, Lieutenant-Colonel Forde.[92] It had very far-reaching effects. It established English supremacy in that region and enabled the English to separate the Sarkars from the Hyderabad State. Rajahmundry was of great strategic importance to the possessions in the East Coast. With its capture, the whole of the Northern Sarkar regions came under English control.

A new agreement was signed between the English and the rajah by which the territories that belonged to the French on either side of the river Godavari were to be equally divided between them. This treaty raised the status of the English considerably. From being mere auxiliaries of the rajah, they became his equal partners asserting equal rights on the Sarkars.[93] De Conflans and his troops had to retreat to the safety of Machilipatnam Fort. From there, he sent word to Salabat Jung to come to his aid in driving away the English. The Nizam Salabat Jung marched to the relief of the beleaguered garrison, but his progress was very slow. Forde, after laying siege to Masulipatam for more than a month, stormed the fortress in April 1759 after a bitter battle.

This remarkable success gained for England the districts that had constituted the most valuable possessions of France in Hindustan. On 14 May 1759, Salabat Jung signed a treaty conferring upon the English, as a free gift, the five districts constituting the province of Northern Sarkars—Ganjam, Visakhapatnam, Rajamahendri, Machhilipatanam, and Guntur.[94] It was also agreed that the Nizam should not entertain the French in his service. The English promised not to give protection or assist the enemies of Salabat Jung. Referring to the treaty, the Madras council wrote: "While he (Salabat Jung) continues in our interests, there can be little reason to apprehend that the French will be able to regain their Northward possessions".[95]

Final Submission: The Cession of the Northern Circars

Hostilities erupted again between Salabat Jung and the Marathas. In the battle of Udgir (3 January 1760), the Peshwa, Balaji Baji Rao, defeated Salabat Jung and in the following treaty he had to surrender Ahmednagar, Bijapur, Daulatabad, and Burhanpur—the four Mughal capitals of the Deccan. However, soon after the Treaty of Udgir, the Marathas suffered a crushing defeat in the Battle of Panipat (14 January 1761) at the hands of Ahmad Shah Abdali. Balaji Baji Rao died in 1761 and his death was followed by the appointment of his 16-year-old son, Madhav Rao, as the next Peshwa with his uncle, Raghunath Rao, as the regent. By this time, Nizam Ali, though holding the office of the diwan, had usurped the real power at Hyderabad. He kept Salabat Jung as a nominal ruler. The eclipse in the fortunes of the Marathas on the field of Panipat and the subsequent death of the Peshwa and the dissensions that ensued between Peshwa Madhav Rao and his uncle, Raghunath Rao, gave him the much-awaited opportunity.[96] He marched towards

Poona, at the head of a huge army, which caused alarm to the young Peshwa who appealed to the English East India Company for help. The English, in return, desired the Island of Salsette, which the Marathas were reluctant to cede. Nizam Ali proceeded with his march towards Poona and a battle took place at Shrigonda. At this time, Tara Bai, the chief partisan of Nizam Ali among the Marathas, died. A treaty was signed in January 1762, which resulted in the cessation of hostilities. In September 1763, Nizam Ali threw Salabat Jung into prison in Bidar Fort, got him murdered, and proclaimed himself as the Nizam. The East India Company preferred to take the side of the Nizam rather than the Marathas as had been the case in the previous wars between them. The English, comprehending the weak position of the Nizam, seemed to have realised as early as 1762 that he was their natural ally against the powerful Maratha State if they wanted to build up their political and commercial power in India.

The English were anxious to retain the Northern Sarkars at any cost. Their main anxiety was that these areas should not revert to the French. Both the Madras and Bombay governments impressed upon the Home Government the necessity of procuring a contiguous territory from Bengal to Madras. This would be possible only by the acquisition of the Sarkars and Orissa. The Court of Directors wrote, "Ceding their possessions in Orissa, which would join our Bengal Possessions to the Circars, and would afford the means of preventing any hostile attempts of any European enemy who might land in that part."[97]

Clive arrived in Madras about this time and the President of Fort St. George compelled him to obtain a grant for the Northern Sarkars from the Mughal Emperor, which was duly obtained by him in 1765. The Company refrained from publishing this information immediately so that it would not raise the wrath of the Nizam. However, the next year in 1766, when the Nizam was preoccupied with fighting Janoji Bhonslay, chief of Berar, the Madras government published the Sanads (a letter having the force of an edict or ordnance) and occupied the Northern Sarkars. The English Government deputed General Caillaud and General

Smith to negotiate with the Nizam and they concluded a treaty on 12 November 1766. By this treaty, the Sarkars of Rajahmundry, Mustafanagar (Kondapalli), Chicacole, Ellore, and Murtizanagar (Guntur), were given as a free gift to the English East India Company. Since Murtizanagar was given as a *jagir* in 1761 to Basalat Jung, the younger brother of the Nizam, it was decided that the Company should take possession of it either after the demise of Balasat Jung or in the event of the latter proving disloyal to the Nizam.[98]

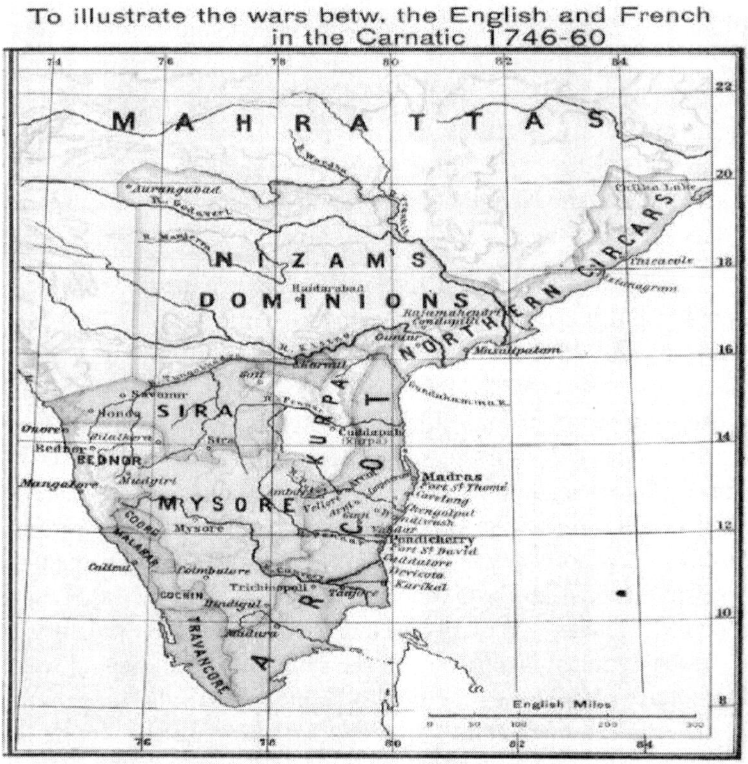

Source: Website of Prof. F.W. Pritchett, Dept. of South Asian Studies, Columbia University. Charles Joppen Open Source.

Map from "Historical Atlas of India," by Charles Joppen (London: Longmans, Green & Co)

The English, in spite of their dislike for the Nizam, were eager to win his friendship since they realised that he could be their ally against the Marathas whose power they dreaded. They readily responded to the proposition of peace from the Nizam and a treaty was concluded at Madras on 23 February 1768.[99] By this treaty, Muhammed Ali, the Nawab of Arcot, was recognised as the rightful ruler of the Carnatic and was released from all dependence from the subedar of the Deccan. The English were given the "Diwani rights" over the Carnatic Balaghat (The Province of Sira). The five Northern Sarkars of Rajahmundry, Mustafanagar (Kondapalli), Chicacole, Ellore, and Murtizanagar (Guntur) were ceded to the Company. The English as a gesture of goodwill agreed to take possession of the Murtizanagar (Guntur) Sarkar after the demise of Basalat Jung. The Nizam in his turn undertook to direct all the zamindars in the Sarkar to obey the English, henceforth, as their lawful masters. Thus, by the treaty of 1768, the Nizam had to give up all claims to the Carnatic and to surrender the Sarkars to the English.[100]

The English at this juncture were clearly conscious of their strength and were thinking in terms of being umpires in India between the various Indian powers which were struggling for control. Clive observed, "Take no open part with these Hindostan princes, but promote quarrelling to all eternity".[101] The Nizam was highly displeased with this agreement and tried to nullify it by entering into a fresh agreement with the Marathas and Hyder Ali against the English. The Bombay government was well aware of the developments. They knew his brother, Basalat Jung, was active in raising troops for Hyder and had started to employ the French troops. The Diwan, Ruccuun-ud-Daula, who helped the English was in the disfavour of Nizam Ali. At the same time, the English were also unhappy about the retention of Guntur by Basalat Jung. With the object of taking over the Guntur Sarkar, the Madras government opened negotiations with Basalat Jung in 1772, but the talks proved abortive, and the question was shelved for several years.

The problem of the Guntur Sarkar became more serious with the outbreak of hostilities between the French and the English in 1778 and the English were very anxious to secure it at any cost.

At the same time, Basalat Jung was facing multiple problems—he was being harassed by his brother, the Nizam, who saw in him a potential contender; Hyder Ali of Mysore was seizing his territory; and the Company wanted him to dismiss his French troops. Basalat Jung started negotiations regarding the Guntur Sarkar with the Madras government and an agreement was signed on 27 January 1779 by which it was agreed that the French would be dismissed, and Guntur would be leased for a specific rent. The English promised to defend his country and assist him with troops.

However, Basalat Jung struck this deal without any reference to the Nizam, his overlord. Adding insult to injury, after obtaining Guntur Sarkar in this manner, the Madras government leased it to the Nawab of Carnatic, Muhammad Ali, an inveterate enemy of the Nizam. When informed about this treaty, the Nizam was greatly enraged against the English. On account of their hostilities with Hyder Ali, the English needed the support and friendship of the Nizam. Warren Hastings, the Governor-General, assured the Nawab of the friendship and good faith of the Company.[102] The Supreme government of Bengal instructed the governor of Madras to restore the Guntur Sarkar to Basalat Jung. This firm action taken by Warren Hastings came at an opportune time. Deeply humiliated, the Nizam was planning an alliance with the Marathas and Hyder Ali against the English and to deprive them of their possessions in Bengal and in the Sarkars. The Nizam gave up his contemplated offensive against the English.

Basalat Jung died in the year 1782 and the Nizam ordered his officers to seize the Guntur Sarkar. The Company demanded the restoration of the Sarkar, as per the treaty of 1768. The Nizam forwarded several proposals which were not acceptable to the Court of Directors and the negotiations concerning the Sarkar were suspended. In the meantime, Warren Hastings left India and he was succeeded by Lord Cornwallis as the Governor-General of India. At the time of sending Lord Cornwallis to India, the Court of Directors had instructed him to take up the question of Guntur Sarkar. Realising that the prevailing conditions were unfavourable to bring up the issue, Lord Cornwallis put off the delicate business until next year when peace prevailed between the Courts of Versailles and London. Tipu was also not in a position to enter into hostilities as he was forced to conclude a treaty with the Marathas and the Nizam. Taking advantage of the interlude, he sent Captain Kennaway and Neil Edmonton to the Nizam's court in July 1788 to demand the cession of the Guntur Sarkar.[103] To make sure that his demand had sufficient force behind it, Lord Cornwallis made necessary military preparations.

Open Source: Painting by Thomas Daniel.

Sir Charles Warren Malet Concluding Treaty in 1790 in Durbar with the Peshwa of the Maratha Empire

Of all his enemies, the Nizam dreaded the Marathas most. The Marathas were the strongest force on the subcontinent at that time. However, it was possible for the Nizam to "buy them off" by making concessions over tax issues. When the delegation of Kennaway reached Hyderabad, the Nizam was in fact trying to reach an agreement with the French at Pondicherry by which he was willing to hand over Guntur to them in return for a guarantee of protection against the British and Tipu. He was very concerned of the newest threat from the south—the rising power of Mysore though he did send an envoy to Tipu proposing an alliance between the two states. However, when negotiations with the sultan broke down and the French failed to give him the guarantee he needed, Nizam Ali accepted Tipu was a much greater problem. Thus, a formal treaty of alliance was signed between the Nizam, the Peshwa, and the Company in 1790. This "Tripartite Agreement" was finally decided upon, permanently changing the face of south Indian politics.

NOTES

1. Thompson, Edward. (1943). *The Making of the Indian Princes-* Oxford University Press. London. p1 (quoted from G B W Forrest, Selections from the State Papers of the Governors-General of India, Warren Hastings, ii.58)
2. Weatherford, Jack. (2004). *Genghis Khan and the making of the Modern World.* Three Rivers Press. New. York. pp 251, 252.
3. Kulke, H. & Rothermund, D. (2004). *op.cit.* p. 227.
4. *Ibid,* p. 227.
5. Khan, Yousuf Hussain (1936). *Nizamu'l-Mulk Asaf Jahl. Founder of the Haiderabad State.* Basel Mission Press. Mangalore.*p235.* Archives. org.>details>in.ernet.dil.2015.63155
6. Schmidt, K. J. (1995). *An Atlas and Survey of South Asian History.* Routledge, New York. p. 24.
7. Wibulslip, Pimmanus. (2012) *"I am Nawab of Arcot"- Reconsidering political history of the late 18th century Kingdom of Arcot through the eye of Nawab Muhammed Ali Wallajah.(r. 1749-1795).* Openaccess. leidenuniv.nl>bitstream>handle> I am Nawab of Arcot.pdf p5.
8. Wibulslip, Pimmanus *op.cit:* 'When in 1744, Nizam-ul-Mulk appointed Anwaruddin Khan of the Wallajah family, conflict arose between the Navayats and the Wallajahs. The Navayat family was known as an elite group of Deccani trading and service people. The most powerful members of this group were those who held high posts under the sultans of Bijapur and other Deccani Muslim sultanates. When these domains came under Mughal rule at the end of the 17th Century, many leading Deccanis were able to seek advancement within the imperial system.' p. 25.
9. Ramaswami, N. S. (1984). *Political history of Carnatic under the Nawabs.* Abhinav Publications. New Delhi, p. 65-67.

10. (i) Muthiah. I. S. (2008). *A 400-year record of the first city of Madras- The Land, The People & Their Governance.* Palaniyappa Brothers. Chennai, p. 122.

    (ii) Records of Fort St. George. Diary and consultation book. Madras.1931. Duke University Libraries. Records of Fort. St George. (Internet Archives)- 'The President acquaints the Board that he had yesterday received an Account from Arcot: That on the 23d. Instant the Son of Our late Nabob Subeder Ally Cawn, named Saib Judda, was murdered there .... at the instigation of Mortas Ally Cawn, the same person who had killed the father in October 1742....' p. 136.

11. 'War of Austrian Succession' is considered as the first real world war. It is a loosely related and indecisive series of struggles fought between two loose and frequently changing alliances involving the leading European states. Here Austria, Great Britain and the United Provinces collaborated against Prussia, Spain, and France. Though fought mainly in central Europe, it also extended overseas to the West Indies, North America, and the Indian subcontinent.

    The three wars between the English and the French, which were fought in India in a span of twenty years between 1744 -1763 are known as the Carnatic Wars.

12. Parker, Geoffrey. (1991). *Europe and the wider world, 1500-1750: The Military balance in The Political Economy of Merchant Empires* Ed. J D Tracy. Cambridge University Press : a small group of Westerners caused the collapse of the mighty Inca and Aztec empires, which had ruled over nearly one tenth of the world's population: Pizarro and his Spanish companions could bring down the Incas in the 1530s with 168 men and 67 horses, p. 176.

13. Parker, G. *op cit.* The total manpower available for the army of the emperor Akbar in the 1590s was estimated at 342,696 cavalry and 4,039,097 infantry- many of them armed with muskets, p. 176.

14. Parker, G. Ed. (1995). *The Cambridge Illustrated History of warfare, The Triumph of the West,* p. 179.

15. Love, H. D. (1913). *Indian Records Series. Vestiges of Old Madras. 1640-1800.*Vol. II, London. 'From Nabob Anwaradean Cawn Bahaudur, Subah at Arcot, July 14th, 1745. Asian Education Service. *1996. Archives.org,* p. 342.

16. Schmidt, Karl J. (2015). *An Atlas and Survey of South Asian History,* Routledge, Oxon. p. 24.

17. Dodwell, Henry. (1989). *Clive and Dupleix, The Beginning of the Empire.* 'Besides three Company's ships taken with rich cargoes from China, Barnett also captured the French Manila ship with 400,000 dollars

aboard, and other vessels returning from Surat, Basra, and Mokha'. Asia Educational Services, p. 8.

18. Bertrand-Francois Mahe, count de la Bourdonnais (1699-1753):French naval commander who took part in the capture of Mahe in 1726. His blockade of Madras by sea enabled the French to capture the port in 1746.
19. Love, H. D. (1913). *Indian Records Series. Vestiges of Old Madras. 1640-1800.*Vol. II, London. 'From Nabob Anwaradean Cawn Bahaudur, Subah at Arcot, July 14th, 1745.Asian Education Service. *1996. Archives.org,* p. 384.
20. Key, John (1993).'*The Honourable Company- A history of the East India Company'*. Harper Collins Publishers: "The superiority of the European arms came as a revelation comparable with the first discovery of a sea route to the East. ... Warfare in India was still a sport; in Europe it had become a science. Officers read Vauban's Memoires and studied the Regulations of the Prussian infantry. Discipline made esprit a corporate responsibility; drill imparted to tactics the irresistible precision of a well-oiled machine", p. 281.
21. Dodwell Henry, *op cit.* p. 20. 'In the 17th century a third of the infantry were armed with pikes, since then every man had been armed with musket and bayonet. By this change alone infantry had become more effective by over a third. The lightest clumsy artillery pieces fired perhaps 15 rounds to the hour. They have been replaced by fieldpieces, probably short 4 –pounders loaded with grape, which could fire nearly as many charges to the minute. Consequently, the minimum unit which could act with success against large bodies of horse had been enormously reduced. The Mughal horse could never charge home against steady infantry. By 1746, the troops which the French and English companies could maintain had become capable of taking the offensive, without being overwhelmed by numbers. This was the truth demonstrated by a Tour's skirmish before Madras and by Paradis' victory at the Adayar'.
22. Parker, Geoffrey. (1991). *Europe and the Wider World, 1500-1700: The Military Balance; in the Political Economy of Merchant Empires, State Power and World Trade 1350-1750.* Edited by James D Tracy, Cambridge University Press, p. 181.
23. Dodwell, Henry. (1989). *Clive and Dupleix-The Beginning of the Empire.* AES, New Delhi, p. 17.
24. Dodwell, H.(1929). *The Cambridge History of India,* Volume V. p. 125. archive.org

25. Britain and France dictated the Treaty *of Aix-la-Chapelle in 1748.* France secured the agreement by promising to evacuate both the Austrian Netherlands and the small portion of United Provinces of Netherlands it occupied. They also agreed to withdraw from the great trading post of Madras in India, which had been captured from the British in return for the fortress of Louisburg on Isle Royale (Cape Breton Island) which New England militiamen had taken possession in 1745.

    'England returned the "Dunkirk of the West" by the Treaty *of Aix-la-Chapelle in* 1748. Since that time, historians have been divided among themselves in assigning motives for the decision of the British ministry. In fact, their evaluations 'England returned the "Dunkirk of the West" by the terms of Treaty *of Aix-la-Chapelle*. Since that time, historians have been divided among themselves in assigning motives for the decision of the British ministry. In fact, their evaluations exhibit a confusing discordance': Sosin M. J. (1957). Louisburg and the Peace of Aix-la-Chapelle, 1748. *The William and Mary Quarterly.* 14(4). pp. 516-535.

    Francis Parkman, American historian, refers to the Tory writer Tobias Smollett in attributing the cession of Cape Briton island to an exchange for the East India port at Madras: 'the British ministers gave up the important island of Cape Briton in exchange for a petty factory in the East Indies (Madras)'. Parkman, F. (1893). France and England in North. America, A series of historical narratives. Little, Brown and Company, Boston, p. 256.

    Colonel John Biddulph in book, *Dupleix* gives the following reason: The Highland Rising that occurred during the war (Battle of Culloden) had forced the English ministers to withdraw their troops from the Austrian Netherlands which had fallen into the hands of the French. The retention of the Low Countries by France would have constituted a perpetual menace for England and their surrender to Austria was the real equivalent for the restoration of Breton to France. (Biddulph, Colonel John. (1910). *Dupleix.* F V White & Co Ltd. London WC. p. 82)

    According to Jonathan Dull, for the French, they were (i) to preserve the rich sugar-producing Caribbean colonies such as Martinique, Guadeloupe and St. Domingue and (ii) to maintain Isle Royale with it the great cod fisheries off Newfoundland and in the Gulf of St. Lawrence. But, here more than the fish its importance was strategical: As the navy could not afford to keep ships at sea during peace time, it was unable to train its own sailors. Instead it conscripted them from the French merchant and fishing fleets during war time. These fisheries with their harsh conditions were considered the best place to train seamen; perhaps they accounted for a quarter of France's 40,000 to 60,000 sailors and trained 2,000 new sailors a year. Without both the fisheries and its Caribbean colonies, France could not hope to construct a navy capable of fighting the British. (Jonathan R Dull. *The French Navy and the Seven Years War,* p. 14)

26. Biddulph, Colonel John. (1910). *Dupleix*. F V White & Co ltd. London. p. 85.
27. Ramaswami, *op cit.,* 101.
28. Regani, Sarojini. (1988). *Nizam-British relations 1724-1857*. Concept Publications, New Delhi, p. 18.
29. Regani, S. *op.cit.,* p. 23: Chanda Sahib, the son-in-law of Nawab Dost Ali Khan, was taken prisoner by the Marathas in 1741, during the latter's invasion of Trichinopoly and was confined at Satara. After becoming governor of Pondicherry, Dupleix established cordial relations with his family who had been sent there when Trichinopoly was besieged by the Marathas. From Chanda Sahib's letters Dupleix formed a shrewd estimate of his political ability and daring nature. Hence Dupleix did not hesitate to interfere on his behalf in the affairs of the Carnatic, which he dreamt of making a French sphere of influence. He raised the necessary ransom of 3 lakh rupees for his release.
30. Regani, S. *ibid,* p. 24.
31. Regani, S. *ibid,* p. 25.
32. Parker, G. (1991). *op.cit.,* p. 182.
33. The loss of Madras in the Battle of Adayar (Oct.1746) had come as a profound shock to the Directors of the English East India Company in London and they immediately initiated several corrective measures.

    First, they persuaded the government to put together 'that secret expedition'. The influence wielded by the East India Company in London was such that an expedition led by Rear Admiral Edward Boscawen, who was acting on instructions not from the Admiralty but from the Company, was sent to the East Indies. The unorthodox nature of his effective subordination to the Company was reflected in his surely unique title of Admiral, General and Commander-in-Chief of all the forces in the East Indies. This was the only instance, investing a naval officer with double command, (except the Earl of Peterborough) of any officer having received such a command from the reign of Charles the Second. On 29th July 1748, he arrived at Fort. St David in command of the greatest marine force (it consisted of more than 30 ships, none of which were of less than 500 tons burden) belonging to any one European nation that had then ever been seen in the East

Indies and the principal object was capture of Pondicherry. (The East India Military Calendar, Containing the Services of General and Field Officers of the Indian Army. Vol. II Naval & Military Press, p. 37)

Second, for their own part the East India Company enlisted about 150 new recruits and hired a Regular Army officer to command them. Armed with the appointment of Major and Garrison Commander of Madras, Stringer Lawrence arrived in India in January 1748. With the 150 recruits he brought out from England he added surviving Madras Europeans, 300 Eurasians and a contingent brought from Bombay. The necessary additional officers were found among departing Independent companies and from young writers and other company officers, whereby Robert Clive gained his first military commission. "Lawrence undertook radical reorganisation of the Company's local troops, replacing the unruly gangs of peons with properly disciplined companies of sepoys, armed and disciplined in the European manner." Reid, Stuart. (2017) *The Battle of Plassey 1757.The Victory that Won an Empire,* Frontline Books.

Stringer Lawrence was born in Hereford 1697 (Clive was a descendent of the local squirearchy of the same place) and obtained his commission as an ensign in Clayton's 14th Foot in 1727 at the age of 30. He advanced to lieutenancy in 1736 and became captain-lieutenant in 1745. He served in that rank at the Battle of Culloden in the following year. The chance for further promotion at his age of 50 was almost non-existent. Without any financial backing to purchase his subsequent promotion he had to rely entirely upon seniority. Moreover, the fact that he got his first commission when he was 30 years old means that he started his career in the ranks. The Company's service therefore was much more attractive.

Battle of Culloden was fought by two opposing armies- on the Hanoverian side (the government or Royal army) led by Duke of Cumberland, the youngest son of King George II, and on the other the Jacobite or Highland Army led by Prince Charles Edward Stuart or Bonnie Prince Charles. It was one of the battles in the contemporary War of Austrian Succession. Most of the senior officers in the Duke of Cumberland's army (also known by the sobriquet 'Butcher Cumberland' for his harsh suppression of the Jacobite rebellion of 1745) came from English or Irish backgrounds or were lowland Scots and after Culloden many of them went on to enjoy solid and in some cases spectacular careers in the British Army because of the patronage of their commanding general. They were Cumberland's men, and they quickly became an identifiable military grouping within the British army when they served in the European, North American, and Indian theatres of Military operations. In doing so, they showed that they had learned the lessons of the Jacobite campaign and remembered them in their operations. At Cumberland's insistence the lines of government infantry men had been instructed in new drills to counter the ferocious charge of claymore-wielding clansmen when they clashed at Culloden, but it was the unrelenting volleys of rapid, accurate, sustained, and disciplined musket fire from the infantrymen that won the day. The officers from Cumberland's Army to forge a successful military career in India were Stringer Lawrence, William Draper, John Cillaud, and Eyre Coote. (Royale, Trevor. (2016) *Culloden: Scotland's Last Battle and the Forging of the British Empire;* Little Brown London. Preface.)

Thus, the commissioning of Stringer Lawrence of 'Battle of Culloden fame' by the East India Company was the result of extensive deliberation and not a random selection.

34. Regani, Sarojini. (1988). *Nizam-British Relations, 1724- 1857.* Concept Publishing Company, New Delhi. Details in pages 18-44.
35. In the Mansabdari system of Akbar, the highest-ranking person was with 7000 horses and horseman and could attend court of the Emperor.
36. Regani, Sarojini. *Nizam-British Relations, 1724-1857.* Concept Publishing Company, New Delhi-110059, 1988, p. 48.
37. Regani, Sarojini. Quoting Henry Dodwell - *Calendar of the Madras Despatches 1744-55.((Despatches from Thomas Saunders, etc. To the Company. Fort. St. David. Feb. 7, 1751. Public Despatches to England,* Vol. 18, pp. 49-83) p. 121.
38. Regani, Sarojini, 50.
39. *Ibid,* 52.
40. Dodwell, Henry. (1989). *Clive and Dupleix The beginning of Empire.* Asia Educational Services. p. 87.
41. Malleson, G.B. Colonel (1885). *The decisive battles of India from 1746 to 1849 inclusive.* W H Allen Co London. Archives.org. pp. 18-19.
42. Ramaswami, 146.
43. The metamorphosis of Robert Clive from an inexperienced young writer to the post of Governor of Presidency of Fort William and Commander-in-Chief of Indian Army had its beginning in the geo-political arena Carnatic. He was appointed as a Writer in the East India Company and reached Madras in 1744. In the Battle of Madras in September 1746, a French force attacked and captured the City of Madras from the British garrison. The Governor and the council were taken as prisoners to Pondicherry and the rest of the English were made to give their parole that they would not bear arms against the French.

Many refused to give their parole and escaped to Fort St David, Clive was among them who volunteered for Military service.

Military training: Impressed by the 'martial disposition' he displayed in these actions Governor Hinde gave Clive an ensign's commission. He had his baptism of fire when the French attempted to capture Fort St David in December 1746. In January 1748 arrived Major Stringer Lawrence who became Clive's military father and mentor. During the months following his arrival there were two further French attempts on Fort St David. 'In defeating the second, a night attack on the Black Town of Cuddalore, Lawrence taught Clive "the ruse of ostentatiously withdrawing one's troops and cannon by day, so as to make the place seem undefended and then returning them after dark." (*Bence-Jones, 24*)

Psychological confidence: The former ruler of Tanjore who had been driven out in 1739, wanted to regain his kingdom and the English agreed to send him troops in return for a grant of Devikottai, a fort in the mouth of River Coleroon (Northern bifurcation of Kaveri river). The first Tanjore expedition under Captain James Cope in March 1749 was a debacle. To redeem this failure, the whole of the Company's forces at Fort St David under command of Stringer Lawrence were shipped to the mouth of the Coleroon and landed together with heavy artillery on an island close to Devikottai. Clive was in charge of a platoon. Lawrence then led his whole army against the fort on which the enemy quickly abandoned it. When, from the ramparts of the fort, Clive saw the Tanjore army of about 20,000 retreating across the plain, it was impressed upon his mind how easily a small but determined European force could put an Indian host to flight. (*Bence Jones, 31*)

Understanding Natives: 'The job of Clive as a commissary was not a sinecure. It took great organising powers to keep a moving army supplied with food and forage. He had to obtain cattle and sheep, together with rice, ghee, and curry-stuffs for the sepoys; he had to find oxen, camels, and elephants to carry guns and stores over rough country and across many rivers. He had to keep peace among the camp-followers and negotiate ad-hoc loans from Indian merchants with which to pay troops. Clive profited from his work as Commissary not just in terms of cash but in knowledge and experience—how to deal with Indians of different types and castes and win their trust. From leading drivers and coolies, he learned how to lead Indian troops into battle'. (Bence Jones, 37)

Background: Clives are country gentry from Shropshire. Robert Clive was born in 1725.The stereotype of Clive is that of an empire builder, but he was also a British politician. 'Clive's life was marked by two climactic victories. One was on the confused battlefield of Plassey in Bengal. The other was on the scarcely less confused and darkling field of the floor of the Westminster House of Commons shortly before his death, and in his absence'. Lenman, B. & Lawson, P. (1983). *Robert Clive- 'The Black Jagir' and British Politics*. The Historical Journal. Vol. 26. Issue 4. Cambridge University Press, p. 803.

According to Mark Bence-Jones, author of Clive of India, 'In trying to learn more about him, I discovered why Clive was the most elusive of the great Englishmen of the eighteenth century- Preface. Dr Gideon Polya, in his book, 'Jane Austin and the Black Hole of British History', (1998) calls this process 'Austenizing', which involves both passive and active distortion of reality. (p. 75) !!

44. Bence-Jones, Mark. (1974). *Clive of India,* Constable. London, p. 37.
45. Bence-Jones, Mark. Clive of India. *op.cit.,* p. 40.
46. *ibid,* p. 42. "*When nearly every horseman had his family and all his possessions with him, when tents, horses, bullocks, camels and elephants were jumbled together in what was more like 'a great confused town than a body of military men encamped', a determined attack by night could cause instant chaos*".
47. Malcolm, Sir John. (1836). *The Life of Robert, Lord Clive: collected from the family papers communicated by the Earl of Powis.* Bibliolife. London, p. 79.
48. Bence –Jones. *op.cit.,* p. 48.
49. Spear, Percival. (1975). Master of Bengal-Clive and his India. Thames and Hudson Ltd., London, p. 51.
50. Mark, Bence-Jones. *op.cit.,* p. 57.
51. Malleson, G. B. The Decisive Battles of India. *op.cit.,* p. 31.
52. One of the younger commanders in the Mysore army was Hyder Ali who lived to displace the Mysore Rajahs and was to threaten the extinction of English power in India. Mark Bence-Jones, *op.cit.,* p. 314.
53. Regani, Sarojini. *op.cit,* p. 6.
54. Malleson, *op.cit,* p. 74. "North of the river and south of the Vindhyan the large territory belonged to the Subhadar of the Deccan, covering almost the entire northern part of the peninsula bounded on the west by the Western Ghats and on the east only by the sea. This important territory was under French influence, being maintained by the presence at Haidarabad of a considerable body of French troops commanded by the Marquis de Bussy. The French held the zamindari rights of the provinces of an area about 17,000 geographical miles

and yielded an annual revenue of 400,000 pounds sterling. (Elur, Srikakulam, Kondapalli, Murtizanagar, towns Ganjam, Vijiyanagaram, Visakhapatnam, Machhilipatanam)

55. McLynn, Frank. 2004. *1759-The Year Britain became master of the World*. Jonathen Cape. London: "...By then the British were fully alerted to the threat to their position posed by Dupleix. From the autumn of 1750, the British East India Company had Dupleix firmly in its sights. Eager to avoid a general war, Louis XV placated the British by a series of conferences in London 1753-54. The end result was a treaty in December 1754 in which the French effectively repudiated the work of Dupleix''. p. 170.

    Keay, John. (1991). *The Honourable Company - The history of the East India Company,* Harper Collins Publishers, 293: "But, at this point the British cabinet stepped in.... negotiations were already in progress... In the course of them the French seemed to have bowed to the demand that Dupleix be recalled. To the Newcastle ministry this seemed a much better solution than having their hands tied by a non-aggression pact which could only favour the French in that it gave them a free hand in Hyderabad and immunity from the attentions of the usually superior British navy", p. 293.

56. Dodwell, H. H. (1929). *The Cambridge history of the British Empire. Vol. IV, British India 1497-1858.* Cambridge. p. 132.
57. Ramaswami, *op.cit.,* 182.
58. Malleson Col. G B, (1899). *Rulers of India. Dupleix and struggle for India by the European Nations*. Oxford 1899.Onlinebooks.library.upenn.edu>book> lookupname. p. 153.
59. *Ibid,* 159.
60. Regani. *op. cit.* p. 83.
61. *Ibid,* 85.
62. Regani. *op.cit.* p. 85, quoting *Orme. A history of the Military Transactions of the British nation in Indostan,* Vol. 1.
63. Regani. *op.cit.,* p. 87.
64. Bruce Lenman; Philip Lawson. (1983). *Robert Clive-The 'Black Jagir' and British Politics.* The Historical Journal, 26,4, p. 805.
65. Roach, John. (1958). *The 39th Regiment of Foot and the East India Company, 1754-1757.* Bulletin of the John Rylands Library.41 (1):102-138. www.manchester.ac.uk/library. pp. 106-107: 'Bagshawe wrote that the revenues of the French acquisitions were fourteen times as much as those of the English, apart from districts which the French had obtained in Golconda. The same note appears over and over again in

the Madras records, particularly in regard to "Golconda", the territories of the Subhadar of the Deccan to the north.'

66. Spear, Percival. (1975). *Master of Bengal- Clive and his India.* Book Club Edition, Thames and Hudson Ltd., London, p. 62.
67. Sen, Surendra Nath. (1928).*The Military System of the Marathas, Orient Longman,* Bombay, pp.169-208.
68. Philips, C. (1940). *The secret committee of the East India Company. Bulletin of the School of Oriental Studies, University of London, 10(2),* Retrieved June 24, 2021 from http://www.jstor.org/stabl/608393: From the beginning of the Company, its executive committee in London consisted of an unwieldy number of twenty-four members. To ensure the safety of the Company's ships and issue secret political orders a smaller trustworthy committee became inevitable. The article gives details of the origin and functions of the Secret Committee over the centuries of its existence, pp. 299-315.
69. Beatson, Robert. (1790). *Naval and Military Memories- Great Britain. From the year 1727, to the present time. Vol. II.* London. Archives. Com. '*His* fleet consisted of the Kent of 70, the Eagle of 60, Salisbury and Bristol of 50 each, Bridge-water of 24, and Kingfisher sloop of 15 guns, sailed from England in February 1754.The Eagle and Bristol got damaged in a storm off the coast of Ireland; therefore, Cumberland of 56 and Tyger of 50 guns were ordered to India. p. 7.
70. H. M's 39th Foot with a complement of about 900 soldiers under Lieutenant Colonel Aldercron, the first King's Regiment to land in India.
71. Regani, *op.cit.,* 89.
72. Hatalkar, V. G. (1958). 'Relations *between the French and the Marathas. (1668-1815).* University of Bombay. *'Tulaji* Angria not only refused to recognize the authority of the Peshwa but had openly defied him by carrying depredations in the territory under his jurisdiction. He controlled a section of the Konkan seaboard (from Bankot to Vijaydurg) in the south. Murarrao Ghorpade, the ruler of Gootti, found a powerful ally in Tulaji. He had always tried to be independent of the Peshwa and envisaged an offensive alliance with all the Maratha chiefs who were jealous of the growing influence of the Peshwa who was a Brahmin. As usual, Tarabai, the inveterate enemy of the Peshwa, promised to lend her powerful support to the projected league. The Peshwa whose spy system was quite efficient was well-posted with the designs of Murarrao.' p. 132.
73. Rodger, N. A. (2004). *The Command of the Ocean. A Naval History of Britain 1649-1815.* Penguin Books, p. 274:'This succeeded, where

all previous assaults had failed, because Watson had adequate charts, surveyed especially for the operation, which allowed him to work his big ships through the shoals and alongside Angria's fortifications. This operational chart-making was to be one of the keys to British success in amphibious operations all over the world.' *(The extensive and in-depth study and utilisation of science and state of art technology of the period is seldom highlighted)*

74. Sen, S. N. (2007).*Textbook of Indian History and Culture.* Macmillan India Ltd.:Professor Sen makes this extremely significant observation: "By seeking foreign assistance against a fellow Maratha, the Peshwa had set a bad example for the other Maratha chiefs. Raghunathrao's appeal to Bombay was not long in coming. The Marathas remained indifferent when Siraj-ud-Daula succumbed to British pressure at Plassey. Even when the British quietly removed their nominee, Mir Jafar, and began consolidating their power in Bengal it caused no concern either at Nagpur or at Pune. The Marathas were then engaged against the Nizam in the south and against Ahmad Shah Abdali in the north. Unaware of the changing pattern of political power in India as a whole, the Peshwa in 1758 asked for British help for the conquest of Janjira and Surat." p. 196.
75. Polya, Dr G.M. (1998). *Jane Austin and the Black Hole of British History: Colonial rapacity, holocaust denial and the crisis in biological sustainability.* Publisher. G M Polya. Dr Polya gives a factual and thorough analysis of the background and impact of this fateful episode in Indian History, pp. 75-87.
76. Malleson, G. B. The decisive battles of India. *op cit.* p. 68.
77. I.O.R. Home Miscellaneous Series, Vol. 809, f.364 et seq. 30th Decr. 1758. British Library. London: In his first letter to Laurence Sulivan, Chairman of the East India Company, Robert Clive wrote: '...The opportunities afforded me by the last revolution have given me a just knowledge of the subject I am writing upon, experience not conjuncture, or the report of others, has made me well acquainted with the genius of the people, and nature of the country, and I can assert with some degree of confidence, that the rich and flourishing kingdom may be totally subdued by so small a force as 2000 Europeans, and the possession thereof maintained and confirmed by the Great Mogul upon paying the sum of 50 lakh per annum, paid by former Subaha. The Moors, as well as Gentoos, are indolent, luxurious, ignorant, and cowardly, beyond all conception, the country itself is full of great and navigable Rivers, is very woody, enclosed by mountains with narrow passes, in short everything conspires to render Infantry formidable, and Cavalry in which the Chief strength of Indostan consists) a mere

bugbear. The Soldiers, if they deserve that name, have not the least attachment to their Prince, he can only expect Service from them who pays them best, but it is matter of great indifference to them whom they serve and I am fully persuaded that after the battle of Placis I could have appropriated the whole Country to the Company and preserved it afterwards with as much ease as Meer Jaffier the present Subah now does, through the terror of the English arms and their influences.'

Clive wrote another letter to the 1st Earl of Chatham, (The Right Hon. William Pitt, one of His Majesty's Principal Secretaries of State) eight days after his letter to Laurence Sulivan, Chairman EIC. (Calcutta, January, 7, 1759.)

"The reigning Subah, whom the victory at Plassey invested with the sovereignty of these provinces, still, it is true, retains his attachment to us, and probably, while he has no other support, will continue to do so; but Mussulmans are so little influenced by gratitude, that should he ever think it in his interest to break with us, the obligations he owes with us would prove no restraint: and this is very evident from him having very lately removed his prime minister, and cut off two or three of his principal officers, all attached to our interest, and who had a share in his elevation. Moreover, he is advanced in years; and his son is so cruel and worthless a young fellow, and apparently an enemy to the English, that it will be almost useless trusting him with succession. So small a body as two thousand Europeans will secure us against any apprehensions from either the one or the other, and in case of their daring to be troublesome, enable the Company to take the sovereignty upon themselves.......I flatter myself I have made it pretty clear to you, that there will be little or no difficulty in obtaining the absolute possession of these rich kingdoms; and that with the mogul's own consent, on condition of paying him less than a fifth of the revenues thereof. Now, I leave you to judge, whether an income yearly of upwards of two million sterling, with the possession of three provinces abounding in the most valuable productions of nature and of art, be an object deserving the public attention; and whether it be worth the nation's while to take the proper measures to secure such an acquisition - an acquisition which, under the management of so able and disinterested a minister, would prove a source of immense wealth to the kingdom, and might in time be appropriated in part as a fund towards the heavy load of debt under which we at present labour."

78. Thomas Arthur, Comte de Lally, baron de Tollendal (13 January 1702 – 9 May 1766) was a French general of Irish Jacobite ancestry.

79. Malleson, Col. G B. *Rulers of India- Dupleix and the struggle for India by the European Nations. Oxford. 1899.* Archives.vog>details-in-enet-dil-2015-77019 p168.

80. 'La Re'giment de Lally' belonged to the Irish Brigade which is an infantry brigade in the French army of Ancient Regime. These regiments were made up of Irish Jacobite exiles. Breaking the Treaty of Limerick, of 1691, the English stripped the Irish Catholics of their land, prosecuted them for their religion and removed every right of citizenship from them. On this note of dishonour and betrayal began the saga of "The Flight of the Wild Geese" and for the next hundred years the French army would include an Irish Brigade. In the paperwork of the ships, the recruits would be listed as "Wild Geese", thus the origin of the name. The fierce and vehement slandering and defaming of Lally by the English may have a lot to do with his Irishness!! 'But, the Irishman, pig-headed as ever, would not listen'. Mc Lynn, Frank. (2004). '*1759- The year Britain became master of the world*'. Jonathen Cape. p. 181.

81. *(i)* Robson, Martin. (2016). *A History of the Royal Navy-The Seven Years War,* p. 78; give details of battle manoeuvres.

    (ii) Rodger, N. A. M. (2004). *'The Command of the Ocean- A Naval History of Britain 1649-1815'.* Penguin Books. Great Britain: The author gives details of the practical problems in the fighting on the Coromondel Coast of Southern India. "Command of the sea during the trading season, April to September, made it possible to trade, blockade and sustain military operations along the coast. To gain it the two admirals fought on 29th April off Cuddalore and 3 August of Nagapatam, p. 275.

82. Mc Lynn, Frank, *op.cit.,* p. 175.

83. *Ibid.,* p. 186. 'The situation had worsened since Clive's capture of Chandranagore in 1757 cut the regular supply of wheat and rice from Bengal ....'

84. McGilvary, George. (2006). '*Guardian of the East India Company- The Life of Laurence Sulivan.*' Tauris Academic Studies London. Laurence Sulivan, Director, Deputy Chairman and then Chairman of EIC, based in London, played a pivotal role during this period. He appreciated that he was in an age of compromise where the views of the British Government ought to harmonize with the Company's commercial interests. 'From India House he took steps to guard Madras by having the defences in the settlement strengthened and military instructions were forwarded. He was in close liaison with the ministry over naval movements; and made skilful use of the Company's Secret Committee'. p. 44.

85. Dull, Jonathan. (2005). *The French Navy and the Seven Years' War.* University of Nebraska Press. Lincoln & London, p. 141.
86. Wylly, Col. H.C (1922). *The life of Lieutenant. General Sir Eyre Coote.* Compiled by Col. H C Wylly. Oxford. Archive.org> stream. pp. 59-78.
87. Cust, Sir. Edward. (1862). *'Annals of the wars of the Eighteenth-Century, compiled from the most Authentic Histories of the Period'.* Vol. III. London 1862. "The French had 300 European cavalry, 2250 European Infantry, 1300 sepoys, and 3000 Mahrattas, with 16 light pieces of artillery. The English 80 European horse, and 250 natives, with 1900 European infantry, 2100 sepoys and 26 pieces of artillery". p. 33.
88. Gleig, G. R. (1848). *The Life of Robert, first lord Clive.* London J Murray. Archive.org. p. 123.

    Clive prophesied: 'The greatest parts of the troops belonging to this establishment are now employed in an expedition against the French in the Deccan; and, by the account lately received from thence, I have great hopes we shall succeeding extirpating them from the province of Golconda, where they have reigned lords paramount so long, and from whence they have drawn their principal resources during the troubles upon the coast. Notwithstanding the extraordinary efforts made by the French in sending out M Lally with a considerable force last year, I am confident, before the end of this, they will be near their last gasp in the Carnatic, unless some very unforeseen event interposes in their favour. *The superiority of our squadron, and the plenty of money and supplies of all kinds which our friends on the coast will be furnished with from this province.* while the enemy are in total want of everything, without any means if any redress, are such advantages as, if properly attended to, cannot fail of wholly affecting their ruin in that as well as in every part of India.'
89. Ford, Col Lionel. (1910). *Lord Clive's Right-Hand Man, A memoir of Colonel Francis Forde.* London James Nisbet & Co. Ltd - Bibliolife. Francis Forde arrived in India in September 1754 as a captain in H M's 39th Foot, the first King's Regiment in India. He was promoted as a Major in 1755. At the invitation of Clive, he resigned his King's Commission to take the post of second in Command of the East India Company's troops in Bengal.
90. Regani. Op cit. 116. 'According to the agreement the revenues of the areas that were not seaports or were not situated at the mouth of navigable rivers were to be enjoyed by the Rajah and the revenues of the seaports and those situated at the mouth of navigable rivers were to be enjoyed by the EEIC. This bold move aimed at the acquisition

of all strategic territories in the Sarkars, leaving to the Rajah only the name of being supreme in the Sarkars.'

91. Malleson, G. B. (1885). For details see: *The Decisive Battles of India. From 1746-1849 inclusive. London.* W H Allen & Co. 1885. pp. 79-87. Archives.org>details> decisivebattleso00malluoft.
92. *Ibid.*, p. 87.
93. Regani. *op cit.*, p. 118.
94. Regani. *op cit.*, p. 119.
95. Regani. *op cit.*, p. 120. quoting Forrest -Bengal and Madras papers Vol. III, 1757-85.
96. Regani. *op cit.*, 121.
97. Regani. *op cit.*, 130.
98. Regani. *op cit.*, 131.
99. Regani *op.cit.*, 135.
100. *Ibid.*, 135. The annual tribute of the Sarkars, was reduced from the original 9 lakhs to 7 lakhs per annum and the Madras Government wrote: "We have also taken care to have the treaty so worded that the payment of this sum does not appear to be by virtue of our holding the Sarkars from the Subah but only in consideration of the friendship subsisting between us". (Quoting Forrest- "Bombay and Madras Papers, Madras Letter, 1757-1790"). The above letter gives a sufficient insight into the minds of the English. *The English are confident the Nizam is in their firm grips !*
101. Mark Bence Jones - *Clive of India,* p. 218.
102. Regani. *op. cit.*, p. 139.
103. Chancey, M. K. (2003). *In the Company's Secret Service: Neil Benjamin Edmonstone and the First Indian Imperialists, 1780-1820.* Retrieved from http://purl.flvc.org/fsu/fd/FSU_migr_etd-3921. p. 36-52.

5

The Marathas

A tripartite alliance against Tipu of Mysore consisting of the English, the Nizam, and the Marathas was formed in 1790. In this agreement the role played by the Marathas was pivotal and momentous. Lord Cornwallis had written to Captain Kennaway, English envoy to the Nizam of Hyderabad: "Without the cooperation of the Marratas I could not flatter myself with a certain prospect of the speedy conclusion as well as the decided success of the war".[1] However, within a short span of about 40 years, from the First Anglo-Maratha War of 1775 to the Third Maratha War of 1818, the Maratha army was decimated, the Maratha Empire was broken up, they lost their independence, and the last of the Peshwas, Baji Rao II, was banished to Bithur near Kanpur.

By 1792, the Third Mysore War (1790–92) went down as the key episode in the late eighteenth century in which the English East India Company decidedly defeated the Indian regime that has been described by Penderel Moon as its most "formidable and most determined foe".[2] Edward Thompson in his classic work *The Making of the Indian Princes* wrote: "Haider and Tipu brought the English East India Company nearer to ruin than any other Indian foes had brought it and nearer than any subsequent foe was to bring it".[3] The striking feature of this defeat of Mysore is that it was accomplished with the help of the Marathas, the only other non-European power on the subcontinent on par with Mysore. "Given that their subsequent conquest by the Company, this decision by the Marathas to back the English against Mysore is puzzling. Did not the Marathas recognize they were next in line?".[4] How did the Marathas come to this predicament and how did the English manage to do it?

The Origin of the Maratha Empire

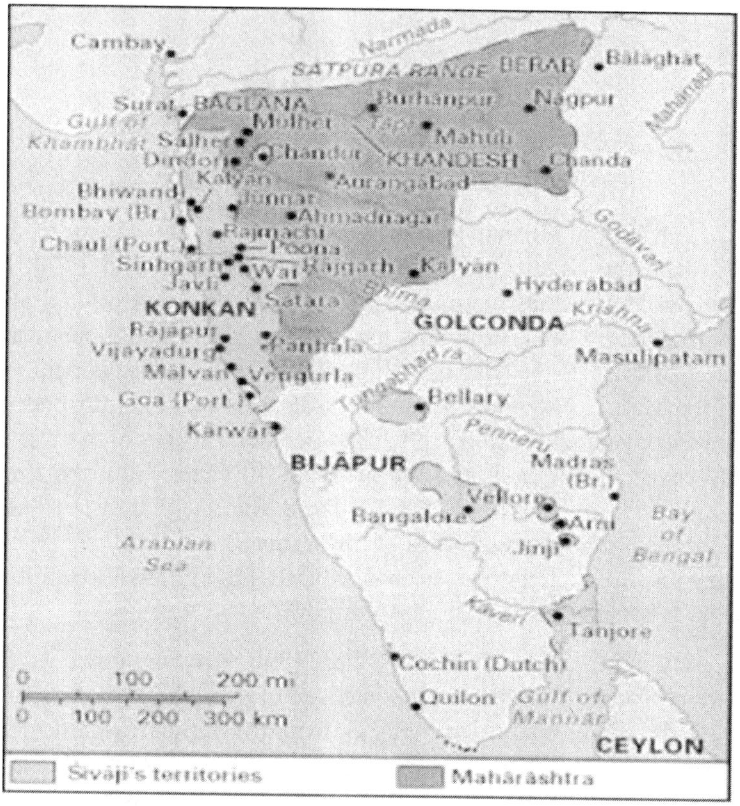

Source: Wikipedia Common.

Maratha kingdom at the time of Shivaji's death in 1680 (shown here in green)

The Maratha Confederacy came into existence as a small principality in the periphery of the north-western edge of the Deccan plateau in 1674 with the coronation of Shivaji as *Chhatrapati*. (Sovereign ruler). In the geopolitical and socio-religious milieu of eighteenth-century India, they played a decisive role in bringing about the fall of the Mughal Empire and came out as a national power before being eclipsed by the British. The most important Maratha warrior clan, the Bhonsles, had held extensive *jagir*s under the Adil Shahi rulers of the Bijapur Sultanate.

As the Sultanate expanded to the south and southwest in the 1630s and 1640s, these regions were amalgamated. Shahaji Bhonsle, the first prominent member of the Bhonsle clan, drew substantial revenues from the Karnataka region. These were territories once controlled by the rulers of Mysore, the Nayaks of Madurai, and other chiefs who arose from the collapse of the Vijayanagaram Empire. Shivaji Bhonsle, one of the sons of Shahaji Bhonsle, emerged as the most powerful figure from the clan in the west, while Vyamkoji, half-brother of Shivaji, who was himself a general in the army of the Bijapur sultan, gained control over the kingdom of Tanjore. Squeezed between the Adil Shahis and the Mughals, the early successes of Shivaji were built on a complex relationship of diverse negotiations and confrontations with his neighbouring states. He directed his attacks not only at agrarian resources, but also at trade. In 1664, he attacked Surat, the important port city of the Mughals in Gujarat. Until the end of his life, Shivaji devoted his time towards extensive expeditions that spread out from Tanjur in the southeast to Khandesh and Berar in the north.

Shivaji, the founder of the Maratha state, was a bold soldier, a clever general and an able engineer. The establishment of an independent Hindu state as a rallying point for all Hindus was his paramount objective. He was not a crusader against Islam as an alien faith. He only wanted to divest it of its political role in India. Crowning himself as the *Chhatrapati*, he succeeded in his resolve and determination. In 1679, Aurangzeb reintroduced the *Jizya* (tax paid by non-Muslim population to their Muslim rulers) in his dominions that had been abolished by Akbar a century earlier. While his subjects were well protected, Shivaji made the enemy subjects pay for his wars against their state by the imposition of the *Chauth*

(A levy of one-fourth of the revenue demand of a district from which the Marathas claimed overlordship or rites of passage). At the time of his death in 1680, Shivaji's dominions extended the length of the Konkan coast—from the Portuguese enclave of Daman to Goa in the south.

Sambhaji, Shivaji's son from his first wife Saibai, ascended the throne on 20 July 1680. At the time of the continuing Mughal aggression in the Deccan, Sambhaji gave refuge to Prince Akbar, the rebellious son of Aurangzeb, who descended into Deccan with a three-lakh strong Mughal army in 1681 and annexed the states of Bijapur and Golkonda. Thereafter, Aurangzeb directed his wholehearted attention to the suppression of the Marathas. Sambhaji continued to resist the Mughals but was finally captured and executed on 11 March 1689. After his death, the capital at Raigad fort fell into the hands of the Mughals. The family members of Sambhaji, including his first wife and chief consort Yesubai (Jivubai) and son Shahu, were captured. From then on Shahu, who was seven years of age, was raised "in gilded fetters" in the Mughal household.

Rajaram, the son of Shivaji's second wife Souarabai, who had been kept in royal captivity by Sambhaji, was crowned as *Chhatrapati* of the Maratha state at Raigad on 12 March 1689. As the Mughals started laying siege to the region around Raigad, Rajaram moved his base to the fortress of Jinji (Ginji) in the Tamil country that had been captured by Shivaji in the seventeenth century. Aurangzeb sent his general, Zulfiqar Khan Nusrat Jung, to capture the Jinji Fort. After three failed attempts, he finally captured Jinji in 1698 after a nine-year siege. Rajaram escaped and fled to Vellore and later to Vishalgad and set up his court at Satara. By this time, the Maratha struggle had been transformed into a full-fledged people's war for liberation, which started to consume all the resources of the Mughal Empire. Rajaram died on 12 March 1700, aged 30. One of his widows, Tarabai, became the regent of her infant son aged four, who was installed on the Maratha throne as the *Chhatrapati*. Contrary to the expectations of the Mughals, the Marathas, under the superb guidance of Tarabai, kept up their pressure with successful raids and liberated substantial parts of their territory. Having failed to stamp out the Maratha war of independence, Aurangzeb gave up the struggle against them and ordered the return of the imperial Mughal court and the troops back to North India in 1706. Aurangzeb died on 21 February 1707 in Ahmednagar.

The death of Aurangzeb plunged the Mughal Empire into a war of succession. His second son, Prince Azam, who was present at the imperial camp, was one of the contenders for the throne in Delhi. Prince Azam had to move to Agra to settle his scores with his brothers, but he realised that the sudden withdrawal of imperial forces from Ahmednagar would create a political vacuum in the Maratha territory. This would help the Marathas under the united power of Tarabai to reclaim their empire. Accepting the advice of his general, Zulfiqar Khan, and some of his Rajput followers, Prince Azam decided to release Shahu from captivity and formally recognize him as the true successor of the ancestral kingdom of the Marathas. The Mughals hoped that this would win them goodwill amongst the Hindus, but, at the same time, by begetting two centres of power—one with Shahu and the other with Tarabai—created discord and distrust amongst the Maratha ranks.[5]

Shahu was released from the Mughal camp on 18 May 1707. He received the support from several Maratha chiefs, the greatest help coming from Parsoji Bhonsle, the ancestor of the later Bhonsle rulers of Nagpur. Tarabai, who had been ruling from Satara on behalf of her minor son, decided to fight the issue, thus creating a situation of civil war between the two descendants of the ruling house of Shivaji as anticipated by the Mughals. At the same time, a failure to reach an agreement amongst the three sons of Aurangzeb on who would be the next to ascend the throne of Delhi led to military conflicts. Prince Azam was killed at the Battle of Jajau on 20 June 1707 and Prince Muazzam ascended the Mughal throne in Delhi. He styled himself as Bahadur Shah. Shahu, who depended heavily on the Mughal support for his very existence, solicited the help of the Emperor Bahadur Shah for his own rehabilitation and Bahadur Shah confirmed him as the *Chhatrapati* of the Marathas.

About this time, Kam Bakhsh, the youngest son of Aurangzeb, who was governing the Deccan, wanted to claim the throne of Delhi. Bahadur Shah promptly marched to the Deccan to settle scores with Kam Bakhsh. As a "vassal" of the Mughal Crown, Shahu supplied a contingent of Maratha troops under the command of Nemaji Shinde to support Bahadur Shah in his war of succession.[6] Kam Bakhsh was defeated in a battle near Hyderabad and later died of his injuries. Feeling obliged to Shahu for the useful service provided by the Maratha troops, Bahadur Shah was about to grant Shahu the right to collect *Chauth* and *Sardeshmughi* (an additional 10% tax on the Chauth) from the six provinces of the Deccan. However, this plan was subverted by the supporters of Tarabai. Adopting a stance of neutrality, the Emperor told Shahu and Tarabai to settle their affairs between them and that these rights would be granted to the one that would emerge successful.

The appearance of two contenders for the throne of the *Chhatrapati* caused great anxiety and confusion among the Maratha community, political leadership, and military hierarchy. To solve the problem of Maratha succession and save the country from the grip of civil war, leaders of various groups conducted extensive parleys with warring factions. Tarabai was adamant in her stance, and this led to a fierce battle at Khed between the two groups in November 1707, in which Shahu emerged victorious. He was crowned Maharaja *Chhatrapati* on 22January 1708. Tarabai continued her fight, but was forced to retreat to Kolhapur, where she settled down to rule over a small principality on behalf of her own son, Shivaji II. However, in 1711, Rajas Bai, the second widow of Rajaram, claimed the throne of Kolhapur for her own son, Sambhaji II. Tarabai and her son were ultimately taken prisoners and Shahu recognised Sambhaji II to be the independent ruler of Kolhapur. The bifurcation of the Maratha kingdom and that of the ruling house of Shivaji was complete. This "dual monarchy" in the *Chhatrapati* line continued to be a "source of perennial evil" that adversely affected the unity and fortunes of the Marathas.[7]

The Rise of the Peshwa

Two personalities came into prominence during this period who were to make an indelible mark on Maratha history—these were Dhanaji Jadav and Balaji Viswanath. Once the troops of Shahu scored a clear victory over the supporters of Tarabai, her *senapati* (military commander) Dhanaji Jadav shifted his allegiance to *Chhatrapati* Shahu. Balaji Vishwanath[8] who held a junior command on the personal staff of the *senapati*, was already acquainted with Shahu and he joined the camp of Shahu. Shahu, following the defeat of Tarabai in the Battle of Khed, established himself as the Maratha *Chhatrapati* at Satara. Dhanaji was confirmed as the *senapati* of Shahu and Balaji Vishwanath received appointment as the *mutaliq* (Assistant) to the *Amatya* (finance minister) of Shahu. By this time, Balaji had won the confidence of Shahu by his wholehearted support extended to him in the consolidation of his position as the *Chhatrapati*.

Two separate developments reinforced the confidence and reliance of Shahu on the abilities of Balaji. *Senapati* Dhanaji Jadhav died in June 1708 and Shahu commissioned his son, Chandrasen Jadhav, as his successor. Chandrasen Jadhav was a sympathizer of Tarabai. Shahu had also chosen Balaji as the *senakarte* or organiser of the Maratha armies. This created resentment in Chandrasen against Balaji. Several Maratha sardars were still indecisive in their loyalty between Shahu and Tarabai. One of them, Dhamaji Thorat, was daring enough to kidnap Balaji Vishwanath, which conveyed a feeling of shock and horror right through the Maratha land. As Mehta claims: "It was a very serious development which posed a danger to the very survival of Shahu as the Chhatrapati. In that hour of trial, Balaji Vishwanath stood by Shahu with steadfastness and proved his tactfulness, organisational skill and diplomatic talent, coupled with bravery and fearlessness in dealing with the situation".[9] Shahu's enemies were dealt with in a forceful and uncompromising manner, and this reinstated order and confidence amongst his soldiers.

Shahu faced danger from another direction. Taking advantage of the confusion in the Maratha polity, Kanhoji Angre, one-time ally of Tarabai and the *sarkhel* or the admiral of the Maratha fleet, overwhelmed a substantial part of the Konkan region. He inflicted a shocking defeat on Bahironji Pant Piglae when he attacked Satara in 1711 and took him prisoner.[10] At this time, the *senapati* also deserted Shahu making his position perilous and insecure. It was at this critical juncture that Shahu made the crucial decision to appoint Balaji as the Peshwa. He was also asked to take over the office of the *senapati*, which he did on 17 November 1713. Unhesitatingly and promptly, Balaji took over the command of the army and marched towards the base of Angre in Lohgarth. The swiftness of the action and the intimidatory stance overawed Kanhoji and he came to terms with Balaji Vishwanath. He tendered his allegiance to Shahu as the overlord of all the Maratha dominions: "This was a great diplomatic victory for Balaji Vishwanath, which stabilised Shahu's position in Maharashtra besides raising the power and prestige of the Peshwa".[11]

The appointment of Balaji Vishwanath as his Peshwa-cum-*senapati* by Shahu in 1713 was a revolutionary development in the history of the Marathas. Being in actual command of the entire civil and military establishment, the Peshwa, thus, became the virtual ruler of the Maratha dominions. He was only nominally answerable to the *Chhatrapati*, who was reduced to the position of a symbolic head of state. His position became hereditary when on the death of Balaji Vishwanath in 1720, his elder son Baji Rao was entrusted with the twin portfolios of Peshwa-cum-*senapati* as a parenteral heritage bestowed by Shahu.[12]

Fractional Politics in the Mughal Empire

Berar, Khandesh, Ahmednagar, Bijapur, Golkonda, and Bidar became the six provinces of the Mughal Deccan and were placed under the overall charge of a Mughal prince or a very prominent officer such as the viceroy. These states were in a state of turmoil after the death of Aurangzeb. Prince Azam had offered the right to collect *Chauth* and *Sardeshmughi* from these areas to Shahu

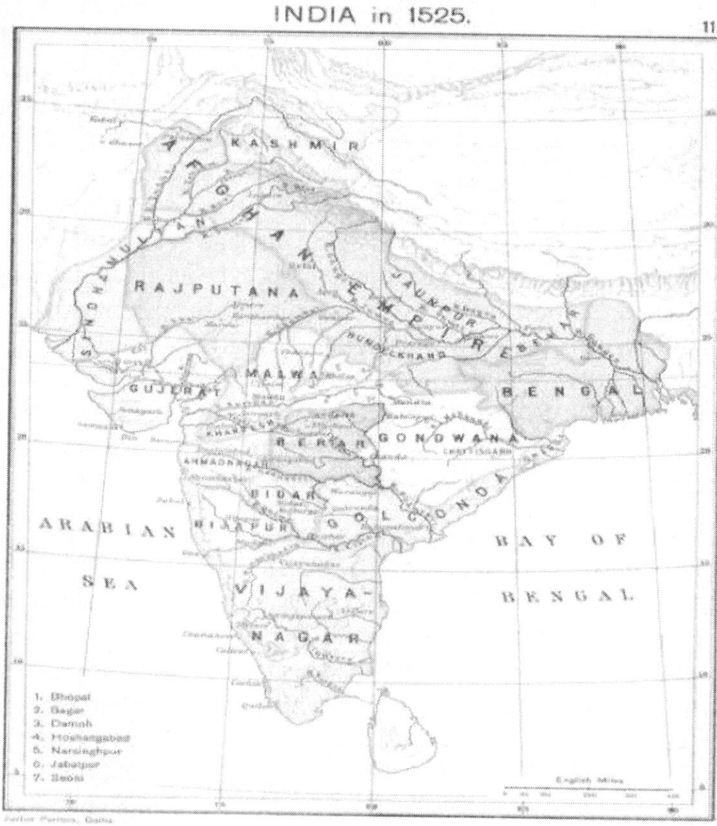

Source: (Joppen, 1907)

Map of India in 1525

in 1707. The Emperor Bahadur Shah who succeeded him did not ratify the above treaty. His death in 1712 also gave rise to a new element in Mughal politics—the hegemony of Mughal nobles as "Kingmakers". In 1712, Jahandar Shah was placed on the throne of Delhi for a brief period by Zulfiqar Khan Nusrat Jung.[13] The next year, Farrukh Siyar ascended the throne of Delhi by eliminating Jahandar Shah with the help of the Sayyid Brothers.[14] In the Mughal Deccan, since 1708, it had been Zulfiqar Khan who had retained the viceroyalty, but his deputy, Daud Panni, was holding the charge with his base in Aurangabad. Emperor Farrukh Siyar deposed Zulfiqar Khan and offered the viceroyalty to Chin Qilich Khan with the title Nizam-ul-Mulk, Khan I Khana, who took charge of his office in 1712.[15] Nizam-ul-Mulk remained the Mughal viceroy of the Deccan for two years in the first instance. His predecessor, Daud Khan Panni, had held a promise to pay Shahu the *Chauth* and *Sardeshmughi* for all the six subhas of the Deccan. Nizam-ul-Mulk refused to adhere to the understanding that had been made by his predecessor. Moreover, he made an attempt to create discord among the disaffected Maratha chiefs by extending liberal patronage to the Maratha renegades. However, before he could do much damage to the Marathas, Farrukh Siyar displaced Nizam-ul-Mulk, much against his wish, from the viceroyalty of the Deccan and shifted him to the insignificant *foujdari* (Military commander with judicial and land revenue rights) of Moradabad near Delhi in 1714.

Sayyid Hussain Ali Khan, the younger of the Sayyid brothers, took over as the new viceroy of the Deccan. Recognising the hostile designs of the Emperor Farrukh Siyar against them because of the dissolution of their administration, he changed his plan of action and decided to win over the Marathas to his own side. In his capacity as the Mughal viceroy of the Deccan and on behalf of the emperor, he negotiated an alliance and subsequently concluded a treaty in July 1718 with Maratha *Chhatrapati* Shahu.[16] Balaji Viswanath, the Peshwa of Shahu, played a major role in formulating this treaty. As Sardesai says:

> His statecraft at once raised Shahu's prestige and established his position as the lawful ruler of the Marathas. It was this legal status which Shahu had all along been trying to acquire since his release...Thus, this treaty enabled the Marathas to be masters of their home and to obtain fresh facilities for expansion outside from their base in the Deccan.[17]

The Mughal-Maratha Interaction

The Mughal-Maratha treaty of 1718 became an important milestone towards the spread of the Maratha power in central and northern India and provided a unique opportunity for them to extend their influence on the Mughal court in Delhi. The Mughal-Maratha treaty, which also markedly strengthened the hands of the Sayyid brothers, caused great concern to the Mughal Emperor Farrukh Siyar. The brothers had gradually seized the powers and the prerogatives of the emperor who became a non-entity in the determination of state policy and in the matter of administration. Farrukh Siyar deliberately supported the Turani and Irani nobles of the court in his manipulations against the Sayyids. This forced the wazir, Sayyad Abdulla Khan, to seek the help of his brother, Sayyid Hussain Ali, placed in the Deccan, from where he marched with all his troops to Delhi. As per the Mughal-Maratha treaty, his army was reinforced with a contingent of 16,000 Maratha troops. *Chhatrapati* Shahu permitted the Peshwa, Balaji Viswanath, to accompany them in person to Delhi on the promise of reward to the Marathas for their valuable services including the confirmation of the treaty from the Mughal emperor (Irvine as cited in Mehta, 2005, p. 79).[18] At Delhi, Raja Ajith Singh of Marwar and Raja Jai Singh of Amber joined Hussain Ali's camp. Farrukh Siyar refused to ratify the treaty made by Sayyid Hussain Ali with the Marathas on behalf of the Mughal crown and called upon his supporters to take up arms against them. The Sayyid brothers, backed by the Maratha and Rajput contingent, defeated Farrukh Siyar who was taken prisoner, blinded, and murdered.

The Sayyid brothers became the de facto rulers of Delhi and in quick succession they created three puppet emperors within a span of one year to keep themselves in power in Delhi. The first of the phantom Mughal rulers, Prince Rafi-ud-Darajat, was installed as emperor on 18 February 1719. He promptly ratified the Mughal-Maratha treaty of 1718. Balaji Viswanath secured firmans from the emperor empowering the Marathas to collect *Chauth* and *Sardeshmughi* from the Deccan. As the legitimate successor of Shivaji, *Chhatrapati* Shahu was confirmed in the possession of the

Maratha Swarajya. The mother, wife, and other relatives of Shahu who were imprisoned by Aurangzeb were also released.

Peshwa as the De Facto Ruler of the Maratha State

Balaji Viswanath, on his return from Delhi, prepared an extensive plan for the consolidation of the Maratha dominions and implementation of the Mughal-Maratha treaty. He set up his base at Poona and made it the administrative headquarters of the Maratha state. The Peshwa acted as the de facto ruler of the Maratha state and carried on the entire business of the state from his headquarters at Poona, in the name and on behalf of the *Chhatrapati*. This willing delegation of royal power and prerogative by Shahu to his Peshwa had far-reaching political and constitutional effects on the Maratha polity in the times to come. Poona became the headquarters of the Maratha state for all practical purposes, although Satara continued to be the ceremonial capital and abode of the Maratha *Chhatrapati*.[19]

Events Related to the Phantom Mughal Emperors

The first two puppet Mughal emperors, Rafi-ud-Darajat and Rafi-ud-Daulah, lasted only for a few months. Towards the end, Muhammad Shah Rangila was enthroned in September 1719 as the new Mughal emperor, but the real authority was in the hands of the Sayyid brothers. They commanded immeasurable power and were the virtual rulers of the Mughal dominions, dictating terms to the emperor. Offended and insulted, Mohammed Shah turned to the Turani and Irani nobles for help over again. Well informed of these political intrigues, the Sayyid brothers decided to relocate the ringleader of the machinations, Nizam-ul-Mulk, to Malwa as the governor.

The viceroyalty of the Deccan, previously held by Nizam-ul-Mulk, was entrusted to the younger of the two Sayyid brothers—Sayyid Hussain Ali—who nominated a nephew of theirs, Dilwar Ali Khan, as a deputy to administer the provinces. On the other side, Nizam-ul-Mulk, used the demotion of his status to transfer Malwa to his advantage. After taking effective control of the place, he crossed the Narmada with his combat troops and occupied Khandesh. The rebellion threatened the very survival of the empire, and this called for a huge imperial army commanded by Dilwar Ali Khan to be sent to subdue the offending Nizam-ul-Mulk. However, Dilwar Ali Khan was defeated and killed by Nizam-ul-Mulk in the battle at Khandwa on 10 August 1720.

An imperial force under Sayyad Hussain Ali Khan, accompanied by the Emperor Muhammad Shah, proceeded to the Deccan to fight Nizam-ul-Mulk. On the way, Hussain Ali was assassinated in his army camp at Fatehpur Sikri on 9 October 1720. Sayyid Abdulla Khan, the wazir, marshalled his military contingent and marched out of Delhi but was defeated in the battle at Bilochpur on 15 November 1720. He was taken prisoner and put to death in royal captivity two years later, thus ending the protracted career of the Sayyid brothers. The victorious Emperor Muhammed Shah returned to Delhi and proclaimed Muhammed Amin Khan, now styled Intimad-ud-Daulah, as the new wazir. He also conferred viceroyalty of the Deccan to Nizam-ul-Mulk with an additional title Asaf Jah.

The Mughal emperor had given legal sanction to the title of *Chhatrapati* of the Marathas to Shahu as the legitimate successor of the heritage of Shivaji. Balaji Viswanath died on 12 April 1720. *Chhatrapati* Shahu installed his son, Baji Rao, as the Peshwa as well as the commander-in-chief of the Maratha army. He also issued a proclamation by which the office of the Peshwa as head of the civil and military government of the Maratha state was made hereditary for all times to come. Baji Rao energetically continued the domestic and external policies of his father, especially those aimed at the consolidation of the Maratha state and expansion of the Maratha empire. However, the homeland of the Marathas was scattered with many pockets of territory held by uncooperative Maratha sardars, Mughal nobles, and other disaffected feudal elements. Many refused to recognize the sovereignty of Shahu over the Maratha Swarajya itself. Thus, the priority of the state policy of Baji Rao was to acquire complete control and consolidate Shahu's hold over the Swarajya.

The political vacuum caused by the fall of the Sayyids was filled by the nobles of foreign pedigree of Turani and Irani origins. As before, the position of Muhammed Shah as a puppet emperor remained unchanged. This resulted in gross indiscipline and corruption in the bureaucratic ranks. The administrative infrastructure collapsed. Disaffected landlords refrained from paying dues. Irregular payment of salaries of soldiers caused desertions among them, which led to the demoralisation and disintegration of the imperial army.

Intimad-ud-Daulah, the first wazir of the Deccan after the Sayyids, died in January 1721 and this position was offered to Nizam-ul-Mulk who took over as the wazir on 22 January 1722 though as an additional assignment. He retained his viceroyalty of the Deccan as his primary responsibility, but, on 18 December 1723, he left the imperial capital Delhi for the Deccan to set up his independent state there. Mubariz Khan, the Mughal governor of Hyderabad State and Gujarat, took up arms against him under the decree of Muhammed Shah and was defeated in the battle of Shaker Kelda on 11 October 1724. Nizam-ul-Mulk shifted his capital from Aurangabad, which, due to its proximity to Satara and Poona, was vulnerable to attack from the Marathas, and set up a base at Hyderabad. Thus, he laid the foundation of the first succession state of the Mughal Empire, although he did not disown the nominal suzerainty of the Mughal Crown during his lifetime.[20] This marked the end of the imperial Mughal rule in the Deccan for all time to come.

This campaign of Nizam-ul-Mulk shook the very foundation of the Mughal Empire. Following his example, Alivardi Khan, the Mughal viceroy in charge of Bengal, Bihar, and Orissa, and Sadat Khan, the governor of Awadh, too asserted their independence. The Mughal governors of Kashmir, Sind, Lahore, Multan, the Jats and the Rohillas all set up their own independent states at the heart of the empire. At the periphery of the empire, the Persian adventurer, Nadir Shah, had already conquered Afghanistan and detached it from the Mughal Empire.

The Conflict between Baji Rao and Nizam-ul-Mulk

Baji Rao regarded the Nizam as an independent ruler of the Deccan and not as a representative of the Mughal government. The Marathas and the Nizam now became serious contenders for the establishment of their individual supremacy in the Deccan. The Mughal emperor had granted the right to collect *Chauth* and *Sardeshmughi* from all the six provinces of the Mughal Deccan to the Marathas, but Nizam-ul-Mulk refused to abide by the terms of the Mughal-Maratha Treaty of 1718 and expelled all the Maratha agents who were deputed by the Peshwa to collect the tax from his dominions. Moreover, Nizam-ul-Mulk attempted to revive the traditional enmity between the two ruling houses of Shivaji, which were based in Satara and Kolhapur, respectively. By extending liberal patronage to the disaffected Maratha chieftains, he set the stage for the antagonists to fight for their overlordship in the South and fill up the vacuum caused by the disappearance of the Mughal imperialism.

Soon, Nizam-ul-Mulk made a successful entry and carried out a surprise attack on Poona and hurriedly proclaimed Sambhaji II of Kolhapur as the sole *Chhatrapati* of the Maratha territories. However, as he was quickly making his way back to his own base, he was confronted by the Peshwa's vast army in the hilly tract of Palkhed. After a brief but bloody battle, the Nizam suffered a humiliating defeat and was forced to sue for peace. According to the "Treaty of Mungi Shevgaon" signed on 6 March 1728, the "Nizam acknowledged the sovereignty of Chhatrapati Shahu as the sole inheritor of all the Maratha dominions and promised to give up the cause of Sambhaji II of Kolhapur. He also recognised the claim of Shahu to levy Chauth and Sardeshmughi upon his territories, comprising the bulk of six erstwhile provinces of the Mughal Deccan".[21]

The Growth and Spread of Maratha Power

The victory at Palkhed marked a watershed moment in the history of the Deccan in the post-Mughal era and was a pivotal moment for the Marathas. It dealt a serious blow to the power and prestige of Nizam-ul-Mulk and shattered his ambition to establish his absolute dominance over the Deccan. It cleared the path for the rapid spread of Maratha power and influence in south India. It gave them the confidence to challenge their foreign foes including the Siddis of Janjira and the Portuguese. It also gave credence to the cherished "forward policy" of the Peshwa regarding the spread of Maratha influence in northern India.

Baji Rao began his northward expansion beyond the Narmada by marching upon Malwa at the head of a large army commanded by his younger brother Chimnaji Appa. He was assisted in this undertaking by his brilliant lieutenants—Ranoji Sindhia, Malharrao Holkar, and Udaji Pawar. It is these subordinate commanders who subsequently laid the foundation of the respective states of Gwalior, Indore, and Dhar. The Mughal army commanded by Giridhar and Daya Bahadur was defeated in a battle at Ajmer in November 1728. The Mughal emperor initially nominated Sawai Raja Jai Singh of Amber and later Muhammad Khan Bangash as governors of Malwa, but they failed to dislodge the Marathas from there making them the de facto rulers of Malwa.

The maritime territory of Gujarat was a centre of attraction for Maratha raiders and plunderers. Khanderao Dhabade, one of the emerging sardars, inflicted an overwhelming defeat upon the Mughal armies. As reward for his bravery, he was promoted to *senapati* by Shahu. Upon Dhabade's death in 1723, his son Trimbakrao was promoted as *senapati*. Two other sardars came into prominence during this period—Pilaji Gaekwar and Kanthaji Kadam Bande. Pilaji laid the foundations of the sovereign power of the Gaekwar family at Baroda. In Gujarat during this period, there was a spell of chaos and confusion resulting in near anarchy and misgovernance. Trimbakrao was killed in a battle at Dabhoi in 1731. Sambhaji II of Kolhapur and other disaffected Maratha allies of Trimbakrao were also forced to surrender. The triumph of Baji Rao against his Maratha antagonists was complete, and the influence of Marathas in Gujarat became more and more pronounced.

Bundelkhand was conquered by Baji Rao in March 1729. The possessions of Baji Rao extended further the frontiers of the Maratha state and served as a base for the concentration of Maratha forces and their advance into the imperial dominions of the Mughals. The Siddis, originally from the east coast of Africa, had made small settlements along the Malabar Coast of India. Gradually, they emerged as a naval power with their main base at Janjira, "an impregnable sea-girt fortress".[22] With the expansion of the Mughal rule in the Deccan, the Siddis recognised the suzerainty of Delhi. Aurangzeb had utilised their services to fight against Shivaji and his successors. Slowly they ventured into the interior of Maharashtra and held several forts. The Peshwa's campaign against the Siddis was a protracted and low-pitched affair. The military and diplomatic preoccupations of the Peshwa prevented him from taking any concerted action against them. Nevertheless, the military power of the Siddis was gradually crippled beyond repair.

Baji Rao's March to Delhi

Baji Rao established Maratha supremacy in Malwa, Gujarat, and Bundelkhand, and became the *de facto* ruler by 1735. After this success, he led a strong army from Poona to Delhi in December 1736. The suburbs of Delhi were plundered and there were several skirmishes with the Mughal forces. As it was not his plan to control the capital, he returned to Poona by March 1737. It familiarised the Marathas with the environs of the imperial capital and opened the way for the northward expansion of Maratha arms and influence in the future. Realising that the Marathas may renew their hostilities, Muhammad Shah summoned Nizam-ul-Mulk to Delhi to protect the collapsing Mughal Empire and installed him as the supreme commander of all the imperial forces. The Nizam was ordered to organise a military campaign to oust the Marathas immediately from Malwa and Bundelkhand. Bajirao reorganised his troops and with the help of his lieutenants—Holkar, Sindhia, Pawar and others in Malwa—closed in upon the Mughal army and encircled and entrapped them. Hard-pressed, the Nizam was forced to sue for peace. The Treaty of Bhopal was signed by Nizam-ul-Mulk at the

Doraha Sarai on 7 January 1738 on behalf of the Mughal emperor. According to the terms of the historic treaty, the emperor granted the whole of the subah of Malwa and ceded complete sovereignty of all lands between the Narmada and Chambal rivers to the Maratha state.[23] Baji Rao's victory of Bhopal over the imperial forces, then commanded by the greatest of all the Mughal generals Nizam-ul-Mulk and the most formidable of all the Peshwa's adversaries in the Deccan, changed the entire political scenario in the country. The Marathas emerged as the major contenders to the domination of India and serious aspirants to the succession of the Mughals as the imperial rulers of the country.

During this push and pull, at a time when Nizam-ul-Mulk—the wazir of the Mughal empire—embarked with his troops on a campaign against Baji Rao, Nadir Shah from Persia carried out his monumental invasion of India. At this time, northern India was left wide open for Nadir Shah's invasion, and he then marched on to Delhi defeating the imperial Mughal army at Karnal on 13 February 1739. Together, these two men—Baji Rao and Nizam-ul-Mulk—could have prevented Nadir Shah's incursion from Persia into India and his sacking of Delhi. After Nadir Shah's campaign and Baji Rao's success, not much was left of the Mughal Empire.[24] The invasion of Nadir Shah proved catastrophic for the already weak and unstable Mughal Empire. The veneration, splendour, and honour of the Mughal ruling dynasty perished forever. For a short period of time, the way was cleared for the rise of the Marathas as a national power.

Baji Rao died on 18April 1740. He deserves due credit for the consolidation of the Maratha state and its transformation into an empire. He protected the budding Maratha state from disorder and disunity and strengthened the position of Shahu as the legitimate successor of Shivaji's heritage. After his death, *Chhatrapati* Shahu installed Balaji Baji Rao, the 19-year-old son of Baji Rao, as the new Peshwa. This nomination of Bajirao was opposed by senior Maratha nobles and experienced bureaucrats, including many members of the *Ashta Pradhan* (Council of Eight of the Maratha Empire). Raghuji Bhonsle,[25] a kinsman of Shahu, had continued to exhibit hostility to the rising power of the Peshwas. Though a feudatory of the Maratha state, he had established himself virtually as the independent ruler of Nagpur (Berar). *Chhatrapati* Shahu had authorised him to carry the Maratha influence into the Carnatic as also into Bengal, Bihar, and Orissa. However, Raghuji did not cooperate with the Peshwa on many of the state policies in an amicable manner and the two Maratha warriors came into conflict with each other over the territories previously mentioned. The Peshwa aimed to exert control over all the Maratha chiefs, but Raghuji Bhonsle was eager to create an independent sphere of action for himself. The Maratha monarch was keen to resolve the differences and he brought about a reconciliation between them by defining their respective spheres of influence. A formal agreement to this effect was signed by Balaji Baji Rao and Raghuji Bhonsle on the dictates of the *Chhatrapati* on 31 August 1743, according to which "all the territory from Berar to the east, right up to Cuttack Bengal and Lucknow, was assigned to Raghuji, with which the Peshwa bound himself not to interfere, and the territories, west of this line, including Ajmer, Agra, Prayag, and Malwa, were to be the exclusive spheres of the Peshwa".[26] However, this differentiation weakened the central authority of the state and hampered its ultimate growth and development as an integrated and all powerful national state.

Death of Shahu and the Reign of His Successors

Before his death in December 1749, *Chhatrapati* Shahu had made the office of the Peshwa, who was the head of the civil and military administration, into a hereditary position. He had already nominated Ram Raja, the alleged grandson of Tarabai, as his successor. He was invested as *Chhatrapati* at Satara on 14 January 1750. However, soon an open conflict developed between Tarabai and the *Chhatrapati* for control over the government of Satara. To bring about a working compromise, Baji Rao met both of them in Poona. He then called an unprecedented summit meeting of the premier Maratha sardars—Mahal Rao Holkar, Jayappa Sindhia, Raghuji Bhonsle, and Sadashiv Rao amongst others. After lengthy mediations, they recognised the supremacy of the

Peshwa as the chief executive authority in the civil and military administration of the Maratha state. However, he was required to exercise powers in the name of the Maratha *Chhatrapati* who was the symbolic head. The *Chhatrapati* signed a written agreement with the Peshwa, known as the Sangola agreement in 1750, which agreed to these terms. This gave constitutional recognition to the abolishment of the historic institution of the *Ashta Pradhan* and also clearly defined the position of the *Chhatrapati* as the titular head of the Maratha state. As Mehta says: "The Sangola agreement effected a complete revolution in the Maratha polity by silently and imperceptibly transferring even the residuary and incidental powers and prerogatives of the Maratha Crown to the Peshwa and made the *Chhatrapati* a mere creature of the Peshwa".[27]

Conquests during the Period of Balaji Baji Rao

The regime of Balaji Baji Rao lasted for 21 years from 1740 to 1761. During this period, the Maratha state reached the high point of its splendour, both with regards to its frontiers as well as its internal management and material prosperity. Balaji Rao is deemed as the founder of the "Maratha Confederacy"—a loose union of Maratha states under the symbolic headship of the Maratha *Chhatrapati*. However, the undisputed real leader of the confederacy was the Peshwa himself. The inception of the Maratha Confederacy can be traced back to the Mughal-Maratha treaty of 1718 which gave them permission to collect the Maratha levies, called *Chauth* and *Sardeshmughi*, from some of the non-Maratha areas referred to as Mughal territories. This task was entrusted to loyal Maratha chiefs who gradually established their own spheres of influence. With the passage of time, their territorial possessions and geographical supremacy began to be passed on as hereditary succession. This created semi-independent states and principalities within the fold of the Maratha Empire and, thus, came into being the confederate units of the vast Maratha dominions. It led to the spread of the Maratha arms and their influence in far-off areas of the country. But their emergence did weaken the power of the Peshwa and diminished the central authority that the Maratha state would have enjoyed in the long run.

The Maratha power and influence over various parts of India increased during the reign of Balaji Rao. He secured the control of Malwa and Bundelkhand from the Mughal emperor. The whole province of Gujarat was already in the possession of the Marathas though a formal grant was lacking.

The Marathas in Bengal

Alivardi Khan was the Nawab of the "successor state" of Bengal, Bihar, and Orissa. The Marathas started their raids into these autonomous states from 1742 onwards. Colluding with Mir Habib, the deputy governor of Orissa, Raghuji Bhonsle of Nagpur raided and ravaged parts of Bengal, Bihar, and Orissa. The Peshwa Baji Rao was furious when he learned that Raghuji had gained permission for the military campaign in Bengal from the *Chhatrapati* without his knowledge. The Mughal Emperor Muhammed Shah, having received information from intelligence sources that Raghuji was acting independently of the Peshwa, called upon him to drive back Raghuji's troops from Bengal in return for the recognition of his claims over Malwa and Bundelkhand.[28] Thus, compelled, the Peshwa led an expedition to Bengal with a 75,000-strong army. Realising the impending endangerment, Raghuji made a hurried retreat from the domain of the Nawab and strongly protested with the *Chhatrapati*. Exerting his personal influence in bringing about a compromise between the warring factions, Shahu obliged them to sign an agreement on 31 August 1743. According to the treaty, the provinces of Bengal, Bihar, and Orissa were assigned to Raghuji Bhonsle. Thus, the long-cherished aspiration of the Peshwa to assert central control over the territories acquired by the Marathas and regulate the activities of all their sardars remained unfulfilled.

Raghuji had been at perpetual war with the Nawab Alivardi Khan from 1745 and the incessant invasions of the Marathas ruined the economy of Bengal. To end this stalemate, a treaty of peace was signed between them in 1751. According to this treaty, Alivardi Khan ceded Orissa to Raghuji and Raghuji in turn agreed to withdraw his troops from the territories of Bengal and Orissa. This brought to an end to the protracted hostilities between the

Marathas and the Nawab of Bengal. But this opened up a pathway for the English traders to consolidate their position and fortify their factory at Calcutta. 'The withdrawal of the Marathas from Bengal and Bihar left the field open for the rise of the English power there and they readily moved in to fill the political vacuum thus caused.'[29]

The Marathas in the Carnatic

Source: (Joppen, 1907)

Political map of India in 1751, at the height of French influence in India

The Mughal power declined in Carnatic after the death of Aurangazib in 1707 where it was divided into numerous states. Provinces like Arcot, Shira, Kadappa, Karnola and Savnur were controlled by Muslim Nawabs who modified their imperial assignments into hereditary rule. Ancient Hindu ruling houses governed places like Mysore, Bedanur, Trichinopoly, Madura and Raidurg. By the mid-1740s the Carnatic passed back into the control of the Nizam. The death of Nizam-ul-Mulk in 1748 resulted in various succession disputes among the heirs of the Nizam. These conflicts from 1748 to 1758 became part of a larger war between the English and the French for control of the Coromandel Coast. Throughout the 1750s, the strength of the Nizam depended on the strength of the French support available to him and this varied according to the French fortunes in the Anglo-French war. According to Gordon: "As they had for decades, the Marathas treated the Karnatak as a suitable hunting ground for treasure, with some hope of longer-term revenue arrangements".[30]

The Marathas in Gujarat

Beginning with the expedition of Shivaji in 1664 to the seaport of Surat, the Marathas repeatedly plundered Gujarat. During the period of Raja Ram and Tarabai, Khanderao Dabhade was making frequent incursions into Gujarat. In 1717, Shahu elevated Dabhade as the *senapati* and a member of the *AshtaPradhan*. On his death, his son—Trimbakrao Dhabade—inherited the title. However, in 1731, Trimbakrao was killed in a tussle with the Peshwa Baji Rao in the Battle of Dabhoi. Shahu granted his title to his son, Yashwantrao Dhabade, but he along with Dhamaji Gaekwar took up arms against Balaji Baji Rao. Yashwantrao was stripped of his titles and Dhamaji Gaekwar was made the sole Maratha representative in Gujarat on 30 March 1752 after signing a written agreement with the Peshwa: "[T] he Peshwa's authority as the supreme manager of the Maratha state was formerly acknowledged by Dhamaji Gaekwar in the same way as Raghuji Bhonsle had done in the case of Nagpur, and as Sindia, Holkar and others were doing in Malwa and Bundelkhand".[31] In 1753, Ahmedabad and Kathiawar, excluding Surat, were taken possession of by the Marathas. By 1757, the Peshwa took complete control of the whole region of Gujarat and Kathiawar.

Maratha Relations with Rajputs and Jats

Following the invasion of Delhi by Nadir Shah, the imperial Mughal authority in Rajputana almost vanished. At the same time, Malwa came under the control of the Marathas and their territorial influence became very close to the boundaries of Rajputana. The Marathas wanted to take over the role of the Mughals as a pan-India power. The Marathas looked upon the inhabitants of the non-Maratha regions as their subjects and attempted to assert their authority over them as their masters.

> His [Baji Rao's] Newai expedition was for money…. This policy, whatever its monetary gains, led to the wholesale alienation of the Hindu allies of the Empire and the through denationalisation of the Maratha army. The Rajputs were systematically plundered and though in the beginning they had welcomed the rule of the Marathas as the rule of their Hindu Brethren, they were soon convinced that the Maratha supremacy meant for them nothing better than a change of masters and for the matter of that a change for the worse. This result of the short-sighted policy deprived the Marathas of the valuable help of the Rajputs in the hour of their urgent need in the Panipat campaign.[32]

The Jats comprised a substantial population of north-western India and they had been equally divided into three major religious denominations—Hinduism, Islam, and Sikhism. Their political awareness took shape during the reign of Aurangzeb at the time of his religious intolerance. It was Raja Churaman who established the first state of the Jats. His nephew, Badan Singh, laid the foundation of a new ruling dynasty of the Jats at Bharatpur. After Badan Singh's death in June 1756, his adopted son Suraj Mal proved to be an able ruler and statesman. The Marathas were ever eager to bring the former Mughal territories under their own control. The Jats were keen to liberate themselves from the Mughal domination, but they did not want it substituted by Maratha supremacy and they resisted the intrusion of the Marathas into their domain. They picked up arms against the Marathas as they had earlier against the Mughals. Suraj Mal tried to maintain a cordial relationship with them, but by the time the third Battle of Panipat ensued, their relationship had irreversibly deteriorated.

The Marathas in Delhi

Meanwhile in Delhi, the Mughal Emperor Muhammed Shah Rangila died in April 1748 and within the next 11 years, four princes ascended the Mughal throne. The Marathas started to get involved in the politics of Delhi during the reign of Muhammed Shah Rangila's son, the Mughal Emperor Ahmad Shah (1748–1754). The Nawab of Awadh, Safdar Jung, was his wazir (prime minister) who sought the help of the Maratha troops garrisoned in Malwa, Bundelkhand, and Rajasthan to suppress the uprising of the Rohillas. At the same time, Ahmad Shah Abdali, the ruler of Afghanistan, set out on his third invasion of India and the Emperor Ahmad Shah also wanted the support of the Marathas. A treaty entrusting the task of protecting the emperor and the imperial capital, Delhi, was signed with the Maratha sardars, Malharrao Holkar and Jayappa Sindhia. However, during the intervening time, the Emperor Ahmad Shah made peace with Abdali and ceded the provinces of Lahore and Multan. Ahmad Shah Abdali then departed for Afghanistan via Sind and Baluchistan.

The Mughal emperor refused to ratify the treaty once the threat of invasion ceased to exist. Safdar Jung fell out with the emperor for not honouring his words and the Maratha sardars charged both of them with the breach of trust. This created intense animosity between the emperor and Safdar Jung with disastrous consequences for both of them. Meanwhile, the Peshwa ordered the Maratha generals back to the Deccan to support Ghazi Uddin, the son of the late Nizam-ul-Mulk to claim his office as the Nizam of Hyderabad. As the military agent of the Peshwa for the Mughal emperor, a nominal force of about 10,000 Maratha troops under the command of Antaji Mankeshwar were left behind at Delhi.

In June 1754, the phantom Emperor Ahmad Shah Bahadur was deposed and imprisoned by his wazir, Imad-ul-Mulk (Ghazi ud-Din Khan Feroze Jung III). He enthroned another Mughal prince, Alamgir II, as the emperor (1754–1759). At this time, Ahmad Shah Abdali set out on his fourth invasion of India. He reached Lahore in December 1756 and proceeded to Delhi. The defence of the capital was assigned to the wazir, Imad-ul-Mulk, and the faujdar of Saharanpur, Najib Khan Rohilla. They were assisted by the Maratha commander, Antaji Mankeshwar. At this critical point, Najib betrayed his emperor and the wazir by changing sides and joining Abdali who entered Delhi in January 1757. The Maratha sardar, Antaji, was forced to withdraw to Faridabad first and then to Mathura.

To support the emperor, the Peshwa Baji Rao dispatched a suitable Maratha force under the command of Raghunath Rao and Malharrao Holkar. However, there was inordinate delay in the progress of the expeditionary force, which resulted in considerable destruction and devastation of the Jat territories by the Afghan raiders. They also plundered and ravaged Delhi and the towns of Mathura and Agra.[33] Abdali returned to Afghanistan in April 1757 before which he released Alamgir II from detainment and reinstalled him on the throne of Delhi. Imad-ul-Mulk continued as the wazir and Najib Khan Rohilla was declared as the plenipotentiary of Abdali in Delhi.

The Maratha army commanded by Raghunath Rao reached Agra in May 1757 with his deputy Malharrao Holkar. He dispatched a contingent of Maratha troops and recovered all their lost possessions in the Doab without any fight. He then proceeded to Delhi, which was under the control of Najib Khan Rohilla and both—the Mughal Emperor, Alamgir II, and the wazir, Imad-ul-Mulk—were Najib's virtual prisoners. After a fortnight of struggle, the Marathas took possession of Delhi and captured Najib Khan Rohilla in September 1757. However, by this time Najib had lured

Malharrao Holkar and started dealing directly with him. The author of *Siyar-ul-Mutakherin*, Sayyid Ghulam Husain Tabatabai, wrote:

> Najib wormed himself into Malharrao's bosom.... Holkar received large bribes from Najib Khan and earnestly pleaded with Raghunath Rao to release the Khan.... Raghunath Rao could not resist Holkar and yielded to his pleading allowing Najib to depart unscathed to his home on a verbal promise never again to interfere with the concerns of Delhi and surrender all his fortified posts in the Doab to the Marathas. The serpent's tail was merely trodden upon.[34]

After the departure of Najib from Delhi, Raghunath Rao formally installed the Mughal Emperor Alamgir II on the throne again and confirmed Imad-ul-Mulk as the wazir. The Afghan chieftain, Ahmad Khan Bangash, was appointed as Mir-Bakshi (head of military administration) and Antaji Mankeshwar became the governor of the province of Delhi. Thus, the Marathas became the *de facto* rulers of Delhi. By December 1757, the whole of Upper Doab also came under Maratha control. Raghunath Rao was jubilant with the setup of Maratha influence at Delhi and expansion of their power in the Doab. However, there were serious flaws in the defences and administrative setup of the territories taken over by the Marathas. There were not sufficient numbers of Maratha troops to man the major strongholds of strategic importance in the Doab. Najib Khan Rohilla, the inveterate enemy of the Marathas, was still very active and lingered around the eastern banks of the Ganga. The sardars and political observers brought these deficiencies to the attention of the Maratha general, Raghunath Rao. However, he was comforted by deceptive appearances and false assurances given to him by the Holkar.

The Marathas in Punjab

Ahmad Shah Abdali made his first foray into Punjab in 1748 and within the next decade annexed up to Sirhind through successive invasions. The Sikhs were fighting against Mughal rule ever since the days of Aurangzeb and they fought against Abdali with equal fervour and force. Adina Beg, the former Mughal faujdar of Jalandhar Doab, was already working with the Sikhs to fight the Afghans. Together they made an appeal to the Marathas to help them end the rule of the Afghans. During this period, Abdali was finding it difficult to hold on his own. He was threatened by the Persians from the west and his own nephew, Abdur Rahman, rose against him by setting off to Poona to seek the Peshwa's support. The three Sikh chiefs—Jasasinh Ahluwalia, Alasinh Jat, and Jasasinh Ramgadia—successfully fought and resisted the onslaught of Abdali. Responding to these developments, Raghunath Rao marched to Punjab with a large force at the end of February 1758. Within the next two months, he was able to establish his command over the whole of Punjab and north-western India.

The Maratha invasion of Punjab was the outcome of their understanding with the Mughal emperor and his wazir and they utilised the local machinery of the government to carry on the administration and collection of revenues. Half of the tribute was to be paid to the wazir and the emperor and the other half was to be retained by the Marathas. Raghunath Rao appointed the former Mughal officer, Adina Beg, as the governor of Punjab while ignoring the claims of the Sikh leaders. The Afghan migrants and emissaries of Abdali promptly changed their loyalties to Adina Beg who readily absorbed the soldiers who were taken as prisoners by Marathas during the fight on the banks of the Chenab into his army. Abdus Samad Khan, former governor of Kashmir, who had been taken as captive by the Marathas, secured his liberation by changing sides. Meanwhile, Abdur Rehman, nephew of Abdali, arrived at Poona with a handful of his associates. His intellect and schemes of conquest impressed the Peshwa so much that he sent him to Raghunath to make use of his services as best as possible. With the concurrence of Holkar, he assigned the whole of the trans-India region to Abdur Rahman with headquarters at Peshawar; he took Abdus Samad Khan as his deputy and was allowed to raise a large army to execute his plan of conquest. Thus, finding the Maratha leadership completely off their guard against their potential adversaries, intruders and abetters infiltrated the ranks of their supporters. They grabbed important administrative and military assignments and presented a totally false picture regarding the stability of the Maratha rule in Punjab and the north-western frontier.

The Sikhs had very bitter memories of the Mughals and they resisted such a political arrangement, which was to perpetuate the same rule in Punjab with the connivance of the Marathas. Moreover, the Sikhs had set their heart upon the pursuit of conquests and held firm belief that they would rule over Punjab sooner or later. There was no formal treaty or agreement between the leaders of the Sikhs and the Marathas regarding the pursuit of their political objectives. In the military action against the Afghans, there was a marked lack of coordination. The Marathas had failed to befriend the native inhabitants of Punjab, particularly the Sikhs and, as a consequence, they were placed in the midst of a hostile population that regarded them as aggressors and plunderers, no better than the Afghans, Uzebeks, or Quizalbashi followers of Ahmad Shah Abdali.[35] Thus, the Marathas failed to discriminate between their friends and potential foes and presented a rosy picture of their political and military achievements in the north to the Peshwa.

The Marathas remained in Punjab only for a brief period from April 1758 to October 1759. At this critical juncture, the Peshwa recalled Raghunath Rao and Malharrao Holkar from Punjab. To him the affairs in the Deccan appeared more important. The Peshwa was conspiring to end the French influence in the court of the Nizam by fermenting an internal revolution there through the agency of the chief minister, Shah Nawaz Khan. Nizam Ali, who was slowly usurping power, also resented the dominance of the French in the court of the Nizam, Salabat Jung. Nizam Ali caused the murder of Hyder Jung, the chief native assistant of Bussey.

Suspecting that Shah Nawaz Khan and his sons were the instigators of Hyder Jung's murder, Bussey dispatched a strong French contingent to seize them. In the resulting turmoil, the Diwan along with his son were killed. Thus, in a real sense the intrigues and manoeuvres of Nizam Ali helped to reduce the French as well as the Maratha influence on the Nizam's Court.[36]

Raghunath Rao and Malharrao Holkar began their departure from Lahore in May 1758. All the political and military experts and advisors of Raghunath Rao and well-wishers of the Maratha cause appealed to him not to think of returning to the Deccan in a hurry. They wanted him to stay put in or around Delhi to give stability to the arrangements just made and to exercise a check on evildoers.[37]

Third Battle of Panipat and its Impact

The Third Battle of Panipat (17 January 1761) is unique in Indian history in respect of the loss of life, magnitude of destruction, and the fortunes of the adversaries, competitors, and collaborators. The political and military developments resulting from this battle adversely affected the fortunes of all the three contenders—the Afghans, the Mughals, and the Marathas.

Ahmad Shah Abdali was unable to perpetuate his imperial designs in India. He withdrew from India and returned to his kingdom in Afghanistan within weeks of his phenomenal victory over the Marathas. The martial societies of the north—the Jats, Sikhs, Bundelas, and Rajputs—and two of the major powers—Shuja-ud-Daula of Awadh and Najib-ud-Daula of Rohilla, the representative of Abdali—retained their authority and control to a large extent. The holocaust of Panipat demolished the halo of invincibility built around the Marathas. They lost their manpower, prestige, and credit. The magnificent army of the then greatest political and military power of India was broken up and dispersed. The battle eliminated a group of gallant young military leaders and statesmen of the regime. The defeat inspired rebellions by local armed lineages, invasion and subversion by neighbouring powers, and fractionisation and bids for power at the centre.

Peshwa Balaji Baji Rao died at the age of 39 in June 1761 within weeks of the defeat of Panipat. His eldest son, Vishwas Rao, had already died fighting in the battlefield. His second son, Madhav Rao, was installed as the fourth Peshwa, and during this period when he was still a minor the control of the government was held by his uncle Raghunath Rao as his regent. Slowly but steadily over the next decade after Panipat, the military strength, effective leadership, and revenue areas of the Marathas gradually recovered under the capable stewardship of Madhav Rao. The Marathas brought back the fugitive Mughal Emperor, Shah Alam II, from his exile and installed him on the throne of Delhi in January 1772. For the next 31 years, the Marathas were the *de facto* as well as *de jure* rulers of Delhi on behalf of the Mughal emperor.[38]

Two themes dominated in the following years—the first being the shifting power relations between the centre and the Maratha "states" (Shinde, Holkar, Gaikwad, and Bhonsle); and second, the emergence of the English as the main competitor in the subcontinent.

Shifting Power Relations at the Capital

The factional conflicts in the Deccan affected the functioning of the areas which the Marathas controlled. In the long run, it resulted in the weakening of the power of the Peshwa and gaining of the power by the nobles.

In the Deccan, Salabat Jung, the fourth Nizam of Hyderabad, had been comprehensively defeated by Balaji Baji Rao in the historic battle of Udgir in February 1760. He was deposed and imprisoned by his younger brother, Nizam Ali, who ascended the *masnad* (throne) of Hyderabad as the fifth Nizam in July 1761. Almost at the same time, Madhav Rao was installed as the fourth Peshwa at Poona. Raghunath Rao as the regent tried to usurp power from the Peshwa, Madhav Rao. This gave birth to factional politics at the Maratha court, which became worse as Madhav Rao began to assert his power. A civil war followed, but realising the consequences of a fratricidal conflict, the young Peshwa reconciled with his uncle through the mediation of the Maratha sardar, Malharrao Holkar. Simultaneously, many leaders including the Bhonsles of Nagpur, the Nimbalkars of Satara, and the Patwardhans of southern Maharashtra opposed the dominance of the government by Chitpavan Brahmans and they joined the Nizam and invaded Maharashtra. However, in a shrewd move, Raghunath Rao bribed Jankoji Bhonsle (son of Raghuji Bhonsle) and extricated him from the alliance with the Nizam, Nizam Ali. In August 1763, the Marathas inflicted a crushing defeat on the Nizam in the battle at Rakhshasbhavan. According to the Treaty of Aurangabad that followed, Nizam Ali was forced to surrender all the Maratha territories that had been acquired by him since the battle of Panipat. Additional areas were surrendered to Bhonsle also. This treaty settled the relations between the Peshwa and the Nizam for the next 30 years. It marked the end of the regency of Raghunath and the beginning of the independent career of Madhav Rao as the supreme authority of the Maratha state.[39] More importantly, it was the first settlement of a successful campaign in which the largest share of the gains went to other nobles rather than the central government (of the Peshwa). *This event marks the beginning of a shift in power between the centre and the periphery, which was to become more serious in a decade.*[40]

Raghunath Rao continued his machinations against the Peshwa and in the civil war that followed, he was openly supported by Hyder Ali, the Nizam and Bhonsle. He was finally defeated in a battle near the fort of Dhodap near Nasik in June 1768. He was in house arrest at Poona for many years till the death of Peshwa Madhav Rao in November 1772.

Shifting Relations at the Periphery

Damaji Gaikwad of Gujarat, after returning from Panipat, got involved in the factional warfare in the Deccan and continued his support of Raghunath Rao. By the late 1760s, the Peshwa was able to dominate the Gaikwad family. In Rajasthan, following the Battle of Mangrol to the northeast of Kota in late 1761, Malharrao Holkar restored Maratha power. In the area around Delhi, the Jats, the Rohillas, and the Muslim forces under Najib-ud-Daula fought endlessly through the decade after Panipat. As directed by the Peshwa, his lieutenants at Indore and Gwalior—Tukoji Holkar and Mahadji Sindhia—proceeded to the north in 1768. They were joined by the main Maratha force from Poona commanded by Ramachandra Ganesh and Visaji Krishna. By February 1771,

Delhi fell to the Marathas. The Emperor Shah Alam II was invited to come back from Allahabad to reoccupy the throne of Delhi by the Marathas. Led by Mahadji Shinde and Visaji Krishna, Emperor Shah Alam II entered the Red Fort in January 1772. Delhi remained under the control of the Marathas for the next two decades.

Alivardi Khan had captured the Bengal *masnad* (throne) in 1740 by toppling the Nasiri dynasty of Nawabs, even as the Maratha infiltration into Bengal, Bihar, and Orissa continued. Eventually the Nawab of Bengal and the Maratha court of Nagpur concluded a treaty in June 1751 agreeing to pay 12 lakh rupees annually out of Bengal revenue as *Chauth.* This treaty had assigned the revenues only and did not cede Orissa to the Marathas. However, utter confusion prevailed due to the adverse effects of the death of Alivardi Khan in 1756. The successor government of Bengal could not keep Orissa under control, and it was gradually annexed to the Kingdom of Berar (Nagpur). At the same time Plassey, Buxar, and the Diwani of 1765 were transforming the political destiny of Bengal. The Marathas with their growing control over Orissa were becoming a menace to the English in Bengal and they wrote to the Selective Committee in Bombay asking to attack the Marathas from their side,

> The routing them out of Cuttack seems to be the only effectual means of preventing their continuing their ravages. The execution we believe will not be very difficult, nor do we apprehend it can be attended with any bad consequences, but on the contrary, will be a step towards giving a check to the overgrown and dangerous power of the Maharattas, from which the civil commotions in their Government, by the death of Ballaje, offer a fair opportunity.... .[41]

Various British initiatives, thereafter, mainly followed attempts by Bombay to gain some advantage from the conflicts between Madhav Rao Peshwa and his uncle, Raghunath Rao. However, Sheo Bhat Sathe, the Maratha governor of Orissa, continued to remain there and a Maratha controlled Orissa remained a sphere of disturbance for the English. Towards the South, Karnataka was considered as a sphere of personal interest by Peshwa Madhav Rao, and he led four expeditions against Hyder Ali who had seized power of the Mysore state. Nonetheless, the Marathas were never able to control more than the border areas and extract some tribute from the rest.

The Emergence of the English as the Main Competitor on the Subcontinent

The collapse of the Mughal authority in central and peninsular India gave rise to a new generation of rulers. The British presence was overwhelming in Bengal, Bihar, Orissa, and in the Carnatic. The British could lay the solid foundation of a maritime empire in India taking advantage of the Maratha withdrawal from the North after the Panipat disaster of 1761. The Battle of Panipat removed the only formidable obstacle in the path of the English expansion westward.[42] Subsequently, the decisive British victory at Buxar in October 1764 destroyed at one fell swoop all the three main scions of Mughal power in north India. Nawab Mir Kasim died in obscurity and abject poverty. Emperor Shah Alam was forced into English control and supervision. Shuja-ud-Daula, eventually surrendered to the English.[43]

Clive returned to India as governor for the second time in May 1765. North India presented a diplomatic problem in itself. The battles of Panipat and Buxar created a power vacuum that had been unprecedented for more than three centuries. At Panipat, the Marathas had suffered a devastating defeat at the hands of the Afghans. The Peshwa himself died and the Marathas did not venture north in force again for another 10 years. The Afghans refused to take the responsibility of administering the conquered territories. Thus, Delhi and Punjab were left without a government. The only powers left were the Rohillas, Shuja-ud-Daula of Oudh, and the Emperor. Clive could have marched to Delhi and set up a "sponsored empire". However, he had already had more than enough of such experiments.[44] Clive's maxim was that the Company should "take no open part with these Hindostan princes, but privately promote their quarrelling to all eternity".[45]

These considerations led Clive to an accord with Shah Alam in August 1765 at Allahabad. He anticipated the ultimate resurgence of the Marathas and their renewed invasion into northern India. The other external threat was from the Afghans in the northwest. Clive, therefore, resolved to create an inner-ring fence as a means of dealing with fresh Maratha incursions and a possible Afghan revival. Shuja-ud-Daula was restored to his old province of Oudh, which was to serve as a buffer between the territories controlled by the Company and the turbulent powers to the north-east. Shah Alam's claims as emperor were recognised and the districts of Korah and Allahabad assigned to his direct control. His authority over Bengal was recognised and the Company promised to pay him an annual tribute of 26 lakhs out of the Bengal revenues. In return, he granted the *diwani* or revenue collecting power to the Company in Bengal, Bihar, and Orissa.[46] The grant of the *diwani* signalled the beginning of the British Raj.

The Death of Madhav Rao, Ascension of Nana Fadnavis, and the Expansion of the English

Madhav Rao, who was at the helm of the Maratha empire, died childless at the age of 27 in November 1772. His death introduced profound changes in the destiny of the Marathas: "The next thirty years are marked by a revolution in the character of the Maratha government, which, joined to the relative growth of forces outside, brought about the loss of Maratha independence and the breakup of the solidarity of the Maratha dominions".[47] The Peshwa died after nominating his 17-year-old younger brother, Narayan Rao, to the Peshwaship. Two days before his death, Madhav Rao released their uncle Raghunath Rao from captivity and entrusted his minor brother to his care. Thus, Raghunath Rao became the regent, and this provided him an opportunity to plot against the young Peshwa under his protection. Within nine months of investiture, Narayan

Rao, was murdered in cold blood. Raghoba (Raghunath Rao) was suspected to be a party to this cowardly and despicable act, but he set himself up as the Peshwa and began to administer the state. He then launched a combined campaign against the Nizam and other enemies who had started invading the Maratha territories. The assassination aroused the extreme anger and frustration of the entire Maratha leadership and the people against Raghoba. As the supreme judicial authority to the Council of *shastris*[48] in the Peshwa's court, Ram Shastri immediately started a full and impartial enquiry into this affair and traced the murder of Narayan Rao to Raghoba as its prime architect.

The ministers of the murdered Peshwa and other prominent Maratha chiefs, led by Balaji Janardhan Bhanu and Nana Fadnavis,[49] came together to bring the culprit to justice. To prevent Raghoba from seizing the Peshwaship, they formed a Council of State of twelve senior Maratha elders called Bara Bhais[50] headed by Nana Fadnavis. 'On February 1774, a proclamation was issued from Purandar in the name of the *Chhatrapati* to the effect that Raghunath Bajirao, having committed the gross sin of bringing about the ruin of Peshwa Narayanrao and of forcibly exacting robes of that office from the Chhatrapati, had now been deprived of that position"[51]. Meanwhile, the wife of Narayan Rao, Ganga Bai, gave birth to a posthumous son at Purandhar in April 1774. He was named Madhav Rao Narayan and the Bara Bhais at once declared him to be the new Peshwa and undertook the running of the administration in his name. This spoiled all chances of Raghoba of making any compromise with the ruling elite of Poona.[52] Deserted by his commanders, soldiers, and most of the Maratha loyalists including Holkar and Sindhia, Raghoba retreated westwards, hoping to find a solid ally among the warring brothers of the Gaikwad family of Gujarat. After extended negotiations, Raghunath Rao finally found a new ally in the English in Bombay.[53]

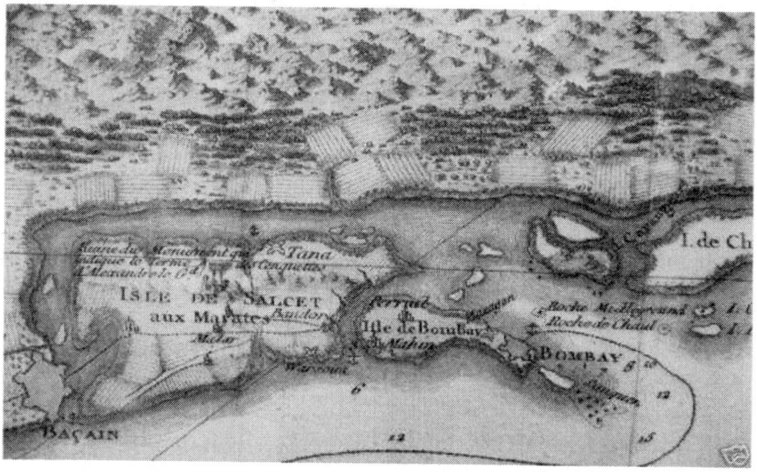

Source: Pierre de Pages 'Voyages Autour Du Monde', Paris, 1782.

An overview of the Bombay region:
From a Surat-to-Bombay map by Benard

Mehta rightly points out: "The day the seniormost member of the Peshwa's ruling house betrayed the interests of the Maratha State and bartered away the honour and self-respect of the country to the foreign adventurers, the sun of the Maratha fortunes set in the western horizon for ever."[54] For the English, commerce was their primary focus on the Western coast of India for a long time. The possession of Bombay[55] and the castle of Surat[56] gave them an advantage in the market of raw materials and maintaining that dominance was an important aim for the English.

> Amongst the foreign dependencies of the British Crown none are of greater and more increasing importance than Bombay.... It is however essential to her prosperity that she should preserve her Indian Empire, and every year strengthens the conviction of thinking men, that whether that Empire be regarded from a political or commercial point of view, its most important possession is the island of Bombay".[57]

It was the Bombay docks that the English wanted to defend at all costs. It was the only place belonging to the English in India where large vessels could be repaired and it was found that it was chiefly owing to the assistance of the docks at Bombay that the English had been able to maintain their naval superiority.

The Court of Directors[58] directed the Bombay government to seize every opportunity of acquiring Salsette, Bassein, Kenery, Hog, Elephanta, and Karanja. In March 1768, they wrote, "We cannot directly point out the mode of doing it, but rather wish they could be obtained by purchase rather than war".[59]

Meanwhile in Delhi, the Mughal Emperor Shah Alam II, after 14 years of exile, returned to his ancestral throne in 1772 under the protection of the Marathas. He conveyed his gratitude to the Maratha sardars and to the Peshwa for their expression of loyalty and attachment and promised "to out-rival the Wazir and the English in serving the interests of our Empire". The emperor had been dissuaded by his close associate Nawab Munir-ud-Daulah and the English from undertaking the enterprise. Almost all the Afghan and the Rohilla sardars were against his "falling into the clutches of the Deccanis".[60] However, Shah Alam disregarded their advice. The policy of establishing an alliance with Shah Alam had the full support of the Poona government. The Peshwa, Madhava Rao, was conscious of the British ambitions in India and wanted to check their expansion in northern India with a Mughal alliance. However, the Marathas who returned to north India were neither feared nor loved. The internecine quarrel amongst the leading Maratha personalities—Ramachandra Ganesh and Visaji Pant, Mahadaji Sindhia and Tukoji Holkar—resulted in disunity and discord amongst them from the very start. Mahadaji Sindhia, who recognised that the Marathas were unpopular all over the north, knew that they would not be able to establish their rule in those parts unless it was enveloped in the gilded packaging of Mughal sovereignty.[61] This alliance led to serious apprehensions in the minds of both Shuja-ud-Daulah, the Nawab of Oudh, and the English regarding the ultimate motives of the Marathas.

In 1772, the English could no longer afford to remain indifferent to the rapid advance of the Maratha forces towards their own frontiers. Claiming the suzerainty over the provinces of Korah (Kora Jahanabad, Fatehpur) and Kara, near Kanpur, a Maratha army under Visaji Pant and Tukoji Holkar inflicted a severe defeat on the Ruhella (Rohilla) forces near Ramghat in March 1773. Soon, the Nawab-Wazir of Oudh, Shuja-ud-Daulah, and the British troops under General Barker moved up the Ganges to meet them, but at the very approach of the well-trained English detachment, the Maratha armies—which had struck terror into the hearts of the Rohillas—timidly withdrew. All the fordable ghats of the Ganges were now strongly guarded by the forces of the English and Shuja-ud-Daulah. The Marathas then set for the Deccan, broken in spirit and utterly discredited, by way of Etawah and Kalpee never to return to Ruhelkhand (Rohilkhand).[62] Both Visaji and Tukoji blamed each other for the irreparable failure of the Maratha enterprise in Hindustan after three years of effort.

The Anglo-Maratha Cooperation and Conflicts

An era of cooperation between the English and the Marathas was inaugurated by the treaty of Bassein in 1739. Principally of a commercial nature, this was the first treaty between the English and the Marathas and conceded to the English the rights of free trade throughout the dominion of the Peshwa. In the ensuing years, by actively cooperating with the Marathas, the English made a determined effort to suppress coastal pirate activity.

In March 1755, a combined naval force commanded by Commodore William James of the East India Company and a Maratha fleet of Peshwa Baji Rao defeated Tulaji Angria capturing Suvarnadurg and Bankot. Suvarnadurg was given to the Marathas while Bankot was taken over by the English and named Fort Victoria. Tulaji Angria who retreated to Vijaydurg was defeated by a combined force of Admiral Watson, Robert Clive, and the Marathas. A treaty was signed in October 1758, which provided commercial advantages to the English.

The three British Presidencies of Madras, Calcutta, and Bombay acted independently of each other till the Regulating Act of 1773. The ambitions of the Government of Bombay on the west coast were thwarted by the powerful Peshwas, whose conquest of Bassein in 1739 was a proclamation of the power of the Marathas. The Government of Bombay tried to win over the Poona Durbar to their side by means of diplomatic negotiations and three English embassies were sent in 1759, 1767, and 1772.[63] The first embassy was sent to the Maratha court at the request of Baji Rao in August 1759 and was headed by W. A. Price and Thomas Mostyn, council in the service of the Honourable United East India Company, at Bombay. There was much deliberation, but nothing was settled.

Then came the Abdali invasion of Delhi in 1761, the Third Battle of Panipat, which was a great setback to Maratha power. However, slowly but steadily Peshwa Madhav Rao reconsolidated his power, which created serious concerns in the minds of the English. If the Marathas joined Hyder Ali and the Nizam against their protégé, the Nawab of Carnatic, their own position on the Coromandel Coast was likely to be exposed to serious danger.[64] In order for such an alliance to not take shape at any cost, the second embassy of Mostyn was sent to Poona by the English in November 1767. Grant Duff wrote, "Mr. Mostyn was sent to Poona by the Bombay government for the purpose of ascertaining the Peshwa's views, and of using every endeavour, by fomenting the domestic dissensions or otherwise, to prevent the Marathas from joining Hyder and Nizam Ali".[65] He was not able to achieve much during his stay for three months there by way of diplomatic success, but he was able to collect a good deal of information regarding the Poona affairs.

In 1772, Mostyn led his third embassy to Poona that originated from the Court of Directors in London with instructions to penetrate into any design of the Marathas that might affect the Company's possession in Bengal and in the Carnatic and try to obtain the cession of Salsette, Bassein, and Karanja. The English were willing to cede Fort Victoria to the Marathas and promised not to oppose their annexation of the Siddi Island of Rajpuri. Mostyn was also to placate the Peshwa's ministers and to become fully acquainted with the intrigues of the Peshwa's court and the Peshwa's temper.

The stay of Mostyn till February 1774 was charged with significant events:[66]

1. The British attempt to secure Bassein, Salsette, and Karanja
2. The capture of Broach
3. The death of Madhav Rao
4. The short-lived Maratha supremacy in Delhi
5. The Maratha defeat in Rohilkhand
6. The contest for the government between Mudaji and Sabaji Bhonsle
7. The murder of Narayan Rao
8. The first months of Raghoba's Peshwaship
9. The beginning of the Bara Bhais' plot

The English had applied much restraint in their dealings with the Marathas, realising that the Maratha state was the largest and strongest of the imperial powers of India. As in the Carnatic and elsewhere in India, internal quarrels among the Indian princes and chiefs offered an opportunity to the English to interfere in Indian affairs. The murder of Peshwa Narayan Rao resulted in a war of succession between the two rival factions of the ruling Maratha elite. The English used the same strategy that was in use throughout India—support one candidate in a succession dispute in hopes of extracting major territorial gains if he won.[67]

In April 1774, Mostyn, the British envoy in Poona, was approached by Raghoba for armed assistance to fight against his political rivals in Poona. Mostyn wrote: "As for security he is willing to make over any lands along the Sea Coast that is that might be agreeable, such as Guzerat, the country about Saringham (Srirangam in Trichy) and the Islands near Bombay, until the Company be fully reimbursed their Expenses and money they might advance".[68] Because he had withdrawn too far off Surat, Raghoba found it impractical to carry on his negotiations with the English through Mostyn at Poona. He approached them through Robert Gambier, civil governor of Surat, to furnish him with a force to carry him "to Poona and establish him in the government, for which he would defray the charges of expedition, make very considerable grants to the Company, and enter into any terms of friendship and alliance the President and Council at Bombay might choose".[69] The Bombay government was of the opinion that some assistance to Raghoba would bring considerable advantages to the Company and immediately entered into negotiations with him. The English had long been waiting for a suitable opportunity to carry out their aggressive designs on the west coast. In the contest between the Ministerial party in Poona and Raghoba, they got the long-awaited chance, and it was just the crisis that the Company was hoping for.[70] While the Poona government was engaged in dealing with Raghoba, the English planned an attack on the island of Salsette, which they captured on 31 December 1774.[71]

The English Offensive in Gujarat

The Maratha chief of Gujarat, Damaji Gaikwar, died in August 1768 and there started a dispute of succession amongst his sons. The Peshwa Madhav Rao entered into a compromise and allowed Sayaji Rao, his eldest son by his second wife, to retain his succession by assigning him with a small *jagir* (grant of power to administer a district and collect tax) Fateh Singh, his youngest son by his third wife, was allotted the Gaikwar territory as well as the army. As long as Madhav Rao was alive, the two brothers kept peace between them. After Narayan Rao's murder and Raghoba's succession to the office of the Peshwa, the claim of Govind Rao, second son of first wife of Damaji, was again recognised. Thus, the family feud between the two Gaikwar brothers assumed an unexpected political significance. The conflict between Raghoba and the ministers shifted from Poona to Gujarat and a new champion, the East India Company, entered the lists at the request of Raghoba.[72] Their combined army met at the outskirts of Baroda and later moved towards Ahmedabad. Raghoba was defeated in a battle fought at

Sanvel in February 1775 by the Maratha forces led by Haripant Phadke. He retreated in the direction of Cambay and Bhavnagar and boarded an English ship to Surat where he threw himself under the shelter of the English.

Negotiations between Raghoba and the English had been started during the last stages of his flight following his defeat at Sanvel. Raghoba appealed to the English to aid him with sufficient force to carry him to Poona and establish him in the government there. In this diplomatic contest, the Bombay government proved itself the shrewdest of merchants and extracted from Raghoba a heavy price for their help. After extensive discussions the fifth and the final draft was signed by Raghoba at Surat on 6 March 1775 and ratified by Bombay on 16 March. The terms of the Treaty of Surat ceded a large area in Gujarat, the islands near Bombay, and 150,000 rupees per month to the maintenance of 2,500 regular troops including artillery. The Court of Directors in their despatch in December 1775 approved the session of these places and asked the Bombay government to adopt such measures as might be necessary for their preservation and defence.[73]

An English army under Colonel Keating was sent to assist Raghoba for re-establishing him in the Supreme Government of the Maratha Empire. The combined forces left Surat on 15 March 1775, and, after several encounters, the armies finally met on the famous plains of Arras (Adas). The Maratha troops under Haripant Phadke were defeated and had to retreat from Gujarat, leaving the entire Maratha territory to the north of the Narmada under the authority of the English and their allies. This came about mainly because Haripant was not sufficiently supported by Mahadaji Sindhia and Tukoji Holkar and this betrayal assisted the English in their effort to win over Fateh Singh Gaikwar. Having shielded Raghoba, the next diplomatic step before the English was to separate Fateh Singh from the ministerial party in Poona. For Fateh Singh there was no option left but to take the initiative of establishing friendship with the English. After lengthy negotiations, a treaty was signed between Raghoba and Fateh Singh and this treaty was a great triumph for the Bombay government.[74] Thus, though the English did not attain their main objective of installing Raghoba on the throne of Poona, they gained an upper hand against the Marathas. Their exit from Gujarat left the English and their allies, Raghoba and Govindrao Gaikwar, free to follow their plans. The net gains of the Bombay government by the cessions made by Fateh Singh and by conquest were very considerable and strategically they were very significant. From Bassein to Chaul, they now had land forming a deep bay, in which were situated the islands of Salsette, Bombay, Karanja, Hog, Elephenta, and Kaneri.

The Maratha Reverses

The Marathas were in a desperate situation as Mahadaji Sindhia and Tukoji Holkar withdrew their armies to their own domains and became inactive and indifferent. They also lost the Gujarat region when Fateh Singh Gaikwar and Appaji Ganesh went over to the English. Meanwhile Sabaji Bhonsle's death gave a chance to his son, Mudaji, to unite the whole state of Berar under him. His attitude of independence forced the Marathas to appease the Nizam who became unreliable in his support of the Maratha state. Moreover, they were in extreme financial difficulties. At the same time, the ministerial party in Poona had to confront internal dissensions and revolts. Friction and fighting began to crop up in the south, especially between the chiefs of Kolhapur and Ichhalkaranji. The *Jagirdars* (the feudal class who collected taxes as a form of revenue) of Kolhapur and Kittur were in open revolt against the Maratha state. Taking advantage of all this uncertainty, Hyder Ali attacked and ravaged Dharvar. The finances of the state were breaking apart and the "Bara Bhais" seemed to be in disintegration. Deprived of allies and distressed by financial difficulties along with defeats on the battlefields of Gujarat, the ministers' party concluded that they could turn the tide around only by taking possession of Raghoba from the English.[75] With this in mind, Sakharam Bapu and Nana Fadnavis started their negotiations with the English who were also getting tired of Raghoba.

Warren Hastings and the Marathas

Under the Regulating Act of 1773, a new government took charge of the administration of Bengal in October 1774 with powers to superintend and control the presidencies of Madras and Bombay—therefore, Bengal became the Supreme Government. Warren Hastings was appointed the first Governor-General of Bengal. The actions of the Bombay government against the Maratha state were contrary to the contents of the Regulating Act and this action was roundly condemned by Calcutta. The Supreme Council declared the conduct of them "as unreasonable, unpolitic, unjust and unauthorised".[76] The Bombay government tried to bring around the Supreme Government to their point of view resulting in a great dilemma in Calcutta. There were clearly two viewpoints in the Council. One, represented by Philip Francis, believed in the unequivocal denouncement of the Bombay government's policy and in issuing immediate orders to them to stop all hostilities. The Governor-General, on the other hand, believed that Bombay had to be furnished with both men and money, but he failed to mobilize majority support for his opinion. The main difficulty in implementing his views was that the British lacked adequate resources to carry on a war of such magnitude. In May 1775, the Supreme Government informed the Poona government that they had communicated to the Bombay government to cease all hostilities between the two forces. They also expressed their desire to depute a trusty person to Poona with a view of settling the differences between the two governments.

Colonel Upton was subsequently deputed to Poona and started his negotiations in December 1775.[77] He was told that the purpose of his embassy was to negotiate and conclude a treaty of peace between the Maratha government and the Presidency of Bombay and to obtain a confirmation regarding the administration of the islands of Salsette and Bassein. They wanted a settlement with the Maratha state to secure a legal sanction for their acquisitions and a diplomatic opening for their objectives on the west coast of India.[78] There were repeated changes in his instructions making it clear that the English wanted to secure all the advantages from the distracted

Maratha state, which was just short of a war. 'After protracted negotiations, the Treaty of Purandhar was signed on 1 March 1776 between Colonel Upton and the ministers, Sakharam Bapu and Nana Fadnavis. The preceding Treaty of Surat was formally annulled. The treaty ended hostilities, returned the cessions in Gujarat, awarded the British Salsette and Bassein and the revenues of Broach, and some immediate cash. In return, the British withdrew all support from Raghunath Rao, who received an annual stipend.[79]

The Bombay government was determined not to implement the treaty and in open defiance of the Supreme Government's order, they gave full protection to Raghoba. With impunity, they flouted the conditions of peace. Their entire thinking was in terms of military preparations and military reinforcements. Part of their thinking was governed by the likely danger from France, but they were mainly attracted by the "confused and unsteady administration" of Poona.[80] They wanted to capitalise on it and their idea was to install a government favourable to the Company under Raghoba, which would bring peace and stability to the empire. Thomas Mostyn of the Bombay Civil Service was appointed as the British resident much against the wishes of the Poona government.

Almost at the same time of Mostyn's arrival at Poona, St. Lubin, a Frenchman,[81] landed in Chaul, near Bombay, in March 1777 and declared himself an accredited agent of the French King, Louis XVI. St. Lubin had been officially deputed by the French ministry to investigate the state of affairs in India, establish contact with the Maratha court with whom the relations of the English were getting strained and to report on the possibilities of the French drawing some advantage. St. Lubin had been widely accepted by the French authorities in India. The reception given to St. Lubin by Nana Fadnavis and Sakharam Bapu was a grand affair and in contrast to the chilly welcome that Mostyn had received previously. Nana Fadnavis seemed to have been sincerely convinced, such as Hyder Ali, that with the help of France, he might be able to offset the growing British aggression in India. However, the historian, S. P. Varma, rightly observes:

> Nana did not seem to know, what Warren Hastings could clearly see, that the English had "nothing to fear from the exertions of a nation who have no sure footing in India and who must transport every soldier that they are to bring into the field from a distant country across a wide ocean. Having lost their footing on the Indian soil and their naval superiority, and too much involved in European commitments, the French had become incapable, after 1763, of rendering any decisive help to any Indian power against the English".[82]

The St. Lubin affair provided the English an excellent pretext for breaking their recent treaty with the Maratha state with which the Bombay government had been annoyed for a long time.

The initial reaction by the Supreme Government at Calcutta to the news of the signing of the treaty at Purandhar between the Marathas and Colonel Upton was its complete acceptance. They immediately withdrew the permission granted to Bombay to give Raghoba sanctuary. Early in July 1776, they instructed Colonel Upton to reassure the Poona government that they would make every endeavour to maintain peace, cultivate friendship, and remove distrust. They called upon the Bombay government to keep a good understanding with the Maratha government. However, the succeeding months witnessed a growing tension between Bombay and Poona as certain outstanding points of dispute were not settled. William Taylor, the agent of the Bombay government in Calcutta, succeeded in his attempt at changing the mind of the Calcutta government in favour of the Bombay stand.[83] Taylor further impressed the Supreme government that a war with the Maratha state was inescapable since the latter was preparing for it.

These arguments were beginning to take some effect. By early November, a definite change came over the attitude of the Calcutta government. A series of events emboldened the governor-general to revive his efforts to regain Bassein, even if that meant the use of force.[84] However, it was the extraordinary favour shown by the Poona Ministers to St. Lubin, an agent of the Crown of France and

Mr. Bolts, a representative of the House of Austria, which caused extreme apprehension in the minds of the English.[85]

By the end of 1777, the Maratha state was in a better position to face the challenges of the English. However, fresh difficulties and complicated problems were confounding them. This was an inevitable outcome of the circumstances in which the government at Poona had been organised. There was no constitutional precedent for the pattern of government that the "Bara Bhais" had set up. For all practical purposes, authority had been consigned to the hands of Nana Fadnavis and Sakharam Bapu. Moroba, one of the members of the council and a cousin of Nana, had declared sympathies with Raghoba. The English resident, Mostyn, formed a secret project with Moroba to convince Raghoba to come to Poona for which the English would support him. The Bombay government was looking for a change of administration at Poona to protect the Company from the dangers and consequences of an alliance between the French and the Marathas.

Warren Hastings regarded the English as bound by the orders of the Court of Directors to give support to Raghoba as long as it was not in violation of the treaty. He accepted the Bombay government's contention that the demand for British help was an application for "the ruling part of the administration of the Maratha State". In relocating Raghoba to Poona, they could not in any way be accused of violating the treaty of Purandhar.[86] Hastings' proposals were accepted and the decision to launch a war upon the biggest political power in India was taken in February 1778.

The Poona government made serious efforts to avoid a feud, but nothing could hold back the determination of the English to initiate a war with the Marathas. Philip Francis, in the internal councils of the Supreme Government, drew the attention of the governor-general to the news of the surrender of General Burgoyne in Saratoga. However, Warren Hastings scorned any connection between the events in America and Europe and the apprehensions of the English in India. He was very confident about the superior advantages that the English possessed, both on land and sea.[87] He wrote, "on the contrary, if it be really true, that the British arms and influence have suffered so severe a check in the western world, it is more incumbent on those who are charged with the interests of Great Britain in the east to exert themselves for the retrieval of the national loss".[88] Hastings prepared comprehensive plans to strike against the various centres of Maratha power, simultaneously, in the name of Raghoba. Accordingly, Bombay was authorised to prepare to storm the Western Ghats while a supporting contingent of the Bengal army was ordered to march out of Oudh. In February 1778, the Calcutta government ordered the formation of an army unit consisting of six of their best battalions under the command of Colonel Lesliefor the assistance of Bombay. Colonel Leslie decided to proceed there by the Bundelkhand route.[89] The objective of selecting this route was to create distraction for Mudaji Bhosle and other northern chiefs and to restrain them from going to help Nana Fadnavis and Haripant Phadke. This would relieve the pressure upon the Malwa chiefs, Bachaba Purandhare and Tukoji Holkar, and give them liberty to play whatever part they pleased in the support of Raghoba. The progress of the battalion was slow as the conditions in Bundelkhand were both chaotic and tempting. Colonel Leslie had an initial success in a battle in Mau and this provoked the local sardars to unite and fight back. For once, the Marathas and the Rajputs forgot their old quarrel and united in a common desire to oppose the English. Leslie's battalion, which reached Rajgarh in August 1778, was checked in advance. Colonel Leslie died on 3 October 1778 and the expedition was entrusted to Colonel Goddard.

Goddard resumed his march from Rajgarh and reached Bhopal in November. He followed a policy of compromise and was keen to strengthen diplomatic ties with neighbouring kingdoms. Hastings wanted a close alliance with Berar and to utilise it as an effective counterpart to the coalition of the Poona government, the Nizam, and the French, which seemed to him threatening the English possessions on the Bombay coast, Awadh, and Bengal.[91] However, negotiations with the Rajah of Berar, Mudaji Bhonsle, did not succeed. On the news of the failure of the Berar mission reaching the Supreme Government, they decided to abide by the treaty they had agreed on with Raghoba and asked Goddard to proceed to Poona to assist the Bombay forces. On 30 January, Goddard reached Burhanpur on the Tapti River where he received the news of the rout of the Bombay army. In view of the defeat sustained by the Bombay government, Goddard thought it all the more necessary for his forces to reach Bombay as early as possible. He was convinced that his presence in Bombay would offset the lost balance between the English and the Marathas.

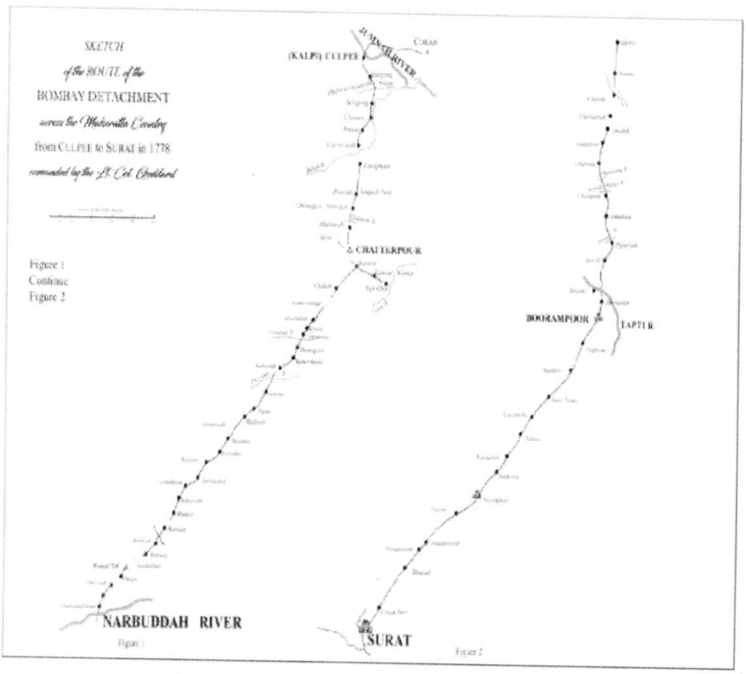

A modified Sketch of Colonel Goddard's Route[90]

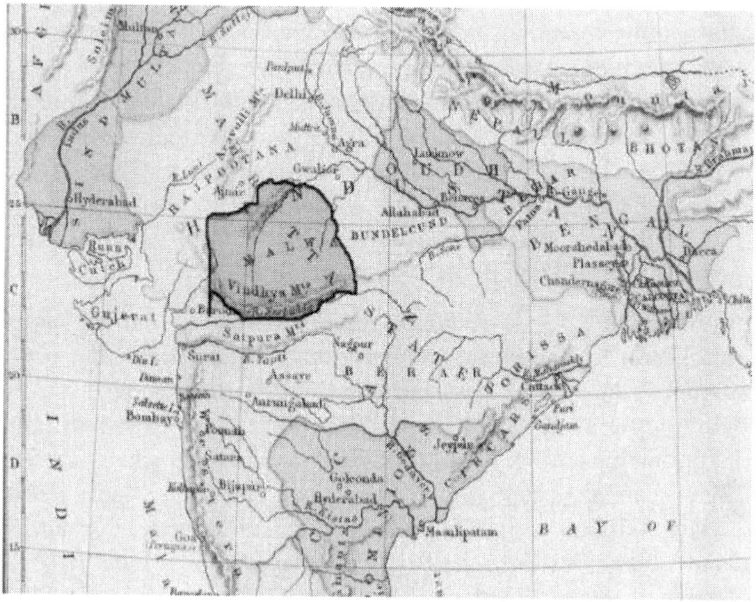

Malwa in 1780 ***Open Source***

The Battle and the Convention of Wadgaon and the Aftermath

Pointing to the director's orders in favour of Raghoba, the Bombay government signed a new agreement with him to install him as regent. The Bombay government dispatched a well-equipped English army under the leadership of Carnac, Egerton, and Mostyn to bring Raghoba to Poona. The army commenced its operation on 7 December 1778 by crossing the Western Ghats. Meanwhile the group in Poona, under Shinde, Holkar, and Nana Fadnavis assembled a large army and by the third week were able to defeat the British forces. The humiliating treaty of Wadgaon was signed on 18 January 1779 by which they promised to surrender Raghoba, besides restoring all the Maratha territories that they had acquired since 1773.[92] The Bombay Select Committee refused to accept the treaty on the basis that Carnac and Egerton had no authority to conclude any treaty or engagement binding on the Company. At the same time, Hastings launched a vigorous war of diplomacy against the Poona government with friendly overtures and tempting offers to the Maratha sardars to wean them away from the Poona government and create dissensions amongst themselves. He sent envoys to the courts of all major Maratha chiefs, including Holkar, Sindhia, Bhonsle, Gaikwar, and others to arouse their sympathies to the English cause. His diplomatic efforts did meet with expected success. Fateh Singh Gaikwar was won over to the English side through the diplomatic manoeuvres of Mostyn. Mudhoji Bhonsle gradually backed out of the "Maratha Confederacy".

Meanwhile Goddard continued his march. He did encounter opposition from several independent Hindu chiefs, but none attempted to block his passage. The English troops moved briskly by avoiding all fortified towns and military posts and without disrupting the normal life of the people. Goddard reached Surat on 25 February, covering 300 miles between Burhanpur and Surat in 20 days. Within a span of four months, he had covered a distance of about 1,000 miles, criss-crossing the subcontinent of India. Warren Hastings wrote to Lawrence Sulivan (Fort William, 18 April 1779):

> The successful and steady progress of a part of the military force of Bengal from Jumna to Surat, has contributed more than perhaps our more splendid achievements to augment our military reputation and to confirm the ascendant of our influence over all the powers of Hindustan. To them, as to ourselves, the attempt appeared astonishing and impractical, because it had never before been made or suggested. It has shown what the British arms are capable of effecting, and it has afforded a most seasonable aid to the Presidency of Bombay when it stood in need of a foreign support.[93]

The task of Goddard was not only to make up for the loss of English military prestige, but also to strengthen the diplomatic relationship. The Supreme Government invested him with full powers as their public minister to negotiate with the Peshwa and the ministers of the Maratha state. The English were ready for the confirmation of the Treaty of Purandhar, provided the Marathas withdrew what they had acquired through the Treaty of Wadgaon. However, if the ministers rejected these proposals, the English were ready for an open war to defend their rights and interests. The plan created at Bombay contemplated a partnership with the Gaikwar of Baroda, Mudaji Bhonsle of Berar, and if possible, a separate secret alliance with Mahadaji Sindhia. Thus, the Supreme Government devised an outline for a network of alliances with the subordinate collaborators of the Maratha Confederacy and with the view of ultimately bringing down the entire superstructure of the Marathas.

Goddard started his negotiations with the Poona government, who put forward two conditions. The first was to deliver Raghoba who had escaped the custody of Sindhia and second was the island of Salsette be returned to the Maratha government. Goddard found these conditions dishonourable and destructive to the interests of the Company and broke off the negotiations. The English moved ahead with the idea of launching an offensive on the Gujarat front, which was a sensible decision from a military, diplomatic, and political standpoint.[94] The chain of mountains, which defended Poona from Bombay, terminated in the Gujarat country. Through this path, an English army could easily penetrate by different routes and reach the heart of the Peshwa's territories. Without control over Gujarat, an attempt on the citadel of the Maratha power was bound to be dangerous. Above all the English hoped to widen the internal dissensions of the Poona court.

British Alliance with Fateh Singh

In the middle of December 1779, the English opened their negotiations with Fateh Singh Gaikwar. For all intents and purposes, this was to force him into a sort of subsidiary alliance which would help them carve out a buffer state between the English and the Maratha states. Goddard backed up the negotiations by mobilizing the army and crossed the river Tapti. Fateh Singh was pressured into signing a treaty of alliance on 26 January 1779. The English compelled him to cede to them much of the revenue of southern Gujarat, which was so far being paid to the Peshwa. The treaty with

Fateh Singh was not only a diplomatic victory, but also a prelude to large-scale military conquests that would play out in the future.[95]

Goddard, who by now had been promoted to general and appointed as the commander-in-chief of the Bombay army, kept up the pressure on the Marathas. He captured the fortress of Dabhoi and then proceeded to Ahmedabad, the capital of the Poona administration in Gujarat. The resistance that the Marathas offered at Ahmedabad was quite stiff, but the ceaseless firing from the English artillery threw the Maratha forces into confusion. A battalion of 100 European grenadiers and 16 companies of sepoy grenadiers under Lieutenant-Colonel Hartley[96] defeated them. The English and the Gaikwar forces occupied Ahmedabad in February 1780.[97] He also conquered Bassein after a long and bloody encounter in December 1780. Encouraged by this spectacular victory, Goddard prepared to advance upon Poona through Borghat as they had done two years ago. With Hartley, he ascended the ghats in February 1781; however, the Marathas were able to inflict several defeats and losses upon the enemy. Goddard was forced to retreat with severe losses and privations. The failure of Goddard, their ablest general who was well-equipped with ammunition and supplies and efficient artillery, discouraged the British beyond measure.[98]

Opposing the English in distant Gujarat, whose Maratha chief Gaikwar had already joined them, was a difficult task for the Poona government. To counter the English aggression, a Grand Quadruple Alliance against the British power was suggested, the four members being the Peshwa's government, the Nizam of Hyderabad, Hyder Ali of Mysore, and the Bhonsle of Nagpur.[99] The idea of this comprehensive alliance against the British was first put forward by Nizam Ali. In the 1760s, when the British became masters of Madras and Bengal, they found that the communication between these two provinces was blocked by two intervening tracts—that of Orissa belonging to Bhonsle of Nagpur and the Guntur district, part of the Northern Circars, belonging to the Nizam. With hostilities against the Marathas and the French flaring up, the east coastline became of vital importance for the free movements of armies of the two Presidencies of Madras and Calcutta. Guntur was assigned by the Nizam to his brother, Basalat Jung, who was forced to cede to the British by the Madras Governor, Thomas Rumbold. As the real owner of his state, Nizam Ali vehemently opposed this move. Realizing the danger of this strong anti-British combination, Warren Hastings restored Guntur to Nizam Ali, thereby detaching an important member from the Confederacy. Thereafter, Nizam Ali remained entirely neutral.

Nana Fadnavis became the moving spirit of the anti-British confederacy as he was singularly well-posted with correct information from all the Indian courts. He assigned specific duties to each member: Bhonsle was to attack the English in Bengal; Hyder Ali to pounce upon them in Madras; the Poona forces to oppose them in Gujarat and the Bombay Konkan; while the Nizam was to menace them on the east coast.[100] However, Mudhoji Bhonsle's elder son, Raghuji Bhonsle, backed out at the critical moment following negotiations with Hastings. Thus, two of the four stipulated members of the alliance backed out. The skill of Nana Fadnavis' diplomacy was soon to become manifest to the English of Madras. To Hyder Ali, Nana offered to cede all the lands actually occupied by his troops between the Krishna and the Tungabhadra Rivers.

Colonel Thomas Goddard, when he first marched across Central India in 1778, reported to Warren Hastings that unless the Maratha strength in Malwa was severely disabled, the war in Western India would not come to an end. Through successful diplomacy, Hastings forged an alliance with the Rana of Gohud (Gohad) who had long been subjugated by the Marathas.[101] Hastings despatched Major William Popham with a force of about 2,500 men equipped with artillery to assist the Rana, the ultimate object of the alliance being to make inroads into Sindhia's country and to disengage Sindhia from the western side of India. Hastings felt that once Sindhia found his dominions were in danger, he would detach himself from the confederacy of which he was the principal associate. This would relieve pressure on Goddard who was trying to overrun Gujarat and help the English to deal with the Marathas on a stronger footing. Popham invaded Sindhia's territory, took the fort of Lahar, and then moved against the capital Gwalior and captured the formidable fort on 4 August 1780.[102]

The fort of Gwalior was considered very secure and unassailable. The cheeky and audacious manner of obtaining the possession of the fort is detailed in a letter written by Captain Jonathan Scott, at that time the Persian interpreter to Major Popham.[103] He solicited the help of a tribe of banditti from the region of the Rana of Gohud who were accustomed to robbing about that town, for scaling the steep rock face. Following the victory, Hastings dispatched Carnac to support Popham and the English marched southwards with the aim of striking Mahadaji himself. In the battle near Mahadpur, they inflicted a crushing defeat on Mahadaji. Thus, during the summer of 1781, while the Poona forces were beating Goddard between Panvel and Kalyan, Mahadaji's position became precarious in Malwa. At this critical juncture, he got support from Ahalyabhai of Indore. A contingent of troops from Poona also turned up. Thus, improving his position, Mahadaji kept up his fight stubbornly and inflicted a severe defeat upon Colonel Muir near Sipri (Shivpuri).[104]

The Battle of Pollilur—Its Impact on the Policy of Hastings and the Treaty of Salbai

The triumph in the whole Maratha war, especially the spectacular accomplishment of Popham, was completely overshadowed by a disaster of the great magnitude: "Unfortunately for Warren Hastings, at the very moment when his courage and fortitude were beginning to fetch its reward, he found himself suddenly called upon to engage in a new struggle, not for the aggrandizement of the British Empire in India, but for its very existence".[105] A combined army of Sir Hector Munro and Colonel Bailey was decimated by the forces of Hyder Ali supported by his son Tipu on 10 September 1780 in the Battle of Pollilur. 60 out of 86 British officers and about 2,000 British and Indian troops perished and about 1,000 more were taken as prisoners. This battle was a wake-up call for Warren Hastings and evidence that India's native armies were no longer easy prey. The Mysore troops had been trained by British officers in the service of Mohammed Ali or by French officers under Chanda Sahib and the Nizam. The words of command were given in English; native cavalry, instead of making fruitless charges against the British guns, were now cleverly deployed to outflank them. In Madras, the proportion of the king's regiments, mostly Highlanders, to Company regiments was higher than ever and they were led by distinguished officers. Reputations easily won in previous decades were now proving hard to sustain against the new generation of opponents.

News of Pollilur made Warren Hastings recognize that only "the most instant, powerful, and hazardous excursions could possibly save Madras and thus prevent the French from snatching this golden opportunity to re-establish themselves in the peninsula".[106] Realising that he had to concentrate his whole energy upon Hyder Ali, he moved in all directions for effecting a settlement with the Marathas. Hastings dispatched General Coote to Madras by sea along with 4,000 troops and 1.5 million rupees. Colonel Pearse was ordered to march overland from Bengal to Madras with a force of 5,000. On the diplomatic front, Hastings ensured the neutrality of the Bhonsles of Berar on Bengal's border. At the same time, he persisted in the negotiations with the Maratha government of Poona.[107] It was clearly impossible for the English to carry on war both against the Maratha state and Hyder Ali successfully. They had to choose between their position in the Karnatak and their designs on the Bombay coast. The danger of losing Karnatak was great and if it was lost, Hyder Ali would be immovably established there. He would be able to attack at the vitals of the British hold in Bengal, besides raising enemies on the western and northern frontiers. The loss of Bombay could never be such a severe blow. The enormity of the threat posed by Hyder Ali of Mysore is clearly palpable in Hasting's letter to his friend and a major political diplomat of the East India Company, David Anderson:

> It is not peace with conditions of advantage that we want but a speedy peace; and we would rather purchase it with the sacrifice of every foot of ground that we have acquired from the Marathas, excepting Salsette and the little islands adjacent to Bombay, than hazard the loss

> of the present opportunity by contending for more. I am afraid of nothing but delay.[108]

The directors of the Company were alarmed by the turn of events and called upon the governor-general to initiate the process for the termination of all hostilities in India. The initiative for peace, therefore, was taken by the English. Thus, the First Anglo-Maratha War lasted over seven years and it took seven months of diplomatic parleys, discussions, and hard bargaining on both sides to bring it to a close by the Treaty of Salbai, which was signed on 17 May 1782.[109] It is highly significant that this treaty was signed between the Governor-General Warren Hastings and Mahadaji Sindhia, one of the sardars of the Maratha Confederacy and not by Nana Fadnavis, the prime minister of the Peshwa.[110] Hastings approved the treaty at Fort William on 6 June, but the final adjustments were delayed by Nana as he was striving for the restoration of Salsette and was secretly conspiring with Hyder. The death of Hyder Ali obliged Nana Fadnavis to ratify the treaty, which he did not do until 24 February 1783.[111] The treaty contained 17 clauses and in the first instance it provided for the restoration of all Maratha territories. This included Bassein, which had been ceded to the British according to the treaty of Purandhar, the only exception being Salsette and three small islands that were retained by the Company. All the territories of Mahadaji Sindhia were restored to him. Madhav Rao Narayan was recognised by the British as the rightful Peshwa. All the Maratha territories, forts, and towns in Gujarat that were granted by him to the Company were restored to the Poona government. Fateh Singh Gaikwar was recognised as an independent ruler, but under the suzerainty of the Peshwa. The cause of Raghunath Rao was given up and the English agreed to surrender him. He was to be paid a monthly allowance and was to reside in Gwalior. Article 9 was related to Hyder Ali, which provided that the Peshwa would restrain him from continuing his hostilities against the British. He was to give up the territories which he had won from the Nawab of Arcot, who was under the shelter of the British. The treaty also restrained the Marathas from having relations with any other European power and the British in turn were to guarantee not to assist the enemies of Marathas directly or indirectly.

The Treaty of Salbai forms a historic landmark in the political history of India. According to Lieutenant-Colonel Luard:

> The importance of this treaty, which placed the political relations of the English and the Marathas on an entirely new and definite footing, cannot be overestimated. It formed the turning point in the history of the English in India. It secured peace with the Marathas for twenty years, and, without the acquisition of any fresh territory, it established beyond dispute, the dominance of the British as controlling factor in India politics, their subsequent rise in 1818 to the position of the paramount power, being an inevitable result of the position gained by the Treaty of Salbai.[112]

Warren Hastings took a more realistic view when he described it as "a successful negotiation of peace ... in the most desperate period of my distresses".[113]

Practically for the English, the Treaty of Salbai was a clear acknowledgement of failure. The English had spent considerable energy in the subjugation of the Maratha Empire, but in this effort they notably failed. Thus, the Marathas were able to hold back the rising tide of English aggression for a period of time. However, in the long term, (there were far reaching disadvantages and shortcomings in the treaty of Salbai) there were limitations to the victory of the Marathas in the Treaty of Salbai. The Marathas were "a war like people with claims, real or pretended, on almost every power in Hindustan".[114] The murder of Narayan Rao in 1774 initiated the First Anglo-Maratha War, which dragged on for seven years. However, even as this war raged, the Marathas were hoping to re-establish their control over the Rajputs, the Jats, the Bundelas, and over Delhi. Mahadaji wanted to drive out the English from Atarveda and push them back into Bengal and finally expel them from there also. The Treaty of Salbai brought an end to these dreams and to the entire process of Maratha expansion, which had been going on for more than half a century. Mahadaji also tried to confine the English to Bengal, but here too he could not succeed. He was forced to acknowledge Nawab Asaf-ud-Daulah as a protégé of the English in the north, just as he had to acknowledge Nawab Mohammed Ali Khan as their protégé in the south.[115]

The Marathas received a guarantee from the Supreme Government of Calcutta against the aggressive designs of their presidencies. The English on their part also agreed not to assist any nation of Deccan or Hindustan opposing the Peshwa. On their behalf, the Marathas gave the English a guarantee that they would not allow any factories of other European nations to be established in their territories. They also agreed not to have any dealings or friendship with other European nations. Nonetheless, this treaty proved to be a one-sided affair in the long run, which severely curtailed the power of the Marathas in inflicting any emphatic injury on the English interest in India. Once the ratification of the treaty was completed, Mahadaji tried to persuade the English into an offensive and defensive alliance of a general nature. The English refused to get involved to that extent, but they were keen to join the Marathas to attack Tipu. Mahadji fell for this idea and persuaded Nana to dispatch forces as soon as possible, but as an architect of the Maratha-Mysore alliance against the English, Nana could not easily decide to turn his forces against Tipu. By the middle of February 1784, the Poona government was able to dispatch an army towards Mysore. By this time, the English directly entered into a treaty with Tipu, which forced the Marathas to fight Tipu on their own. The Maratha-Mysore war ended in April 1785 following the Treaty of Gajendragad. Malet in his letter number 68, to the Governor-General, Poona, on 27 June 1787, says: "Every information I can collect relative to the late peace tends to persuade me it has been highly advantageous to Tippoo. He has dissolved a formidable confederacy and dissipated an immense army".[116]

Nana Fadnavis and Mahadaji Sindhia dominated the post-Panipat period of Maratha history. They played a decisive role in winning the First Maratha War and won a credible peace treaty. But in the aftermath of peace, they lost heavily. As the negotiations dragged on, the weakness of the Maratha state was exposed more and more. The attention of Sindhia concentrated on the establishment of the Maratha power at Delhi and in northern India, in taking the imperial affairs under his control and in subduing the Jats and the Rohillas, the Sikhs and the Rajputs. On the other hand, Nana was focused on the "desha", the home province of the Marathas. According to Sarkar: "He knew not that the old Maratha policies of war and diplomacy which had succeeded under Baji Rao I and Baji Rao (1720-1760) were now hopelessly outdated and that an entirely new orientation of Maratha policy in Hindustan and a new genre of Maratha generals and administrators are required for carry out the new policy".[117]

The All-India vision of Mahadaji and Nana was biased and distorted in many ways. According to Professor Shanti Prasad Varma:

> The English with Awadh as their foot stool were getting ready to jump at Delhi and they had another foot stool at Carnatic, and they threatened Poona both from the south-east and from the west. Mahadaji never seems to have understood the danger to the "home" provinces fully. The British expansion was equally dangerous to the Maratha power, whether it came from Lucknow or Arcot. Mahadaji took a long time and Nana still longer to realise the magnitude of the English designs and the assiduity with which they were determined to push them on.[118]

Preparations for the Final Blow, the Arrival of Lord Cornwallis, and the Tripartite Alliance

Warren Hastings shaped events in India for a period of 13 years from 1772 and he left the country on 5 February1785. On his voyage home, he drew up an analysis of the prevailing political condition there. Hastings saw only two genuinely independent powers in India—the ruler of Mysore Tipu Sultan and the Maratha Confederacy, which extended across central India and now reached far into the north, controlling Delhi itself. It was certain that sooner or later war would break out between these two powers and the British.

> Lord Cornwallis assumed charge of the Company's affairs in India in September 1786. From the very outset he fixed on the idea of isolating Tipu by drawing the Nizam and the Peshwa into an alliance of mutual benefit against him; but almost ineradicable jealousies and irreconcilable interests separated these two Powers. The task of coordinating and reconciling the clashing interests of Lord Cornwallis's coveted allies was placed in the hands of two of the ablest British diplomats. C W Malet and J Kennaway, the Residents at Poona and Hyderabad respectively.[119]

The Purpose of Appointment of Charles Malet at Poona

Malet started his career in Cambay in 1774 as the head of the English factory and resident at the court of the local nawab. He was appointed as resident minister at Poona in 1785 by Warren Hasting and assumed charge of his office at Poona on 3 March 1786.[120] From the very beginning, Malet was intimately involved in the political intrigues in the west coast. In Cambay in 1775, he gave shelter to the fugitive Peshwa Raghoba and helped him to reach Surat. It was the support of Raghoba's cause by the British that led to the First Maratha War. The Treaty of Salbai propelled Mahadaji Sindhia into greater prominence in the affairs of the Maratha state. He was to be a guarantee for the due observance of the stipulations of the treaty, both on the part of the English and the Court of Poona. David Anderson who negotiated the treaty was appointed as a permanent British resident representing the governor-general at the Court of Sindhia. The increased importance of Mahadaji Sindhia in the Maratha politics annoyed Nana Fadnavis who was then conducting Maratha affairs in the name of the boy Peshwa. Nana wanted an opening to directly deal with the governor-general, dispensing with the medium of Sindhia. The result was the appointment of Malet in Poona.

Lord Cornwallis and the Tripartite Alliance

Lord Cornwallis succeeded Warren Hastings as Governor-General on 12 September 1886, where he continued for seven years till October 1793. During this period, he introduced a radical change in British-Indian politics and administration. The Indian overlords hardly realised what this meant, being totally ignorant of European history and politics that were quietly shaping India's destiny.

Lord Cornwallis on his arrival in India spent his first two years patiently studying and observing before initiating a decisive course of policy. He noticed Hastings' administration had generated a lot of hostile feelings all around. The Council of Southern Presidency was thoroughly rotten. The Treaty of Mangalore had discredited the British name and lowered its prestige. In the north Sindhia had become powerful at the Mughal capital; in the south Tipu Sultan had assumed a domineering style towards the British Power. The Nizam, the Nawab of Arcot, the Wazir of Oudh and the Emperor himself had all become restless and distrustful, threatening the position of the English. The French became once more aggressive and tried to work their way in India through Tipu.[121]

The Marathas, the English, and the ruler of Mysore were then obviously the three main powers competing for supremacy in India, all practically evenly balanced, so that any two of them combined could be easily stronger than the third. The Nizam was of little account and threw his influence always on the winning side. The traditional antagonism between England and France was considered favourable to strengthening Tipu's position. Tipu had great hope from his French connection. He energetically tried to keep friendly relations with the Marathas and prevent their cooperation with the British against him.

Lord Cornwallis was as keen as Hastings to establish British supremacy in India but bearing all the factors in mind he wisely refrained from interfering with any Indian power. He carefully improved the finances by strengthening the economy in the various branches of the Company's administration, putting down corruption, and stopping the prevalent practice of making presents on ceremonial visits and other occasions. By the end of 1788, when he found himself well provided with capital, he turned his attention to external affairs, among which he found it necessary first to crush the power of Tipu Sultan. To that end he worked strenuously for another year and half building up an alliance with the Nizam and the Marathas. In this, he pushed his way cautiously and slowly through an intricate maze of secret diplomacy worked by his trusted agents Malet at Poona and Kennaway at Hyderabad.[122] Malet worked subtly upon Nana's sentiments and gained his goodwill. He was able to bring about a disaffection between Nana and Mahadaji. In 1788, Lord Cornwallis instructed Malet to negotiate an alliance with the Peshwa and entrusted a similar mission to his own trusted agent Kennaway, whom he despatched as the first British resident to the Court of Nizam with instruction to organise a tripartite alliance. Malet formed personal friendships with most of the Maratha gentry of Poona and thereby prepared a favourable atmosphere for engaging the Peshwa's power in a war against Mysore. Mahadaji was not at all enthusiastic about the British move encouraged by Nana. Malet had extensive discussions with the governor of Bombay during the end of 1788 and early 1789. On his return to Poona, he succeeded in drawing up a treaty of alliance with the Peshwa's government, of which a draft was sent to Hyderabad. The subject was under consideration for more than one year.

The rapid growth of the British power, which now menaced the security and independence of India, was causing an agitation within Indian politics. The Marathas and the Nizam were anxious to put down Tipu's aggressiveness, but the other Indian powers were not naturally enthusiastic about the destruction of Tipu. His continuation, with the possibility of French power proving a check on the English, was considered essential in India's interest. But under the able direction of Lord Cornwallis, the astute diplomats Malet and Kennaway were able to bring about a solid contract between the three powers after two years of hard work and resolute energy and force. In order to disarm Maratha suspicion, Lord Cornwallis went to the lengths of placing the Company's Bombay contingent under Maratha command during the period of the war.[123]

A treaty containing 14 articles was concluded on 1 June 1790. The Maratha army of 10,000 horses was to accompany the British troops.[124] The territories and forts conquered during the war were to be divided equally about the allies. The Nizam was the weakest of the three powers in the Deccan. He was afraid that once the strength of Tipu was weakened and the power of the Marathas rebuilt, he would be exposed to their aggression on account of the huge arrears of *Chauth*, which he had accumulated over many years. He tried to obtain a guarantee from Lord Cornwallis of British protection against Maratha claims, but Lord Cornwallis only offered to use his friendly offices in adjusting the dispute if it should arise. Nizam Ali, after a good deal of hesitation, signed the Poona Tripartite Treaty on 4 July 1790.

NOTES

1. Ray, N. B, Ed. ((1937). *Poona Residency Correspondence.* Vol. 3, *The Allies' War with Tipu Sultan. 1790-1793.* Bombay. Cornwallis to Captain Kennaway, Fort William, June 7, 1790, p. 157.
2. Oak, M. and Swamy. (2010*). Commitment and Conquest-The Case of British Rule in India.* (Moon, 1990, p. 291).www/.williams.edu> economics> oakswamycommitmentandcare. p3
3. *Ibid.,* p. 3. quoting Edward Thompson (1943), 'The making of the Indian Princes'.
4. *Ibid.,* p. 3.
5. Joshi, V. V. (1941). *'Clash of Three Empires- A study of British conquest of India with special reference to the Maratha people'*. Archives.Com . 'The history of the Marathas may practically divided into two separate eras: The first was the Royal period which lasted till the return of Shahu from the Mughal camp, which was distinguished by the growth and fulfilment of the Maratha nation state and the second was the Peshwa period which began with the rise of Balaji Viswanath as the virtual head of the Maratha state. In this Peshwa period the Maratha state was transformed into an Empire'. p. 49.
6. Mehta, J. L. (2005). *'Advanced Study in the History of Modern India 1707-1813'.* New Dawn Press, Inc. New Delhi, p. 58.
7. *Ibid.,* p. 62.
8. *Ibid.,* p. 66. Balaji belonged to the Bhatt family of Chitpawan Brahmins whose forefathers were hereditary deshmukhs of Srivardhan on the

Konkan coast. He started as a clerk in the salt works in Chiplun. Later he took to soldiery and worked as a mercenary trooper under various Maratha sardars. After the fall of Sambhaji he was employed as a revenue official in the Maratha court at Raigarh.

9. *Ibid.*, p. 69.
10. Piglae was the younger son of the first Peshwa of Sivaji, Moropant Pingale.
11. Mehta, J L.(2005). *op.cit,* p. 72.
12. *Ibid.*, p. 71.
13. Amir-ul-Umara (noble of nobles) of Mughal Empire & Governorship of Deccan.
14. Farrukh Siyar was actively supported by the Sayyad brothers, Abdulla Khan and Hussain Ali Khan, in his accession to the throne of Delhi eliminating Jahandar Shah. In return for their valuable service the Emperor made Abdulla Khan as his wazir (Prime Minister) and Hussain Ali Khan as the Salah salar (commander in chief).The rise of Sayyad brothers as kingmakers aroused the jealousies of other prominent Mughal peers, particularly the Turani and Irani nobles, who constituted the backbone of the hereditary Mughal aristocracy including (future Nizam-ul-Mulk) Chin Qilich Khan. Mehta, J. L. (2005). *Op.cit,* p. 20. William Irvin in his classic work, '*The Later Mughals*', analyses the composition and character of the two rival factions of the Mughal court which emerged during the reign of Farrukh Siyar, 'everyman from beyond the Oxus or from any of the provinces of the Persian kingdom was called a Mughal. If his home was in Turan, north of the Oxus, he was a Turani, if south of it, in the region of Iran, he was an Irani Mughal.' The Turanis were the Sunni sect...came from the old house of the reigning dynasty.....For these reasons they were highly favoured by the Indian emperors...The Iranis were Shias, —they included among them men of good birth and great ability..... The faction led by the Turani and Irani nobles was thus composed of the foreign immigrants and their immediate descendants. On the contrary the Hindustani Mughals, as they were called, were Indian Muslims born and bred in India; they were either Hindu converts of Islam and their offsprings or remote descendants of the foreign immigrants. *Quoted* Mehta, J L. (2005). *Op.cit,* p. 21.
15. G S Sardesai. (1946). *New History of the Marathas. The expansion of Maratha Power (1707-1772). Vol II.* Digitallibraryindia. Internetarchive. 'About this very moment Balaji Vishwanath was invested with Peshwaship, so that these two great men and their descendants between them made up the history of the Deccan for

nearly a century, developing relations, sometimes of amenity, at others of enmity towards each other..., p. 32.

16. *Ibid.* Sardesai gives details of the treaty: Sivaji's original dominions (Swarajya) should be delivered to Shahu, the recently conquered territories by the Marathas should be ceded to them, Marathas should be allowed to collect Chauth and Sardeshmughi from all the six Mughal subhas, Shahu should not harm Sambhaji of Kolhapur, Marathas should pay a tribute of Ten lakhs Rupees to the Emperor, and Emperor should release his family held in Delhi, p. 41.
17. *Ibid.,* 42.
18. Mehta, J. L. 79-quoting Irvine.
19. Mehta, *op cit.* p. 82.
20. Mehta J. L. *op cit.* p. 35.
21. Mehta, J. L. *op cit.* p. 97.
22. Chhabra, G. S. (1971). *Advanced Study in the History of Modern India Vol.1(1707-1813).* Sterling Publishing Pvt Ltd. New Delhi, p. 25.
23. Mehta, J. L. *op cit.* p. 118.
24. Kulke, H. & Rothermund. (2004). *A History of India,* Routledge, p. 214.
25. Mehta, J. L. *op cit.,* p. 173. Sagunbai, the youngest queen of Shahu and the wife of Raghuji Bhonsle were sisters. 'Raghuji has established himself as an independent ruler of Nagpur (Berar). He belonged to the Bhonsle clan of Marathas, although his ancestral family had no blood-relations with the ruling house of Shivaji.'
26. *Ibid.,* p. 174.
27. Mehta, J. L. *op.cit,* p. 189.
28. Mehta, J. L. *op.cit,* p. 198.
29. Mehta, J. L. *op.cit,* p. 201.
30. Gordon, S.(1993). *The new Cambridge history of India- The Marathas 1600-1818.* Cambridge University Press 1993. pp. 135.
31. Sardesai, G. S. (1946*). New History of the Marathas. The expansion of Maratha Power (1707-1772). Vol. II.* Digitallibraryindia. Internetarchive. p. 312.
32. Nadkarni, R. V. (1966). *The rise and fall of the Maratha empire.* Bombay Popular Prakashan, Bombay, pp. 358-359 Archives. org>stream. In.ernet.dil/2015/117970.
33. Sardesai, G. S.(1946*). New History of the Marathas. The expansion of Maratha Power (1707-1772). Vol II. Phoenix publications.* Digitallibraryindia. Internetarchive. p. 389: Sardesai narrates the appalling acts of cruelty inflicted on civilians by the invaders.

34. Sardesai, G. S.(1946*)*, p. 397.
35. Mehta, J. L. (2005). *Advanced study in the history of Modern India. 1707-1813.* New Dawn Press Inc., New Delhi, p. 238.
36. Shejwalker, T. S. (1946). *Panipat: 1761.Deccan College Monograph Series Deccan College Poona.* archives.org> details> in.ernet. dli2015.126833. p. 8.
37. Mehta, J. L. *op cit.*, p. 240.
38. Mehta, J. L. *op cit.*, p. 308.
39. Mehta, J. L. *op cit.*, p. 455.
40. Gordon, S. *op cit.*, p. 156.
41. Datta, K. K.(1949).The Marathas in Orissa. *Proceedings of the Indian History Congress, 12,* 299-301 www.jstor.org/stable/44140557-quoting Select Committee's proceedings,11 September 1761
42. Varma, S P.(1956). *A study in Maratha Diplomacy (Anglo-Maratha Relations 1772-1783).* Shiva Lal Agrawala & Co Agra. A Thesis. archive.org> stream> in.emet.lli.2015.100293. p19. He quotes Sardesai (*New History of Marathas, Vol 2, Ch. XXI p456):* 'The Battle of Panipat was fought on 14th January 1761. The very next day the Mughal Emperor Shah Alam, in his effort to recover Bengal, sustained a serious defeat on the river Son at the hands of the British forces led by Major Carnac. The day after this event, on the 16th January, Pondicherry, the rival of Madras, fell into the British hands, thereby smashing the French power in India. These three days proved momentous in determining the future fate of this country.'
43. Keay, John. (1991). *The Honorable Company*. Harper Collins Publishers, London, 374.
44. Spear, P. (1975). *Master of Bengal, Clive and his India.* Thames and Hudson Ltd., London, p. 149.
45. Bence-Jones, Mark. (1974). *Clive of India.* Constable, London, p. 218.
46. Spear, P. (1975). *op.cit.*, p. 153.
47. Sardesai, G. S.(1946). *New history of the Marathas Vol. III.* Phoenix Publications. archives.org> details> in.emet.dli.2015.56808p11.
48. *Shastri:* An honourable designation to the names of Brahmans versed in any Shastra.
49. Mehta, J. L. *Op cit.*, Nana Fadnavis held the charge of the Huzur Daftar or Imperial Secretariat at Poona in his capacity as the Chief Auditor (Fhadnis or Farnavis) and Secretary to the Peshwa since the days of Madhav Rao, p. 534.
50. *The Bara Bhais (Barbhai) Council was an alliance of influential Sardars (Generals) led by Nana. Other members of the council were Haripant*

Phadke, Moroba Phadnavis, Sakharam Bapu Bokil, Trimbakraomama Pethe, Mahadji Shinde, Tukojirao Holkar, Phaltankar, Bhagwanrao Pratinidhi, Maliji Ghorpade, Sardar Raste and Babuji Naik.

51. Varma, S. P. (1956). *A study in Maratha Diplomacy (Anglo-Maratha Relations 1772-1783 A.D).* Shiva Lal Agrawala & Co Agra. archive. org> stream> in.emet.lli.2015.100293. retrieved 3.9 2020 p61
52. Mehta, J. L., *op cit.*, p. 534.
53. Gordon, S. (1993).*The new Cambridge history of India. The Marathas 1600-1818.* Cambridge University Press, p. 163.
54. Mehta, J. L. *op cit.,* p. 534.
55. Wadia, R. A. (1955). *'The Bombay Dockyard and the Wadia master Builders.'* Published by R. A Wadia, Thakur Nivas, Jamsetji Tata Road, Bombay 1.archive.org>details> in.gov. ignca.4870:Under the treaty of Marriage of 1662 between Charles II and the Infanta Catherine of Braganza the King of Portugal ceded and granted to the crown of England the Island and Harbour of Bombay in full sovereignty, p. 8.

    Beyond the generally represented Royal dowry, there was another purpose behind it. (S. P. Varma, p. 45). A secret article of the treaty mentioned the objective as (quotes Forrest- Collections App A), 'the better improvement of the English interest and commerce in the East Indies....'
56. Shejwalker, T. S.(1947). *'The Surat episode 1759.' Bulletin of the Deccan College PG And Research Institute 1947.Vol. 8.* Dikshit Memorial Volume (1947), p. 173-203. Jstor.org/stable/42929590: gives detailed analysis of the whole episode
57. Anderson, Philip. (1854). *The English in Western India being the Early History of the factory at Surat, of Bombay.* Smith Taylor and Co. London. Archive.org. p50
58. The administration of the English East India Company was managed by a body of 24 directors called The Court of directors. They were elected by shareholders of the company on an annual basis.
59. Sen, S. N. (1959). *Origin of the first Anglo-Maratha war. Proceedings of the Indian History Congress Vol. 22,* pp. 400-402. Published by Indian History Congress. Jstor.org> stable
60. Varma, S. P. (1959). *A study in Maratha Diplomacy (Anglo-Maratha Relations 1772-1783).* Shiva Lal Agrawala & Co Agra. A Thesis archive.org. p5 quoting G S Sardesai, New History of the Marathas Vol. II, p. 514.

61. *Ibid.,* p, 18. Varma argues that Sindhia was guided by motives of personal gains only and in raising Shah Alam to the imperial throne he merely wanted to cover for the enhancement of own power which he could not have exercised in North India as a mere vassal of the Peshwa. The phantom sovereignty had a psychological appeal. Warren Hastings had called Shah Alam, 'this wretched king of shreds and patches, this idle pageant, an idol of our creation continued to profess open loyalty and devotion to him and send him nazars and received khilats from him.'
62. *Ibid.,* p. 24.
63. Gense, Rev. G. H. & Banaji, D. R. Ed. (1934). *'The Third English Embassy to Poona, comprising Mostyn's Diary.' (Sep.1772-Feb.1774) and Mostyn's Letters (Feb- Nov, 1774).* Bombay: Taraporevala and Sons. Archives.org: Mostyn proved for the British Presidency of Bombay a useful agent for the purpose of checking the Maratha power, as demonstrated by his three diplomatic missions to Poona.
64. Forrest, G. W. *Selections from the letters, despatches, and other state papers preserved in the Bombay secretariat- Maratha Series. Vol. I.* Bombay Castle 18th November 1767. Thomas Hodge etc. "The growing power of the Marathas is a subject much to be lamented, and has not failed to attract our attention, as well as that of the Presidencies of Madras and Bengal, inasmuch that nothing either in their power nor ours would be omitted to check the same as much as possible........" p. 141.
65. Gense and Banaji. *Op cit.* Introduction, p. X.
66. Gense and Banaji. *Op cit.* Introduction, p. XIII.
67. Gordon, S. (1993). *The new Cambridge history of India - The Marathas 1600-1818.* Cambridge University Press. p. 163.
68. Gense and Banaji. *Op cit.* 1774. Secret and Political Department Diary. Reply of Thomas Mostyn, p. 343.
69. Varma, S. P. *op cit.* p. 64.
70. Varma, S. P. *op.cit.* p. 70. The Bombay Government complemented their action by a legal claim to these islands. They held that these were included in the grant of Bombay which they had received in dowry from the Spanish King on the occasion of Charles II's marriage with his daughter. Then they lost it to the Marathas. As an immediate cause they pointed out that the Portuguese were planning to capture it. The real cause was the revenue from Salsette of about four lakhs per annum. Salsette commanded the principal passes to the island of Bombay and anybody who possessed it could control its trade revenue.

71. Kantak, M R. (1993). *"The First Anglo-Maratha War 1774-1783, A Military Study of Major Battles"*. Popular Prakashan Pvt Ltd. Bombay. 1993: 'The First Anglo-Maratha war is one of the most important events of the eighteenth century from the point of view of history of India in general and of the Marathas in particular. It covers the period of about a decade after the murder of Narayanrao Peshwa in August 1773. The War was precipitated by the political asylum offered by the British to Raghoba at Surat and the wanton British attack on the fort of Salsette in December 1774.These two action of the British led to a chain of battles between the Marathas and the British, which were fought on a wide area in Malwa, Gujarat and Maharashtra (Konkan and Khandesh). These battles and encounters constitute what is known as the First Anglo-Maratha war. The native powers like the Nizam and Hyder Ali were dragged into the War …but the main contenders were the Marathas and the British. The War ended with the Treaty of Salbai in 1783.' Introduction, p. 1.
72. Varma, S. P. *op cit.* p. 79.
73. Varma, S P. *op cit.* details in p. 79 to 81.
74. Varma, S P. *op cit.* p. 96..
75. Varma, S P. *op cit.* p. 102.
76. Varma, S P. *op cit.* p. 107.
77. Varma, S. P. *op cit.* p. 117: Col. Upton suggested that he should take a land route and he should proceed by way of Allahabad to Kalpee (Kalpi). The road from Kalpee to Poona was a high road, which the Marathas always took when going to the upper parts of Hindustan. Passes from the country under a few independent Rajas could be secured through their protégé Nawab Asaf-ud-Daulah of Awadh. The larger part of the country to be passed through by him was either in the possession or influence of the Marathas. And, there was one other significant motive behind this scheme. This was the first opportunity the English had of surveying the peninsula of India and identifying the true distance of the places through which he would pass. Rev. William Smith was appointed 'to survey the country in the most accurate manner he can and by astronomical observations to ascertain the actual situation of the places'. Col. Upton left Calcutta by 21 July and reached Purandhar 29 December 1775.
78. Varma, S. P. *op cit.* p. 119.
79. Gordon, S. (1993). *The Cambridge History of India- The Marathas 1600-1818.* Cambridge University Press, Cambridge, p. 164.
80. Varma, S. P. *op cit.* p. 148.

81. Hatalkar, V. G. (1958). *Relations between the French and the Marathas (1668-1815)*-University of Bombay.p184. The embassy of St Lubin to the Maratha court formed an important episode in the history of the relations between the French and the Marathas. In 1776, war broke out between England and her American Colonies. Thus, the opportunity had come for France to avenge the humiliations of the Treaty of Paris (1763.) Count de Vergennes, the French Minister for Foreign Affairs advised de Sartine, comte d' Alby to establish contact with the Government of Poona. Sartine, in consideration of the several memoirs and plans addressed to him by St Lubin on this subject decided to entrust him with the mission.
82. Varma, S. P. *op cit.,* p. 154.
83. *Ibid.,* p. 158.
84. *Ibid.,* p. 159.
85. Feiling, Keith. (1966). *Warren Hastings.* (Macmillan London).Keith Feiling gives a detailed description of the role of Hastings in the Maratha War of 1777-1779. (pp.194-205).
86. Varma, S. P. *op cit.* p. 165.
87. Varma, S. P. op cit.p167. 'The forces of the Presidency were- Artillery 61, European Infantry 783, sepoys 5621, Irregulars 1231. Warren Hastings pointed out: 'these forces were much larger than what Bengal had possessed at the Battle of Plassey, or when she was occupied in the defence of the province against the Shahzada, or the expedition under Col. Forde against Masulipatam, or at the time of the struggle with Quasim Ali Khan.'
88. Varma, S. P. *op cit.* p. 178. *Quoting Foreign Department: Secret Proceedings, 22nd June, 1778.*
89. Varma, S. P. comments, p.187: Col. Leslie's expedition through Bundelkhand has a twofold importance in Indian history. Firstly, it was part of the first British land drive across the Indian subcontinent. Secondly, it put the Maratha strength to test and showed clearly that the Maratha state was not yet ripe for dissolution. The Bundelkhand expedition of 1778 is the First Anglo-Maratha War in miniature.

    John Keay in 'the Honourable Company – a history of the EEIC', comments, (p. 406): "The idea of marching six battalions clean across the subcontinent was nothing if not bold. The march provided tangible proof that the Company's hitherto isolated settlements now acknowledged a common purpose and formed a single political unit. It presumed a rite of passage through what had previously been regarded as inviolable sovereignties. And it foreshadowed an attitude of mind that would regard the whole of India as one political entity."

90. Archives.org. '*A journal of the march of the Bombay detachment, across the Mahratta country, from Culpee to Surat, in 1788; commanded by Lieutenant- Colonel Goddard: together with the proceedings of the Bombay army, under Colonel Egerton, in their march towards Poonah- with a sketch of Colonel Goddard's route.*' 1779. London. This journal gives extensive details of the audacious undertaking.
91. Varma, S. P., *op cit.,* p. 191.
92. Sardesai, G. S. *New History of the Marathas Vol.3, op cit.,* p. 85 —A tragic consequence at the victory at Wadgaon was the downfall of the senior member of the Poona government Sakharam Bapu who once supported Raghoba. The removal of Bapu and his subsequent death on August 1781 put an end to the Council of Barabhais after a carrier of six years. Hereafter Nana Fadnavis helped by Mahadaji Sindhia, became the sole manager of the Peshwa's Government and wielded full power right up to the death of the young Peshwa in 1795.
93. Greig, G. R. (1841). *Memoirs of the Life of the Right Hon. Warren Hastings, Vol 2.* Internet Archives- new.dli.ernet.in/handle/2015/53324. p*273*
94. Varma, S. P., *op cit.,* p. 216.
95. Varma, S. P., *op cit.,* p. 220.
96. The same army officer won the Battle of Tarvananghurry on December 10, 1790, in Malabar.
97. Varma, S P., *op cit.,* p. 222.
98. Sardesai, G. S. *New History of the Marathas.* Vol. 3, *op cit.,* p. 109.
99. Sardesai, G S. *New History of the Marathas.* Vol. 3, *op cit.,* p. 94.
100. *Ibid.,* 96.
101. Greg, G. R. (1841*). Memoirs of the life of the Rt. Hon. Warren Hastings Vol.2.* Digital Library of India item 2015.53324: Gohud is a small princely state interposed between the territories of Scandia and the Nawab of Oudh, where the English were already the *de facto* rulers. Though the Rana of Gohud was quite incapable of resisting the Marathas, his country, from its position and the natural obstacles it possessed to an invading force, formed a good outwork to the kingdom of Oudh. p. 231.
102. Keay, John. (1993). *The Honorable Company.* Harper Collins, London. 'Gwalior, a classic table-top fortress elevated several hundred feet above the surrounding plain, was probably the strongest natural fortress in all India .... such was its strategic importance astride the main roads leading south from Delhi and Agra that no government claiming dominion over both the north and the peninsula had ever been able to ignore it.' p. 408.

103. William Hodges, R. A. (1793). *Travels in India during the years 1780-1783. London.* Archive. pp. 139-142: The assault on the fort of Gwalior is given in detail.
104. Sardesai, G. S. *New History of the Marathas. Vol. 3, op cit.,* p. 110.
105. Greg. G R. (1841). *Memoirs of the life of the Rt. Hon. Warren Hastings Vol.2.* Digital Library of India item 2015.53324: p. 234.
106. Keay, John (1993). *The Honorable Company*. Harper Collins, London. p. 413.
107. Varma, S P. (1956). *A study in Maratha diplomacy -1712-1783 First Ed. Archives. Org.* 'The Marathas were definitely the less dangerous of the two enemies of the English had to face in India in the last quarter of the 18th century. During the last war they themselves had struck certain decisive blows at the Maratha hegemony. The war had financially crippled and broken the Maratha power. But what was more welcome from the British point of view, the Maratha empire was now definitely broken into separate states.' p. 349.
108. Gleig G. R. *'Memoirs of the life of the Right Hon. Warren Hastings. Vol II'. Letter to David Anderson. Fort William.* 15 March 1782, p. 531. Archives.org
109. Mehta, J. L. *op. cit.,* p. 539.
110. Gordon, Stewart. *Op cit.,* p. 167: "The treaty is an important marker in the Maratha polity. There had been direct negotiations between outside powers and the Maratha 'states' before…but what changed here was that Shinde (Sindhia), formerly subordinate to the Peshwa was guaranteeing the behavior of the whole Maratha polity. The treaty also reflects the direct rivalry of Shinde, who wanted freedom from the English threat in order to expand his territories in the north, and Nana Fadnavis, who wanted to expand to the south. Shinde won and this allowed him to attack and conquer many clans in Malwa and Delhi area. But this process bankrupted Shinde, who largely lost control of Delhi and surrounding area. The new artillery/infantry units were crushingly expensive."
111. Dodwell, H.H. Ed (1929). *The Cambridge history of the British Empire Vol. IV,* British India Cambridge University Press, p. 271.
112. *Ibid.,* p. 271.
113. Varma, S P. *op. cit. A study of Maratha Diplomacy 1773-82,* p. 388 quoting Gleig
114. *Ibid.,* p. 394
115. *Ibid.,* p. 395

116. Sardesai, G. S. Ed. (1936) : *Poona Residency Correspondence, Vol. 2, Poona Affairs 1786-1797 (Malet's Embassy)*: Malet in his letter number 68, to the Governor General, Poona on 27th June 1787 give the details, p. 122.
117. Sarkar, J. N.(1950). *Fall of the Mughal Empire, Vol IV,* M C Sarkar & Ltd. Calcutta. Archives.org. new.dli.ernet.in/handle/2015/17905 *p6*
118. Varma, S. P. *op cit.*, p. 406.
119. Ray, N. B. (Ed). (1937*). Poona Residency Correspondence, Vol. III, The Allies' war with Tipu Sultan 1790-1793. Archives.Org. Introduction pp. v-vi.*
120. Minutes of Evidence taken before the Committee of the Whole House and the Select Committee on the Affairs of the East India Company. Oxford. (1813). Reports &c. (East India Company) First Part. Vol. VII. p. 241. "Were not you also employed on a mission to Poona? —I think it was in the year 1785 that the government general, then under Mr. Hastings, applied to the government at Bombay for its acquiescence in my being sent minister plenipotentiary to the court of Poonah".
121. Sardesai, G. S. *New history of the Marathas,* Vol. III, Archives.Com. p. 182.
122. Sardesai, G. S. *New History of Marathas.* Vol. III, p. 183, *op.cit.*
123. Sardesai, G. S. *op.cit.*, 184.
124. Barua, P.(1994). *Military Developments in India 1750-1850. The Journal of Military History,* 58 (4). pp.599-616. doi: 10.2307/2944270. www.jstor.org/stable/2944270

    Professor Pradeep Barua tries to demonstrate that the victory of the English in some major conflicts in India was not so much because of the inability of the Indians to completely adopt the Western military system, but because of the ability of the British to adapt rapidly to the changing military situation in India.

    Haider's campaigns in the Carnatic during the First and Second Anglo-Mysore wars were masterpieces of light cavalry action. Tipu's tactics during the Third and Fourth Anglo- Mysore Wars mirrored that of his father. In 1791 he let Cornwallis march to Seringapatam without offering battle. However, his cavalry denied the British army any access to forage or to obtain supplies from Madras, forcing Cornwallis to order a precipitate retreat to save his army from starvation. When he returned in 1792, Cornwallis having forged an alliance with the Marathas, had a force of 12,000 superb Maratha light cavalry to protect his foragers and his supply columns. (Note the comments of Marshman in J C Marshman- *The History of India,* Vol. II, p. 25). With the aid of the Marathas, Cornwallis quickly brought Seringapatam under siege and compelled Tipu to sign the crippling Treaty of Seringapatam in 18 March 1792.

Pradeep Barua further comments, 'During the Anglo-Mysore wars the tactics employed were uniquely Indian: the uses of masses of cavalry. By refusing to meet the British in a set piece battle, both Hyder and Tipu managed to fragment the British forces and destroy them piecemeal. But their most favoured tactic was to starve out the British by cutting their supplies and denying their draught-animals access to forage. The British eventually brought the Mysoreans to battle with the aid of Maratha light cavalry and substantially increased their own cavalry forces. (In addition to the Marathas Cornwallis had at his disposal a numerous, if less effective force of 18,000 Hyderabadi cavalry). It was the British ability to adapt to the tactics of their enemy by, first, making use of Maratha cavalry and, second, by giving priority to the problems of supply in the harsh terrain of the Deccan that enabled them to achieve victory in the Anglo-Mysore Wars.'

6

The European Success: An English Lesson

Rasselas, Prince of Abyssinia, the protagonist in the novella by Samuel Johnson, poignantly inquires his philosopher friend Imlac,

> "By what means are the Europeans thus powerful? Or why, since they can so easily visit Asia and Africa for trade or conquest, cannot the Asiatics and Africans invade their coast, plant colonies in their ports, and give law to their princes? The same wind that carries them back would bring us thither".
>
> "They are more powerful, sir, than we," answered Imlac, "because they are wiser; knowledge will always predominate over ignorance, as man governs other animals. But why their knowledge is more than ours I know not what reason can be given but the unsearchable will of the Supreme Being." [1]

The port cities and settlements on the Arabian Sea Littoral-Arabia, Africa and South Asia- traded with each other. In Indian economic and business history, the Arabian Sea had special significance.

> 'Merchants sailed to various regions based on well-established networks that ran through generations and had been in place for centuries. But, there were no armed polities that underwrote their contracts, protected their investments or guaranteed their safety. Sophisticated nautical technologies were developed wherein large sea-worthy vessels crossed the Indian Ocean with large amounts of goods and numerous passengers. They were propelled by dependable monsoon winds and metal free ships.' [2]

Pioneering the search for a sea-route to Asia by the Europeans, Columbus finally arrived in the Americas. Vasco da Gama became the first European to successfully sail to Calicut on the Malabar Coast in May 1498.

> 'With this momentous event, the existing sea-routes of the Mediterranean and the emerging Atlantic world became linked to the centuries old trading routes of the Indian Ocean world. In Calicut, a peaceful trading port where ships from many nations docked to collect spices and textiles, da Gama and his men unleashed violence: robbing the ships and killing the crew, traders and inhabitants of the city, using their cannon-fitted ships.'[3]

The Catholic powers - Spain and Portugal - who had divided the world between themselves in the sixteenth century were surpassed in the seventeenth century by the rising Protestant states of the North, England and the United Netherlands. They were maritime powers to whom mastery of the seas was vital. Though they aided each other sometimes in displacing the Portuguese from India their long term interests conflicted one another and clashes became inevitable. This resulted in a long series of Anglo-Dutch wars in the mid seventeenth to late eighteenth century. The Dutch took an earlier lead as they were superior in seamanship, financial resources and political backing and held it for most of the seventeenth century.[4] They pushed out the Portuguese from Amboyna, the heart of the Clove trade in 1605.Factories were established in Bantam,

Jakarta and Batavia which became the centre of the Dutch Empire in the East. Because of their policy of acquiring only centres of production, the Dutch treated India as a subsidiary interest although it underwrote the success of their other ventures in the East. The English EIC set up factories in Banda and Amboyna but they were driven westward to India by the founder of the Dutch empire in the East, Jan Pietersoon Coen. Following the massacre in 1622, the English abandoned Amboyna entirely and concentrated in the Indian subcontinent. The French, the traditional rivals of the English, established themselves in Pondicherry in 1674. The War of Austrian Succession and the Seven Years War gave opportunity to the English to attack French colonies and trade everywhere and lead them to take control of the subcontinent.

The rise and the dominance of the English in the Indian subcontinent is a remarkable and impressive episode in colonial history. How did , 'A rainy, irreverent, resource-poor archipelago in the north Atlantic, the British Isles, managed to impose its ideas of trade, government, religion and culture across vast swaths of Humanity.[5] Voltaire commented: "Posterity might be surprised that a small island, which has from her own only some lead, tin, fuller's earth and coarse wool, has become, thanks to its trade, powerful enough to dispatch in 1733 three squadrons.... to three uttermost ends of the earth."[6] The extreme imbalance in wealth between India and England in the sixteenth century is striking. "No episode in the life and death struggle of Elizabethan England against Imperial Spain, perhaps no event in the whole of the Queen's reign, so transparently reveals her people and the Tudor system at their best and worst as the capture of the Madre de Dios".[7] English privateers under the command of the Earl of Cumberland and lead by Captain John Burrough along with Sir Walter Raleigh attacked and plundered the Portuguese carrack captained by Fernao de Mendonca Furtado off Flores, one of the Azores islands on 3 August 1592.[8] The capture of the Madre de Dios had a lasting influence on the quest of England for future eastern trade. Richard Hakluyt wrote, 'I cannot but enter into consideration and acknowledgement of God's great favour towards our nation who by putting this purchase into our hands hath manifestly discovered those secrete trades and Indian riches, which hitherto lay strangely hidden, and cunningly concealed from us'.[9] The original value of the cargo just in one ship from India was estimated to be 500,000 pounds when the yearly income of the government of Queen Elizabeth I of England was 250,000 pounds!!

The Rise of the East India Company

The Governor and Company of the Merchants of London trading into the East Indies (first of the several different forms of the English EIC) received its Royal Charter from Queen Elizabeth I in 1600. In contrast, The Treasurer and Company of Adventurers and Planters of the City of London for the First Colony in Virginia received its charter in 1606. "The Virginia company established numerous subsidiary companies to make glass and beads, fish, trade furs, publish an apparel magazine, build boats and even import 'Maids to Virginia to be made Wives'."[10] Here, two of these earliest joint-stock companies demonstrated fundamentally different strategies. The EIC was primarily a 'trading company', intent on making profits through trading in the Far East. They invested their Capital in merchandise rather than in fixed assets such as ships or factories. Permanent settlements were established only to the extent they facilitated trade. 'For the first century and a half the strategy was to court favour with the local rulers. In India there was an extensive well established complex political and economic society and at this stage the EIC had no thought of colonisation. On the contrary, in North America, the Virginia companies faced a diverse social, political and economic environment and therefore brought into play different structures and strategies much more in keeping with a conglomerate than a trading company'.[11]

John Mill identifies the end of the First Carnatic War in 1749, as the year in which the EIC's strategy changed in India. This war was the Indian theatre of the War of Austrian Succession which concluded with the Treaty of Aix-La-Chapelle in April 1748. 'A new scene is now to open in the history of the EIC. Before this period they had maintained the character of mere traders, and by humility and submission, endeavoured to preserve a footing in that distant country under the protection or oppression of the native powers. We shall now behold them entering the lists of war; and mixing with eagerness in the contests of the princes'.[12] The French under the leadership of Dumas and Dupleix had already begun their interventionist policy in the affairs of local rulers. Thus, to protect his territory and to annex his opponents domains the Nawabs and Princes began to depend more and more on the support of the Europeans. The French held an edge until the Battle of Plassey, which according to many historians, identifies the date which marked the dominance of the EIC in Indian politics.

Thus, the EIC, which started as a commercial enterprise primarily concerned with making a profit for the investors, became a major economic force both in India and England and its financial and political dimensions became inseparable. 'The decision to become something more than a 'mere' trading company was not the result of some grand strategy developed in London but rather an 'emergent' strategy which evolved locally because of the competitive forces in India at the time'.[13] The change in strategy and the increased complexity of the operations of the Company required a significant change in the structure of the London office of the EIC. The 1750s saw a significant change in the composition and character of the Court of Directors. Previously dominated by those Londoners with a special interest in trade, like bankers, ship-owners, merchants, experience in India became another important quality.[14] A new department was established to manage the Indian operations, the Department of Indian Correspondence. The Chief Examiner who presided over this department was in charge of the entire Indian operations and he initiated the company's response to events both in India and in London.

'The mercantilists in the company's service became functionaries of the new empire: diplomats, administrators, statesmen and spies replaced in importance the bookkeepers and accountants of the previous age. The first organised, deliberately expansionist government in the Company's history came into being with this generation. They combined for the first time all of the requirements for imperial success- a passionately held ideology, a sound plan to achieve their aims, and more expertise on the sub-continent than any previous generation attained. Theirs was not the haphazard or primarily self-seeking aggrandizement of the mercantile age, but a carefully ordered design intended to found an empire'.[15]

Mapmaking and Imperialism - Mapping an Empire

An important lesson from the innumerable battles in India is the relative insensitivity, ignorance and disregard in keeping pace with the developments around the world in the political, economic and scientific fields in the ruling class in India. A striking example is the closeness of imperialism and mapmaking. The knowledge of a territory is represented by geographic representations and most especially by the map. Geography and empire are thus intimately and thoroughly interwoven. To govern territories one must know them. 'In the hundred years after 1750, the military and civil officials of the EIC undertook a massive intellectual campaign to transform a land of incomprehensible spectacle to an empire of knowledge. At the forefront of this campaign were the geographers who mapped the landscapes and studied the inhabitants, who collected geological and botanical specimens and who recorded details of economy, society and culture. The empire exists because it can be mapped; the meaning of the empire is inscribed into each map.[16]

In the fifteenth and sixteenth centuries, Europeans conceived of Asia as an ill-defined series of exotic and fabulously wealthy countries, namely Cathay, Cipangu, and "the Indies". The impression of Indies originally derived from Hellenistic Antiquity signified all the land east of the Indus, the traditional eastward limit of the Greek world. This image of the Indies was adapted by Renaissance Europe from the Geographies of Ptolemy and Strabo. The Ptolemaic map was supplanted by new maps constructed by Portuguese navigators but the Hellenistic nomenclature survived. *India intra Gangem*—the Indies this side of the Ganges—comprised all the lands lying between the Indus and the mouth of Ganges. *India extra Gangem*-the Indies beyond the Ganges—comprising all the land further west.

By 1700, the English merchants established several trading centres known as *factories* mainly in Madras (Fort St. George), Bombay, and Calcutta (Fort William). Bombay and Calcutta gave access to the markets and produce of the Mughal empire, which dominated the North of the subcontinent. Madras, the principal presidency, lay on the southern fringes of Mughal power so that the English there enjoyed much greater economic flexibility.

European maps accordingly framed the subcontinent into three distinct ways in this early period. Beginning in the early 1500s, general maps showed the traditional region of the Indies, from the Indus to Indochina. Later in the sixteenth century Europeans began to produce maps that framed only the peninsula south of the river Krishna, the area of principal involvement. The third framing developed in the early seventeenth century and focused on the polity of the Mughal empire. These maps emphasized the seat of Mughal power in the Northern plains and also included the Mughal territories west of the Indus: the Punjab, the Hindu Kush and Afghanistan. They omitted the peninsula.[17] The three frames began to merge in the eighteenth century.

J. B. B. d'Anville, the French cartographer published the first inclusive map of India in 1752. But it was the maps of Major James Rennel, the Surveyor- General of Bengal which effectively propagated the new concept of the subcontinent virtually as an actual region. He collected geographical data acquired by the British on their campaigns which allowed him to compile maps of the entire subcontinent. Though the details of many areas were scanty these maps provided the definitive image of India for the British army in their battles, a fact amply exemplified in the Battle of Tarvananghurry.[18]

Empire and Intelligence Gathering

John Marlborough, the First Duke of Marlborough wrote, 'No war can be conducted successfully without early and good intelligence. George Washington agreed: "The necessity of procuring good intelligence is apparent and need not be further argued'.[19] In spite of its great size, information moved with surprising speed over long distances in India. Men and women were always on the move as pilgrims, marriage parties, soldiers or merchants. Like in any sovereign state good intelligence gathering was an integral part of the science of kingship in ancient India and the royal intelligence depended very much on the informal networks of learned and well informed people. The Indian rulers had to assemble stores of information and set up networks of communication before they could venture out on any offensive.

> "Brahmins, the priestly class, and seekers of hidden knowledge were to gather the more sophisticated intelligence and communicate it in writing, but the king also needed the services of people with humbler skills. On campaigns he required runners and trackers, who knew the by-ways, water sources and river fords. The agents should be 'foresters', drawn from the domain beyond arable which was associated with magic, hunting and mysticism."[20]

The knowledge and understanding of the British of the vast hinterland and great regimes of the Indian subcontinent was minimal to begin with. But this was progressively remedied after 1757 when the British gradually came to get involved in the main Indian intelligence system. The speed and effectiveness with which the English expanded their conquests explains their practical approach to the Indian information system. 'Money talked' – so stated by Euripides in the fifth century B.C. and restated by Erasmus. The superior financial resources of the British helped them to secure the services of the once powerful noble families in the services of the Mughals who were suffering from the decline of royal patronage. They staffed many of the important and confidential embassies of various rulers. The British built up an effective and systematic system of news writers and spies around every one of their major residencies at Indian courts.[21] They also bought their way into the news and postal activities, and skilled news writers were paid attractive salaries. The most important native diplomats and informants were given large landholdings in jagir at the termination of their services. These British gentlemen were, moreover, quite skilled at unravelling the chains of cultural connections that ran through Asian aristocracy; like the connections of Gosains and hill Brahmins, as well as that of Mughals and Afghan horse-fanciers. The English were also able to secure the support of the writer-Brahmin connections in both north and south India whose familiarity with the Hindu pattern of pilgrimage made them very good intelligence officers.

The British, particularly the military, learned to manipulate the *harkara* system of India (horse and foot runner for communication)[22] on a massive scale to defend their marching columns from surprise attacks from the light cavalry of the Mysore and Maratha horses. Major William Fullerton of the Madras Infantry was among the first Company officers to fully recognize the importance of *harkaras* in fast cavalry warfare. From John Sullivan, the resident at Tanjore, and from the Nawab of Arcot he procured trustworthy middlemen who later employed harkaras on a personal basis. Fullerton then had these controllers compete with each other, threatening to kill them if they deceived him! The harkaras were sent out to observe different roads and later examined in the presence of their chief. Fullerton, fully briefed, then interrogated them himself.

In order to render this intelligence still more certain, Col. Fullerton had procured from Tondaiman, (Rajah Raghunatha Tondaiman, Ruler of Pudukkottai kingdom 1769-89) a body of Colleries (Kallars), who were perfectly acquainted with all the bypaths of the country. These were stationed in pairs as a Tappal or Dawk (postal service) at regular distances along the roads in different directions round the Passes of the Gauts, in all the principal towns in the Coimbatore country and in the passes at Srirangapatnam and Mysore. Individuals were also setup under various disguises in shops and in the Bazaar as Faquirs or Merchants:

> They were ordered to write down everything that occurred at regular intervals. If any particular incident occurred, they were to immediately write a *Cadjan* (document written in palm leaf) or note with the

> intelligence. These notes they gave to the Colleries posted on the road, who conveyed them from one to the other, so that they reached camp much faster than any troops could march".[23]

In effect, Fullerton has reconstituted under British control the classic Indian intelligence system which allied the writing skills and knowledge of learned Brahmins with the hard bodies and running skills of tribal and low-class people. Following new rules for 'intelligence, movement and supply' Fullerton marched the army from 'the Coromandel to the Malabar coast through the most difficult and before untried roads', thus scoring one of the first Company successes against Haider and Tipu.[24] These tactics were later extended to Northern and Western India where the British faced an equally mobile and enemy in the Marathas. Runners and spies were also recruited from the indigenous contacts -like the Bedas of the central Indian Plateau, Bhils and Kolis in the west, and Kurumbas in the southwest.

It is all important to appreciate that the English did not merely utilise the pre-existing information systems. On the contrary they made extremely significant conceptual changes in the sphere of surveillance and espionage in its political relations with the Indian States. The size and importance of the Intelligence and Postal departments of major residencies and of the Company's army were augmented. In the conquered and ceded territories the native *dawk (*postal service*)* were suppressed and were brought under the control of the Presidency government. The Company also prohibited all intercourse by diplomatic officials, post or confidential agents with an enemy power and this infringement was declared illegal.

During the eighteenth century, the ruling Indian powers and the Indo-Muslim literary intelligentsia had built up a vast repository of archival information. The Peshwa's Daftar (Chancellery) at Poona was one of the richest archives in Asia. Massive details on revenue, political and social issues, down to infractions of caste rules at village level are recorded here. Maratha leaders, notably Nana Fadnavis, had some of the most effective personal intelligence systems available to Indian politicians. In addition, the rapid transfer of information was guaranteed by a well-rooted system of public informants, runners and spies maintained by a cess on the villages. They also had the capability and expertise to convey information rapidly across political boundaries. But the Company was able to manage their extensive accumulated information, both from the intelligence and diplomatic systems, in a refined and practical way. Linguists like Neil Benjamin Edmonstone[25] who managed the Persian Department and the Persian branch of the Secret and Political Department of the English was also active in intelligence gathering. Information from newsletters or residents' and the ambassador's reports were sorted into subject files and extensive political biographies were built up. Moreover the Company routinely processed these records into widely disseminated printed packages which marked a decisive break. 'After 1790 periodical literature such as the *Asiatick Researches*, *Asiatic Annual Register*, filling out the government gazettes, fed the products of Indian reports and newsletters to the wider European public. This created an information rich administrative and military service.'[26]

The original idea of just accumulating and publicizing the data also changed. In India, this statistically rich information was generally used for a single purpose of taxing the houses in a bazaar, figuring land revenues or discrete political intelligence. On the other hand, the Company made use of the details to build up banks of multipurpose social data in conformity with the new European science of statistics.

> 'Thus, the British amassed wealth of information and analysed the society more systematically than their predecessors and their knowledge acquired a new territorial three dimensional form. Though the surveys of James Rennel of the territories of the company in the 1760s and 1770s were not quite been maps in the modern sense, they were excellent illustration of various routes, which pinpointed rivers, villages, wells and other geographical features which a military party might encounter on a march through territory.[27]

The British were able to conquer the Indian subcontinent within a period of two generations because they commanded the Indian seas and the Bengal revenues. Equally important was knowledge of the country that enabled the EIC to use these resources to greatest effect. The British in India unequivocally had military superiority over many regional forces. However,

> 'Indian armies were rapidly narrowing the gap in technology in the later eighteenth century. Where the British did have a critical advantage, however, was in their political planning and in cohesion of their ruling group. They were now much more effective at anticipating the alliances and armed resistance of the Indian states. In large measure this was because they were forewarned by increasingly effective systems of intelligence.[28]

The Military Fiscal State

By the late medieval and early modern era, the monarchies of Europe based on dynastic principles gradually substituted the feudal order centred on allegiance to the international institutions of the Pope or Empire in Western Europe. Britain had established multiple colonies in the New World. With the formation of Joint Stock Companies new markets developed. The escalated scale of military competition resulted in the development of larger and more effective bureaucracies and a prodigious increase in the cost of war. The transformation of Britain into a major international power originated from the ability of the government to wage war. As Cicero commented in Orationes Philippicae, 'sinews of War are infinite money'.

Britain raised the funds it needed. How did it do it? Nancy Cohen of Harvard University affirms, 'Through trade, trade and more trade both at home and abroad'.[29] Michael Kimmel recounts: Trade had become 'the life of the state'—as Beattie had called in 1645 (cited in Appleby, 1978:121).[30] What did they Trade? Where did their capital come from?

The most important event which led to the development of commerce and industry in Europe, especially Britain and US were the Trans-Atlantic Triangular Slave Trade. The forced transportation of 12.5 million Africans to the New World between the sixteenth and nineteenth centuries was "one of history's greatest crimes against humanity".[31] William Wood declared in 1718 that the slave trade was "the spring and parent from whence from which the others flow."[32] Malachi Postlewayt, commented in 1745, 'The African Trade is the first principle and foundations of all the rest, the mainspring of the machine which sets every wheel in motion.'[33] The triangular trade gave a triple stimulus to the British industry. In this trade England, France, and Colonial America equally supplied the exports - a cargo of manufactured goods. These were exchanged at a profit on the coast of Africa to purchase Negros, who were traded on the plantations at another profit. The maintenance of the Negros and their owners on the plantations also provided another market for the British industry, New England agriculture and Newfoundland fisheries. The slaves produced sugar, cotton, indigo, molasses and other tropical produce, which was taken back to the home country. The profits obtained by the process, which produced new industries in England, provided one of the main streams of that accumulation of capital in England which financed the Industrial Revolution.[34]

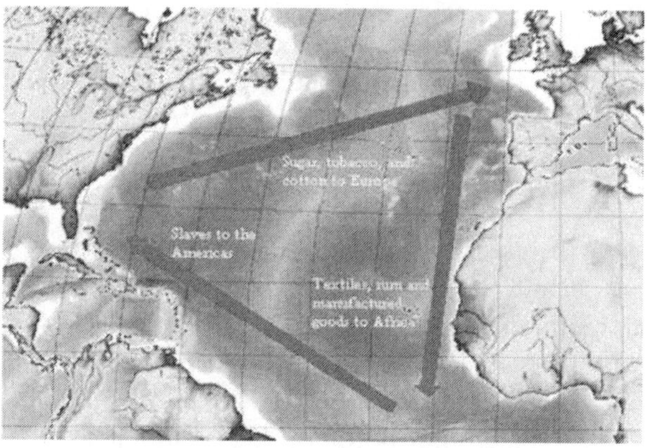

Triangle trade. Modified version, which was created by John Monopoly- open source

Great Britain dominated the buying and shipping of slaves to the Americas during the 60-year period between 1750 to 1807. It reached its zenith in the late eighteenth century, by which time Britain had established itself as the leading slave nation, carrying 40 percent of all Africans transported between 1761 and 1807. As a matter of fact, the exceptional demands of this horrid and detestable operation launched, energised, and invigorated important developments in key sectors and regions of the British economy.

> 'A critical factor enabling the transatlantic slave trade to grow to such dimensions was the ability of the merchants to find ways to mitigate not only the usual risks of trans-oceanic commerce in a pre-industrial age, but also those risks peculiar to the trade itself. The latter included high crew and slave morbidity rates, highly variable loading rates and ocean crossing times and the difficulties of provisioning for these, the moral hazard of crew neglecting their cargoes or trading for themselves, losses caused through shipboard revolts or resistance and a variety of transaction risks including exchange value uncertainties, price volatility and planter credit default in the purchase of new slaves.'[35]

Thus, the regular and growing demand for insurance cover was an important factor in the development of marine insurance in England. The trade also required extension of credit at various stages. The favourable demand conditions created in this way were important for the development of the banking and discount market in England.

The special shipping requirements of the trade stimulated considerable activities in British shipyards for building of a special class of vessel and for the repair and costly outfit of slave vessels. The input requirements of these activities had important linkage effects on other industries, particularly the metal and metal-using trades like copper, brass and iron and hence the mining of metal ore and coal, and their transportation. The manufacture of guns for the purchase of slaves was an important Birmingham industry. The transformation of an agricultural economy into a manufacturing one contributed to urbanisation by creating economic growth and job opportunities that drew people to cities. 'But the British industry whose development was most critically influenced by the slave trade was the cotton textile industry.' [36]

Leading states required substantial economic means and organisational machinery to utilise resources in the cause of national build-ups. Maintenance of the domination of the trade routes and the protection of bases and colonies depended upon troops and a navy which required money and befitting organisations.

> 'The late seventeenth and eighteenth centuries saw an astonishing transformation in British government, one which put muscle on the bones of the British body politic, increasing its endurance, strength and reach. Britain was able to shoulder an ever-more ponderous burden of military commitments thanks to a radical increase in taxation, the development of public deficit finance (a national debt) on an unprecedented scale, and the growth of a sizable public administration devoted to organising the fiscal and military activities of the state'.[37]

Following the Glorious Revolution of 1688 the British military involvement radically changed.

> "In the century between 1680 and 1780 British army and navy tripled in size. During these years Britain fought five major Wars: the Nine Years war (War of English Succession 1688-97), The War of Spanish Succession (1702-13), the Wars of Jenkin's Ear and Austrian Succession (1739-48) , the Seven Years War (1756-63) and American War of Independence (1775-83).[38]

The greater part of this military expenditure of England was financed by state borrowing. The British Treasury raised money by issuing government stock, usually long-term bonds with a guaranteed annual premium. Out of this need originated the Bank of England in 1694.

> 'The formation of the Bank would help meet the need for greater liquidity in the national market place, fuel the increasing overseas trade, and meet the needs of businesses and newly-urban private individuals, as well as the political and military needs of the Crown; it would do this, despite opposition from entrenched interests, by replacing the previous bullion-based economy, with a modern credit-based economy which would provide the stable financial base needed to fuel the growth of Britain's empire'.[39]

Thus, the Bank established a structure of public credit, through the trading wealth of England could be invested in security and stability of government and give that government the power to engage successfully in long range war for political and commercial ends. It was this public credit that made England a world power.

Science and the Empire

The early use of modern science in India was scattered, infrequent and motivated by individual curiosity. The basis of the various histories of British Science in India was their utility for the governance and economic exploitation of India. A basic knowledge of the kinds of animal and plant geography in different areas is fundamental in attempting to understand the regionality of the natural world.

> 'Ever since the great age of European geographical exploration that opened with the epic figure of Henry the Navigator and encompassed Vasco da Gama, Columbus, Cortes, Cabot, Magellan, Drake, and Tasman, leading to the voyages of La Condamine, Pallas, Kotzebue, Cook, Vancouer, Dumont D'Urville, Humboldt, Mengo

> Park, Burton, and Speke and, more particularly after the time of Linnaeus, great emphasis was laid in Europe on comprehending the native fauna and flora of new regions and on bringing specimens back for cataloguing and future assessment.'[40]

The cartographic surveys were a major constituent of useful sciences and maps were cardinal means of administration. The same applies to the Company's botanical, astronomical and geological establishments.

> 'Amassing scientific collections based on systematic principles was the scientific equivalent of mapping the world, making its products available in the imperial centre in a form which was readily accessible and exploitable. For empire is a mental construction- a way of conceiving the world which gives privileged status to the forms of knowledge and canons of rationality that predominate in the metropolitan power.'[41]

Botany interested traders and bureaucrats as in addition to their culinary values, plants also had medicinal, commercial and exotic values. The first western botanist in India was Garcia D'Orta, a Portuguese New Christian (Converted Jew) and physician based mainly in Goa. In 1563 he wrote 'Colloquies on the simples, drugs and Materia medica od India' on the exotic plants of Asia which was published in 1567 by Carolus Clusius. The Dutch followed the Portuguese. The material collected from Malabar from 1669 to 1676, was compiled by Hendrik van Rheed, governor of Dutch Malabar to a 12 volume *Hortus Malabaricus* published at Amsterdam. 'Following the Battle of Plassey, which laid the foundation of the British colonial empire, science began to be pressed into the cause of empire building and institutionalised.'[42] The systematic study of Botany was pioneered by John Gerald Koenig, a pupil of Carl Linnaeus in the Dutch settlement of Tranquebar in the 1770s.

The East India Company initiated its botanical activity with the establishment of a botanical garden in Calcutta in 1787. ' ...by its means the cultivation of the teak and of the Malayan spices might be introduced into a province near one of the Company's chief Indian centres'.[43] Other botanical gardens were established in Bangalore, Madras and Bombay primarily for the introduction of cash crops like coffee, tea and rubber.

Mathematics had a significant role in the development of Indian culture. 'They developed arithmetic and geometry from the mensuration point of view further than the Greeks who had considered geometry from an abstract standpoint. But their greatest contribution is our present number system which came to Europe through the Arabs and hence got its name.'[44] In ancient times, mathematics was mainly used in auxiliary or applied roles.

> 'Thus, mathematical methods were used to solve problems in architecture and construction, (as in the public works of the Harappan civilisation), in astronomy and astrology (as in the words of the Jain mathematicians), and in the construction of Vedic altars (as in the case of the Shulba Sutras of Baudhayana and his successors).'[45]

The classic era of Indian mathematics (500 to 1200 AD) created some of the greatest exponents of Indian mathematics- Aryabhata, Brahmagupta and Bhaskara. But it was the Europeans who exploited mathematical thinking and mathematical methods to support military technology mathematically which helped to change the character and performance of modern warfare.

Niccolò Fontana Tartaglia (1499-1557), an Italian scholar and engineer, applied the science of mathematics in the study of the paths of cannon balls, developing the discipline of ballistics. In 1537 he published the book *Nova Scientia,* a very early example of mathematical physics, where he attempted to utilise mathematical axioms to explain the physical world. He encouraged gunners to use a device called quadrant to measure their gunner's angles of elevation. Tartaglia paved the way for Galileo.

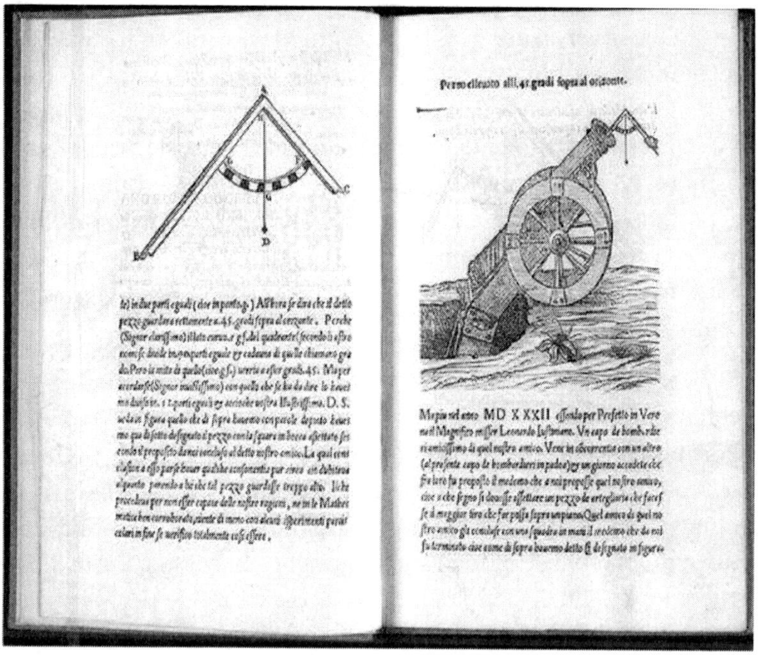

Nova Scientia: Tartaglia. Niccolò, 1557- Internet Archives. Archives.org

Astronomy in India formed one of the most important branches of knowledge from ancient times.

> 'The traditional astronomer performed two very useful functions in Indian society. He computed the annual calendars or *pancangas* which gave the dates both of extraordinary celestial events and of the festivals which depend on the complex computations of the beginnings of local *tithis* or lunar days. Many of the Vedic liturgical performances were regulated by the *tithi,* as were also more popular and local religious observations. Furthermore, the astronomers computed the tables used

by astrologers in casting horoscopes, and often acted as astrologers.'[46]

On the other hand, in Europe, astronomy came to be used for a wide range of highly practical matters. Long sea voyages with their enormous economic and political importance required better navigational instruments for the accurate measurement of star positions. 'The Madras Observatory was established in 1789 to support the astronomical observations of the EIC. Their main aim was to correct and to calibrate the delicate marine chronometers and so to make the determination of the latitude at sea all the more accurate.'[47]

Scientific record keeping was one area where India lagged behind Europe, as succinctly observed by Shejwalker.[48] The study of the documents and publications of the English is an eye-opener for the competence and dexterity they have reached.[49]All their military campaigns, naval fights, and political build-up are found fully written down, reported and thoroughly discussed. From these deliberations and discourses they work out their lines of policy for future guidance. Any tiny amount of knowledge once gained, any upper hand once secured, or any inch of ground once occupied was not wasted or lost by them. The Marathas in their career had to go through many a campaign, to enter into diplomatic talks, to carry on political controversies and to devise various ways and means for securing their end, but scarcely any of these things are found published for public edification, for the use of the younger students in various walks of life. A nation which carried on wars in all directions over a wide continent for more than a century, has not produced a single treatise on warfare. In the very year of the Panipat disaster, the English had published a book with detailed maps, plans of battles, illustrations of the positions of forts giving a visual demonstration of their military situation, naval manoeuvres with drawings of anchored ships, together with their political and diplomatic background.

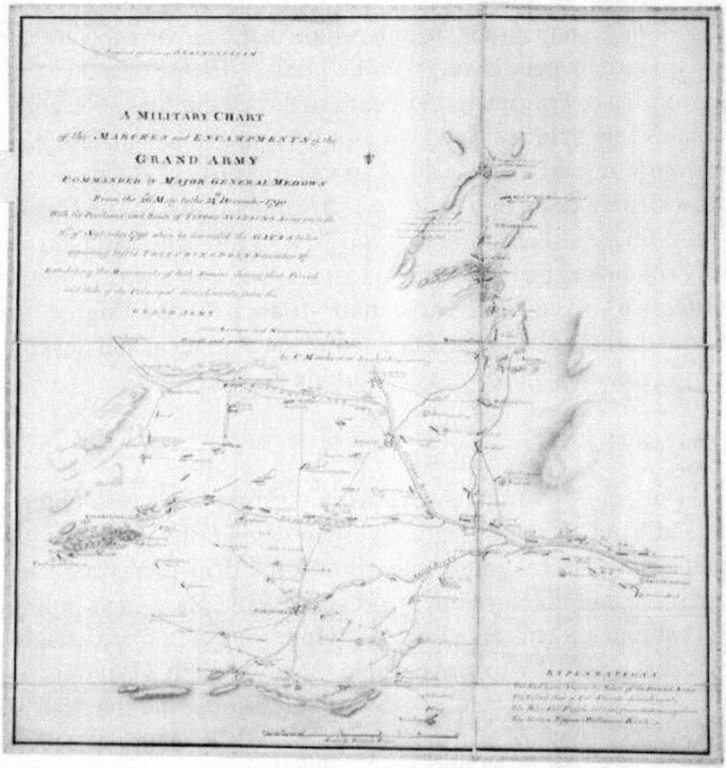

The military chart of the marches and encampments of the Grand Army

The military chart of the marches and encampments of the Grand Army by Colin Mackenzie[50] is a classic example of the art and science of cartography used to convey strategic, operational and tactical movements of armies, analyse their omissions and commissions and plan future means and methods. The decision to supersede General Medows by the Governor General Lord Cornwallis came from such solid evidence.

Where did the Manpower Come From?

The estimated population of England by the end of the

17th century was about five and a half million and they were confronting a population of 200 million in the Indian subcontinent. To boost their manpower, they had one million Scots and three million Irish. Following the death of Elizabeth One, her cousin James VI the King of Scotland also became the King of England, resulting in the Union of the Crowns in 1601. The Kingdom of Great Britain came into being in 1707. Ireland was the first colony of the English. During the period from 1536-1691, Ireland was fully conquered by the English and it was colonised with protestant settlers from England. The cannon-fodder for the English was supplied from Ireland and Scotland with the manual and unskilled toil provided by the lower and working class English.

1. Ireland

The Anglo-Normans who were the first settlers to come to Ireland from Britain, progressively integrated themselves within Irish society. In the fourteenth century the British crown decided to reinforce its colonisation by progressively imposing its political and cultural systems onto Ireland. 'Its aim was not a mere territorial conquest it was also to turn a whole society, namely Gaelic society, into a mirror of England'.[51] Several battles opposed the Irish and the English. One of the most famous was the Battle of Kinsale which saw the defeat of the Irish and led to the Flight of the Earls in 1607 opening up an easy conquest of Ireland for the British. Then the Jacobian Plantations, which consisted in dispossessing the native population of its land and giving it to the new settlers, were implemented by the Act of the Settlement of Ireland in 1652. Thus, the Irish became slaves in their own country. This was enforced with a military force by Oliver Cromwell until the end of the 1650s. Thus, the full-scale colonisation of Ireland got underway in the late sixteenth and early seventeenth century. Jane Ohlmeyer examined a wide range of English policies and practices in Ireland – military, political, administrative, legal, religious, and cultural- and concluded that together 'these strategies, though couched in the rhetoric of civility, effectively amounted to a form of imperialism that sought to exploit Ireland for England's political and economic advantage…'.[52] The introduction of English law which allowed for the confiscation and redistribution of land helped to destroy the economic foundations of the 'old Gaelic order'. Disempowered and disposed Irish Catholics became the main source of white migration to the West Indies during the 1650s in the form of indentured servants and convicts and prisoners of war. Thus, strategically, economically and culturally, English colonialism achieved its earliest triumphs in Ireland, establishing a model for other ventures further afield. Ireland was the laboratory for the empire.

From the mid seventeenth century, the English Parliament exercised strict legal control over the economic activities of colonies, whether in Ireland, the Atlantic, or the East. Priorities shifted from conquest, colonisation and civilisation to commerce and economic protectionism and these years witnessed the emergence of a new concept of Empire, one firmly grounded on English economic and political domination. 'This transformation manifested itself in England's need to regulate Ireland's burgeoning economy with restrictive statutes, such as the Navigation Acts, Cattle Acts or legalisation controlling the woollen industry'.[53]

In 1654, Dr William Petty, Physician to the Cromwellian army was made responsible for mapping all the forfeited land in Ireland. It was known as the Down Survey because it was set down on maps and not just in tabulated form as in some earlier surveys. He viewed Ireland as a testing ground for Baconian principles of improvement.[54] The survey is notable for the sheer magnitude of the work, and the methods of recruitment, training, organisation, and remuneration of the surveyors which allowed the work to be completed in five years.[55]

2. Scotland

Scotland is broadly divided into Highland and Lowland although this is not an official geographical area. Scottish Highlands include the mountainous regions of Scotland north and west of Highland and Boundary Fault between Stonehaven and Helensburgh on the Firth of Clyde. The rest is the Lowlands, the non-Gaelic region.

In terms of language, religion, levels of literacy, social organisation and ethnicity, Scottish Lowlanders had far more in common with the inhabitants of the north of England than they did with their own Highland countrymen. Lowland Scots traditionally regarded their Highland countrymen as members of a different and inferior race, violent, treacherous, poverty stricken and backward calling them savages or aborigines.

The Highland area is sparsely populated but before the nineteenth century it was home to a much larger population. The story of the depopulation of Scottish Highlands has a tragic story behind it.Charles II was formally restored to his kingdoms and proclaimed King of Great Britain and Ireland in May 1660. The Restoration parliament was extremely paranoid that the Stewart kings would present an uncontested line of Catholic monarchs as King Charles II failed to produce a male heir to the throne. His younger brother, James II, a passionate catholic convert, was the next in line, which caused panic among the English nobility. They were desperate to cement Protestantism as the country's religion, with the monarch as head of the church. As William of Orange arrived from his native Holland, James fled, setting sail for France on 23rd December 1688. Welcoming William of Orange as King William III, a group of politicians altered the course of history by wresting the legitimate line of succession for both English and Scottish crowns. The insurgent movement arrived in the form of Jacobites, who stood up against this illegitimate king. From the inception of the Jacobite movement in 1689 to its bloody end in the fields of Culloden in 1745, a variety of grievances were challenged under the Jacobite banner.

The Battle of Culloden was the final clash between the French supported Jacobites and the Hanoverian British government. The Jacobites, the majority of them Highland Scots, supported the claims of James Francis Edward Stuart (Bonnie Prince Charles-the Old Pretender). The English won a decisive victory under the Duke of Cumberland in the Battle of Culloden. The Duke wanted to ensure that the long series of Jacobite uprisings in Scotland, with previous flare-ups in 1689, 1708, 1715 and 1719, should be brought to an end, once and for all. In the aftermath of the battle, Cumberland's troops committed widespread atrocities, killing many wounded, surrendering and fleeing Jacobites, as well as bystanders, residents and anyone else within reach. Worse was to come. Cumberland established his headquarters at Fort Augustus. From there he sent out columns of troops backed by the troops of the Royal Navy. He actually considered shipping the entire population of these areas to the colonies: but in the end satisfied himself with burning every farmstead, croft and house; with widespread murder and rape; and with rounding up and sending south 20,000 head of cattle, effectively wiping out the entire basis of the economy of Highlands.‘ Although a fraction only of the clans had taken part in the last Jacobite rebellion of 1745, all felt the results of its defeat. Bayonet and noose, the proscription of arms, of tartan and kilt, sequestration of their estates, began the destruction of the clan system.[56] For his activities at Culloden, he came to be known as, "Butcher Cumberland". After Culloden the Commissioners of the Forfeited Estates started evictions.

Highland Clearances

Maps of highlands and lowlands of Scotland. Jrockley

The Highland Clearances is one of the sorest, most painful themes in Modern Scottish history.The deliberate dismantling of clans started immediately after the Battle of Culloden was completed in the process of the Clearances. This was done by the successors of the Highland Chiefs themselves, who had brought out their kin for the Jacobite cause in the first place. Landowners, many of them ruined financially by the 1745 rebellion, saw an opportunity to restore their finances by replacing their tenants with sheep. Tens of thousands of men, women and children were violently evicted from their homes to make way for large scale sheep farming.

There were two distinct types of 'Clearance'. The first was forced settlement on barren land near the sea. The Crofts, as these lands became known, had very poor agricultural potential which the gentry wrongly assumed would be compensated for by fishing and kelping (seaweed harvesting). The second type of 'clearance' was prompted by the failure of the crofts to produce a living for the Highlanders. It was a hopeless situation for many. The sheer number of people pushed to the coast coupled with huge rent increases, over-fishing and over-kelping resulted in death from starvation and exposure. Many were reduced to living outside like animals. Many highlanders took service with the British army or emigrated which in large measure account for the wide scattering of Scots around the world today.

The regiments raised in the period from 1746 -1800 have been portrayed as forming an unbroken link with the distinctively Scottish social institutions of Highland clanship and as the living embodiment of a historically authentic past. However, beneath the apparent close association between clanship and kilted regiments, lay entirely new methods and levels of coercion. The threat of Press Acts that were wholly British and imperial in character were always a danger. (The Crown claimed a permanent right to seize men for service in the Royal Navy and the Army. This practice of 'Impressment' was given parliamentary authority during the eighteenth century). 'Thus, the threat of state sponsored impressment combined with the economic leverage controlled by the landlords who were paid up members of the Anglo-British elite made highland recruitment extremely efficient.'[57] During the recruitment of the 75th (Highland) Stirlingshire Regiment (who fought in the Battle of Tervannengarry in Calicut in 1790) a letter, in the possession of Campbell of Dunstaffnage, written by a Mull laird to his cousin who was raising men for a commission, is to the following effect:

> 'I send a recruit who will, I think, make up your number. As he is a very obstreperous man, he is tied in a cart, and you will please give the carter 5s. and 2s.6d. for the rope if you do not return it, as it is new'. Judging from a letter written in 1777, there was an aversion to soldiering in the Lone district of Argyll. ' There are great numbers of idle fellows that transgress the law by wearing the Highland dress and arms (retribution for the Battle of Culloden). I dread it will only be by comprehending (apprehending) them for either of these that I can be of any assistance (in recruiting); however, I'll exert myself to the utmost of my power, and try every fair means first.' [58]

A huge tide of voluntary emigration by the Highlanders followed. This caused great concern to the landlords as they were worried about the loss of manpower in farming and the kelp industry. As for the English, "Westminster worried about the shortage of cannon-fodder; Highlanders were now valued, if only as infantry statistics, in the service of the British state."[59]

3. Enclosure or Inclosure

Enclosure is the process by which 'common land' is taken into fully private ownership and use accompanied by force, resistance and bloodshed. Common land is land, which is owned by one person, but over which other people have certain traditional rights, such as arable farming, mowing meadows for hay, or grazing livestock. Under enclosure, such land is *fenced (enclosed) and deeded or entitled* to one or more private owners, who then enjoy the possession and produce of land to the exclusion of others.

Enclosures occurred to some degrees in Northern Europe but the most well-known Enclosure Movements took place in the British Isles. Since the twelfth century a small number of enclosures were going on in the north and west of England but these enclosures were generally informal. Henry VII in 1544 encouraged enclosures. When enclosure was introduced by Act of Parliament for the first time in 1604 the informal method continued. The English Civil War (1642-51) spurred a major acceleration of enclosures. England was a dramatically changed society after the Glorious Revolution of 1688. "On a local level rich landlords consolidated their powers. In its progress the agrarian revolution engulfed the open field system, the self-governing village and the peasant proprietors, the 'ancient and godly yeoman of England'.[60] The revolution "facilitated the conversion of rural society into a three-tiered structure of big landlords, substantial tenant leaseholders with reasonable security of tenure and landless laborers".[61] There was little fear that the state would upset the influential class by interfering with the economic activities of its members. The English Civil War swept away the main barrier to the enclosing landlord and simultaneously prepared England for rule by a 'committee of landlords'. They gained absolute rights to their estates, institutionalising primogeniture, with the effect of maintaining the stability of large estates. The result was the ever-increasing concentration of land in the hands of the large landowners.

By the 1750s the Parliamentary system became the more usual method and many more Acts were introduced. The Inclosure Act of 1773 created a law that enabled enclosure of land, at the same time removing the right of commencer's access.[62] Thus, the process of enclosure, often accompanied by force, resistance, and bloodshed and which remains one of the most controversial areas of agricultural and economic history in England, created a pool of landless working class.[63] It was this pool of wage labourers who paved the way for the agricultural revolution of the eighteenth century and for the industrial revolution of the nineteenth century.[64] The dispute over enclosures features prominently in some of Shakespeare's plays like Henry VI and Coriolanus.

NOTES

1. Rasselas is a novella by Samuel Johnson which was first published in England in 1759. Johnson was influenced by the vogue for exotic locations. He had translated 'A voyage to Abyssinia' by Portuguese Jesuit missionary Jeronemo Lobo in 1735. *Rasselas Prince of Abyssinia by Samuel Johnson.* Cassel & Company Ltd. London 1889' Project Guttenberg.
2. Singh, Anjana. Early Modern European Mercantilism and Indian Ocean Trade in Strootman, R van den Eijnde & van Wijk R (Eds) (2020). *Empires of the Sea: Maritime Power Networks in World History*. Brill. www.jstor.org/stable/10.1163/j.ctv2gjx041.14. p248)
3. *Ibid,* p. 251.
4. McGinty, A. B. (1946). *Anglo-Dutch Rivalry in India. Current History.* Vol.11 (63) www.jstor.org/stable/45306980. p383.
5. History Magazine (2010 February). *How did Britain come to rule the waves*? p. 23.
6. Crouzet, F. (1990). Quoting Voltaire in: *The sources of England's wealth: some French views in the eighteenth century- Britain ascendant: Comparative studies in Franco-British economic history.* Cambridge University Press, Cambridge, pp. 127-148.
7. Spence, R. T. (1995). The Portuguese carrack from India Madre de Deus was intercepted off the island of Azores by an English fleet in August 1592. The fabulous wealth of just one ship stoked the English appetite for trade with the Far East, giving stimulus to the formation of East India Company in 1600. *The Privateering Earl- George Clifford, 3rd Earl of Cumberland, 1558-1605.* Alan Sutton Publishing Ltd. p. 117.
8. Kessel, Elsje van (2020). The inventories of the Madre de Deus: tracing Asian material culture in early modern England. *Journal of the History of Collections.* OUP 32(2) 207-223: Among these riches were chests filled with jewels and pearls, gold and silver coins, ambergris, rolls of the highest quality cloth, fine tapestries, 425 tons of pepper, 45 tons of clove, 35 tons of cinnamon, 3 tons of mace and 3 of nutmeg, 2.5 tons of Benjamin (aromatic balsamic resin used for perfume) 25 tons of cochineal and 15 tons of ebony. There was also a document, printed in Macau in 1590, containing valuable information on the China and Japan trade, which was "enclosed in a case of sweet cedar wood, and lapped up a hundred fold in fine Calicut-cloth, as though it had been some incomparable jewel".

9. Hakluyt, Richard.(1904). *The Principal Navigations, Voyages, Trafiques & Discoveries of the English Nation Made by Sea or Overland to the Remote and Farthest Distant Quarters of the Earth at Any time within the Compasse of these 1600 years.* Vol. 7. Glasgow, MacLehose and Sons, pp. 116-117.
10. Scott, W.R. (1911). *The Constitution and Finance of English, Scottish, Irish Joint- Stock Companies to 1720.* Cambridge, p. 467.
11. Buchan, B.P. (1994). The East India Company 1749-1800: The Evolution of a Territorial Strategy and the Changing Role of the Directors. *Business and Economic History,* Vol. 23/1, pp. 52. Cambridge University Press.www.jstor.org/stable/23702832.
12. Mill, James. (1858). *The History of British India.* Vol. III, London, Archives.org> in.ernet.dil.2015.65990.
13. Buchan, B.P., *op.cit.,* p. 60.
14. Buchan, B.P., *op.cit.,* p. 53.
15. Chancy, M. K. (2003). *In the Company's Secret Service: Neil Benjamin Edmonstone and the first Indian Imperialists, 1780-1820.* The Florida State University Libraries, Electronic Thesis, Treatise and Dissertation. https://diginole.lib.fsu.edu>datastream retrieved 14/7/2022.
16. Edney, M. H. (1990). *Mapping an Empire- The Geographical Construction of British India 1765-1843.* University of Chicago Press, p. 2.
17. Edney, M. H., *op.cit.,* p. 5.
18. *The Map of the seat of War during the last Campaign in India constructed from a late survey of that of the Malabar Coast by Capt. Montresor; and from the Surveys of the other Countries. By Capts. Beatson and Allan,* Published by Major Rennell in 1792.
19. Keegan, John. (2002). *Intelligence in War.* Vintage Books, p. 7.
20. Bayly, C. A. (1996). *Empire and Information: Intelligence gathering and social communication in India, 1780-1870.* Cambridge University Press, Cambridge, p. 12.
21. *Records of Fort St George. Country Correspondence, Military Department.* 1757. Madras 1911: The Country Correspondence-Military Department, consists translations of those letters received and send by the Government of Fort St George to several native powers and functionaries in Southern India. Washadeva Punt, in the camp of the Nizam Salabat Jung and a spy in the services of the English, sends numerous sensitive letters to the English.
22. The organised Harkara postal system started with Sher Shah and was strengthened by Akbar. Later Aurangazib increased the running

distance of Harkaras to 10 miles, but finally when the English got into power reduced to 5-7 miles.

23. *Fullerton's Hircarrah system*. Home Misc. 84,ff. British Library, pp. 11-23.
24. Wilson, W. J. Lt Colonel (1882). *History of the Madras Army*. Internet Archives. pp. 85-92: Colonel Fullarton of Fullarton was a Scottish soldier and a landed gentry. In May 1782 in Dindugal he took command of H.Ms 98th Regiment which he had helped to raise from his own estates in Scotland. In September two additional detachments (500 Europeans belonging to the H.M's 78th and the Madras regiment; 500 men of H.M's 101st and 102nd Regiments) were sent from the main army to join him which raised his force to about 13,600 men of which 2050 were Europeans. Here Col Fullerton made pioneering changes in the way a large army should march in hostile conditions. Early in October the army marched to Palani and then toward Palghat, reducing several forts on the way. The march through the Anamalai hills was achieved with great difficulty and the Palghat fort was secured in November 1783.
25. Chancy, M. K., *op cit.*
26. Bayly, C A . (1993). Knowing the Country: Empire and Information in India. Modern Asian Studies, 27(1), 3-43. www.jstor/org/stable/3128777.
27. Bayly, C. A. (1993), *op.cit.*, p. 34.
28. Bayly, C. A. (1996), *op.cit.*, p. 56.
29. Koehn, N. F. (1994). *The Power of Commerce.* Cornell University, p. 6.
30. Kimmel, M.S. (1988). *Absolutism and its discontents. State and Society in seventeenth Century France and England.* Transaction Inc., p. 220.
31. Davis, D. B. (2010). *Atlas of the Transatlantic Slave trade*, by David Eltis and David Richardson. Yale University Press, Forward, p. xvii.
32. Wood, William. (1718). *A Survey of Trade.* London, Part III, p. 178.
33. Boston, T. D. Ed. (1997). *A Different Vision, Race and Public Policy*, Vol. 2, Routledge London, p. 225.
34. Williams, Eric. (1994). *Capitalism and Slavery*. The University of North Carolina Press, USA, p. 52.
35. Pearson, R. and Richardson, D. (2019). Insuring the Transatlantic Trade. The Journal of Economic History. 79(2), p. 418.
36. Shepherd, V. A. & Beckles. Ed. (2000). Caribbean Slavery in the Atlantic, A Student Reader- The Slave Trade and the Atlantic

Economies, 1451-1870. Joseph Inikori. Ian Randle Publishers Ltd, Jamaica, p. 293.

37. Brewer, John. (1989). *The Sinews of Power- War, Money and the English State.* Alfred Knopf, Inc., New York, Introduction, XVII.
38. Brewer, John. (1989), *op.cit.,* p. 29.
39. Goodman, Halley. (2009). "The Formation of the Bank of England: A Response to Changing Political and Economic Climate, 1694", *Penn History Review,* Vol. 17: Iss 1, Article 2.
40. Browne, J. (1992). A science of Empire: British Biogeography before Darwin. *Revue d'histoire des sciences, 45*(4), 453-475. www.jstor.org/stable/23632965
41. Gascoigne, John. (1998).*Science in the service of the Empire.* Cambridge University Press, Cambridge, p. 202.
42. Kochar, R. K. (1992). Science in British India. I. Colonial tool. *Current Science, 63*(11). www.jstor.org/stable/24094778. pp. 689-694.
43. *Ibid.,* p. 693.
44. Brown, W. E. (1921). The History of Mathematics. *The Scientific Monthly, 12* (5). American Association for the Advancement of Science. www.jstor.org/stable/6389, pp. 385-413.
45. Murty, V.K. (2007). *A brief history of Indian Mathematics-eSamskriti.* www.esamscriti.com
46. Pingree, David. (1978). Indian Astronomy. *Proceedings of the American Philosophical Society, 122*(6), 361-364. www.jstor.org/stable/986451
47. Edney, *op. cit.,* p. 295.
48. Shejwalker, T. S. (1946). *Panipat 1761.* Deccan College, Poona, p. 122-123.
49. The 14 kilometres of shelves of volumes, files and boxes of papers, together with 70,000 volumes of official publications and 105,000 manuscript and printed maps, are public records comprising the archives of the East India Company (1600-1858), of the Board of Control or Board of Commissioners for the Affairs of India (1784-1858), of the India Office (1858-1947), of the Burma Office (1937-1948), and of a number of British agencies overseas which were officially linked with one or other of the four main bodies. They are complemented by extensive collections of private papers which provide alternative perspectives on official business and insights into individuals' lives, thoughts and interests which often included studying the countries, languages and cultures they encountered. www.bl.uk
50. Mackenzie, C. 'Marches and encampments of Grand Army commanded

by Major General Medows from 26th May to 14th December 1790 with the positions and route of Tippoo Sultan's army from the 11th of September 1790 when he descended the Gauts, to his appearing before Trichinopoly November 27th exhibiting the movements of both armies during that period and those of the principle detachments from the Grand Army. From surveys and measurements of the roads and authentic information on the spot by C. Mackenzie. Lieut. of Engineers'. From Art Collection/ Alamy Stock Photo, dated 08.10.2022- in public domain.

51. Estelle, Epinoux. (2007). *Introduction to Irish History and Civilisation. Texts and Documents on Ireland.* Presses Universitaires de Limoges, 39c, rue Camille Guerin-87031.Limoges cedex-France, p. 35.
52. Kenny, K. (Ed). (2004.) *Ireland and British Empire- An Introduction.* The Oxford History of British Empire Companion Series. p7
53. *Ibid.,* p. 51.
54. Connolly, S. J. (Ed). (1998). *The Oxford Companion to Irish History.* p. 440.
55. *Ibid.,* p. 153.
56. Prebble, John. (1982). The Highland Clearances. Penguin Books, London, p. 13.
57. McKillop, A.(2007). Continuity, Coercion and Myth: The Recruitment of Highland Regiments in the Later Eighteenth Century. *International Review of Scottish Studies* 26. DOI:10.21083/irss.v2610.210 p51.
58. Gardyne, C.G. *The Life of a Regiment-The History of the Gordon Highlanders from 1816 to 1898 including an account of the 75th Regiment from 1787 to 1881* by Lt. Col C G Gardyne. The Medici Society Ltd., London, pp. 183-184.
59. Macleod, John. (1996). *Highlanders- A History of the Gales.* Hodder & Stoughton, London, p. 186.
60. Tate, W. E. (1967). *The English Village Community and the Enclosure Movements.* Victor Gollancz Ltd. p. 79.
61. Stone, L. (1980). The results of the English Revolutions of the Seventeenth Century in *Three British Revolutions,1641, 1688, 1776* (J G. A. Pocock. Ed) Princeton, p. 93.
62. Between 1604 and 1914 there were more than 5200 enclosure bills which amounted to 3 million hectares of land which approximated one fifth of the total area of England. UK Parliament (2021). "Enclosing the Land". London: UK Parliament.
63. The *Midland Revolt* broke out in 1607. The rebels described themselves as 'diggers' and 'levellers' labels later used by radicals during the

civil war. These were well planned actions where the mutineers tore down fences and filled the ditches. The movement was stopped by the landlords and the ring leaders were 'hanged, drawn and quartered'. Though this was a statutory punishment for high treason this ghastly penalty was conveniently used against opponents of authority on any pretext.

64. Kimmel, Michael S. (1988). *Absolutism and its Discontents-State and Society in Seventeenth Century France and England.* Transaction Books, New Jersey, p. 219.

Conclusion

The naval battle of 1503 and the land battle of 1790 of Calicut are minor battles in terms of number of combatants and equipment, the fame of the commanders or the prominence and importance of the terrain. But these were extremely significant battles in the history of Colonialism—how nations with minimal wealth and resources were able to extend their control virtually over the rest of the world in establishing settlements and exploiting the resources, both human and natural. It is fundamental to appreciate that these battles were not spontaneous, voluntary or personal impulsive events. Enormous changes in organisation, tactic, technology and finance occurred between what happened before, during and what came after these battles

Europe developed an ability to influence economy and politics on a worldwide scale through its superior competence in warfare at sea. With their institutional, organisational, and technical development, they were able to enforce a state of monopoly of violence on land as well as the sea. By controlling the maritime lines of communication, they were able to dominate trade and with military power extracted wealth by violence or through protection from violence. This fleet action off the Malabar Coast between the Zamorin and da Gama was not one of those decisive battles of the world but can be seen as both an accurate forecast of what was to come and an example of what had been learnt of sea fighting by the Atlantic nations. Against resolute resistance of the indigenous populace, the weapons and tactics adopted by the Portuguese opened to them the sea lanes of the Indian Ocean and the Far East. The decisive points are that Da Gama and Sodre made sure of the weather gauge, that is, fighting from to windward (the weather gauge is the advantageous position of a fighting sailing vessel relative to another) and they arranged their ships in a line ahead formation. They chose their own range to fight, which initially was both outside the range of the enemy guns and their own swivel pieces but, inside the effective range of their battery guns. This disabled the enemy and helped the Portuguese sufficiently close enough to board rival vessels.

From 1503, the Portuguese sent several fleets of ships to the Indian Ocean and gradually built up a large naval power in the area. This show of force further assisted the Portuguese when the small rulers along the Indian West Coast, primarily Cochin, allied themselves with them. The native overlords provided them with bases, ports for trade, and access to pepper-producing areas along the West Coast. Apart from the pepper trade, Portugal had also established itself as the seller of protection to the Asian seaborne trade by offering *cartaz* (a naval trade licence issued by the Portuguese empire in the Indian Ocean during the sixteenth century). Brutally enforced, the blockade extended to the movement of men and traded goods across the Indian Ocean. This substantially affected the revenues of the Muslim traders along the Malabar Coast, the Zamorin of Calicut, the Mamluk Sultan of Egypt, and indirectly the traders of Venice. 'When Babur, the first emperor of the Mughal Dynasty, made his first forays into India in 1526, where his dynasty established one of the greatest land powers of Asia, Portuguese sea power already controlled the Indian Ocean.'[1] The Portuguese were able to capitalise on the lack of geo-political sense and total ignorance of the intentions and capabilities of the newcomers by the native populations.

The Europeans thus made a better showing at sea to begin with, but there were no substantial territorial conquests before those of the English in India starting nearly three hundred years after the arrival of da Gama. In the early 1500s Albuquerque dreamt of conquering the subcontinent, just as like-minded Spanish thought of acquiring China and Japan. The harsh realities on the ground taught them otherwise. The defeat of the Dutch East India Company by Travancore in the Battle of Colachel in 1741 was an eye-opener that the Europeans could be vulnerable against the natives and that the wars were prohibitively expensive. Still within the span of twenty odd years between the Battle of Austrian Succession and the Seven Years War the English were able to gain an upper hand in Indian politics.

It was during this period a fundamental shift occurred in the relative strength of the EIC and the Indian powers with which it had dealings. The disintegration of the Mughal Empire and Anglo-French rivalry greatly facilitated the foreign conquest of India. The political instability which affected the Europeans directly was on the Coromandel Coast where the Nawab of Carnatic was trying to create a new state. He was opposed by smaller rulers who were also obliged to resist Maratha invasions and the interventions of the Nizams of the Deccan who claimed suzerainty over them. Added to the confusion there was disputed succession for Carnatic and the Deccan. It was in this context Anglo-French rivalry developed to a point that European forces were introduced to India on an entirely new scale. The British quickly built up armies capable of defeating the French and also coercing Indian rulers who were immune from European military pressure.

The Battle of Tarvananghurry on 10 December 1790 is a landmark battle in Indian history. As mentioned earlier, it was the first successful battle for the English in the Third Mysore War (1790–1792), enabling them to achieve their nobler task of redeeming a lost empire. As Oak and Swamy opined: The Third Mysore War is a key episode in the late eighteenth century, in which the Company decisively defeated the India regime (Mysore) that has been described as its most 'formidable and most determined foe'.[2] Lord Cornwallis's war against Mysore removed the most serious danger to the peace of India and freed the rulers of British India from their greatest anxiety for nearly a decade. It rendered possible Wellesley's sensational triumph over the same foe with rapidity, completeness, and small cost seven years later. According to Nirod Bhushan Ray, 'Cornwallis bearded a Tipu, who was the most formidable Indian prince of his time, assisted by a large and efficient French corps, in the fullness of his resources and overflowing with confidence born of past victories over the English and the Marathas.'[3]

In 1792, after Mysore had been defeated by the Company and its allies, French observers in Pondicherry commended that "at last both Nizam and the Marathas must surely have their eyes opened, and begin to see how unwise they have been in warring against Mysore, thereby enfeebling the only power '*qui puisse en imposer aux anglais*' [that would impress the English]".[4] The operations, both diplomatic and military, over a period spanning from the War of Austrian Succession in 1740 to the Third Mysore War in 1792, paved the way ultimately for the Tripartite Alliance, the ultimate cause of Tipu's defeat and a very critical development in the Third Mysore War.

The European attempts to understand India have been pursued from ancient times in a variety of fields. From the very beginning India occupied a central place in the interest of the West. From Herodotus on, Greek and Roman writers who wrote on politics, geography or natural history included material on Asia, particularly India. Even before the triumph of arms in India, fascinated by their great age, their continuing vitality and their practical achievements, the Europeans, especially the English and French, used every opportunity for understanding and exploiting this information. The large number of books that were written and published on the history, religion and art of India is an illustration of this interest and enthusiasm. This vast repertoire of information was readily available for the victors.

Thus, the two battles of Calicut of 1503 and 1790, separated by a span of almost 300 years, are representatives of two different phases of colonialism. It is a fact that the international status of the English changed because of their military heroics, economic growth and global expansion. Undeniably these victories were achieved through superior gun-powder weaponry both in their Ships of Line and on land. What is not properly acknowledged or highlighted is the pre-eminent role played by statesmanship, diplomacy and the all-inclusive utilisation of the latest technological and scientific innovations available at that period to equip themselves with ways and means which made territorial expansion and domination possible by the Western over the non-Western societies.

It is fascinating to go behind the deceptive frontage of captivating and enticing descriptions of battles to explore the real social, intellectual, technological, economic, political, legal and scientific foundations which actually form the bedrock of colonial exploitation. Marshman in his book, *The History of India*, gives a glimpse of the magnitude of the marching column of Lord Cornwallis: In the vanguard marched a hundred elephants laden with treasure, followed by a hundred carts carrying liquor, and 60,000 bullocks carrying provisions belonging to the Banjaras. Following in three parallel columns came the battering train and heavy carriages, the infantry and the field pieces, the baggage and camp followers. The appearance of these vast supplies caused Tipu to exclaim, 'It is not what I see of the resources of the English that I dread, but what I do not see'.[5] Very few rulers of India realised this and the rest is history.

NOTES

1. Kulke, H. & Rothermund, D. (2004). *The History of India*. 4th Ed. Routledge, London & New York, p. 214.
2. Oak, M. & Swamy, A. (2010). "Commitment and Conquest: The case of British rule in India",Centre for Development Economics 2010-05, Department of Economics. Williams College. Massachusetts. p. . 3. quoting from Moon p. . The British Conquest and Dominion of India. 1990. London. Gerald Duckworth and Co., p. 291.
3. Ray, N. B. (1937). *Poona Residency Correspondence, Vol. 3. Op.cit.*, Forward, p. iii.
4. Oak, M. & Swamy, A. (2010). p. 3. *op.cit.*, quoting Thompson E. (1943) *The Making of the Indian princes*. Oxford University Press, London, p. 4.

5. Marshman, J. C. (1868). *The History of India, Part 1. From the earliest period to the close of the eighteenth century*. Serampore Press, Serampore, p. 461.

References

Anderson, P. (1854). *The English in Western India being the early history of the factory at Surat, of Bombay.* Smith Taylor and Co.

Askari, S.H. (Ed.). (1976). *Fort William-India House correspondence and other contemporary papers relating thereto - foreign, secret, and political* (Vol. XVI: 1787–1791). Published for the National Archives of India. By the Controller of Publications. Government of India. Civil Lines, Delhi.

Ballard, G.A. (1998). *Rulers of the Indian Ocean.* Life Span Publishers and Distributors, New Delhi.

Barker, R. (1996). A gun list from Portuguese India, 1525. *Journal of the Ordnance Society* 8, pp. 53-63.

Barua, P. (1994). *Military developments in India 1750–1850. The Journal of Military History, 58*(4): 599–616. Doi:10.2307/2944270.

Bayly, C.A. (1993). Knowing the country: Empire and information in India. *Modern Asian Studies, 27*(1). 3-43. Special Issue: How Social, Political and Cultural Information is Collected, defined, Used, and Analysed.

———. (1996). *Empire and information: Intelligence gathering and social communication in India, 1780–1870.*Cambridge University Press.

Beatson, R. (1790). *Naval and military memories of Great Britain, from the year 1727, to the Present Time* (Vol. II). Gale Ecco, Print Editions, 2010.

Bence-Jones, M. (1974). *Clive of India*. Constable.

Bew, J. (2014). *The Case for Cornwallis.* The National Interest, 134, 58–66.

Biddulph, C.J.(1910). *Dupleix*. F.V. White & Co. Ltd.

Boston, T.D. (Ed.) (1997). *A Different vision, race and public policy* (Vol. 2). Routledge.

Brewer, J. (1989). *The sinews of power: War, money and the English state*. Alfred Knopf, Inc.

Brown, W.E. (1921). The history of mathematics. *The Scientific Monthly*, *12*(5). 385–413.

Browne, J. (1992). A science of empire: British biogeography before Darwin. *Revue d'histoire des sciences*, *45*(4), 453–475. *Especes, espaces: La biogeographie sans frontieres*.

Buchan, B.P. (1994). The East India Company 1749–1800: The evolution of a territorial strategy and the changing role of the directors. *Business and Economic History*, *23*(1), 52-61.

Buckwalter, J. (2009). *The transatlantic slave trade and the creation of the English Weltanschauung, 1685–1710.* https://www.eiu.edu/historia/Historia2009Buckwalter.pdf.

Crouzet, F. (1990). *Britain ascendant: Comparative studies in Franco-British economic history*, Cambridge University Press.

Chancey, M.K. (2003). *In the company's secret service: Neil Benjamin Edmonstone and the first Indian imperialists, 1780–1820*. [Unpublished PhD dissertation]. Florida State University, Florida. https://diginole.lib.fsu.edu>datastream

———. (2006). The making of the Anglo-Hyderabad alliance, 1788–1823. *South Asia: Journal of South Asian Studies*, *XXIX* (2), 181-214.

Cipolla, C.M. (1965). *Guns, sails and empires: Technological innovation and the early phases of European expansion, 1400–1700*. Minerva Press.

Clayton, L. (2001). The Iberian advantage. In G. Raudzens (Ed)., *Technology, disease, and colonial conquests, sixteenth to eighteenth centuries. Essays reappraising the guns and germs theories*. Brill Academic Publishers Inc., pp. 211-236.

Conolly, S. J. (Ed). (1998). *The Oxford companion to Irish history*. Oxford University Press.

Das, H. (1959). *The Norris embassy to Aurangazib (1699–1702)*. Firma K.L. Mukhopadhyay.

Datta, K.K. (1949).The Marathas in Orissa. *Proceedings of the Indian History Congress, 12*, 299–301.

Eltis, D. and Richardson, D. (2010). *Atlas of the transatlantic slave trade*. Yale University Press.

Diffie, W. (1977). *Foundations of the Portuguese empire, 1415–1580*. University of Minnesota Press.

Diffie, B.W. and G.D. Winius. (1977). *Foundations of the Portuguese Empire 1415–1580. Europe and the World in the Age of Expansion* (Vol. 1). University of Minnesota.

Dirom, Major. (1997). *A narrative of the campaign in India which terminated the war with Tipu Sultan in 1792,* W.Faden, London. 1793. Indira Gandhi National Centre for Arts, New Delhi.

Dodwell, H.H. (Ed.). (1929). *The Cambridge history of the British Empire* (Vol. IV, British India). Cambridge University Press.

Dodwell, H. (1989). *Clive and Dupleix: The beginning of the empire.* Asia Educational Services.

Dull, J. (2005). *The French navy and the Seven Years' War*. University of Nebraska Press.

Durant, W. (1954). *Our oriental heritage*. Simon and Schuster.

Dutt, R.(1969). *The economic history of India under early British rule* (Vol. 1). Publication Division. Ministry of Information and Broadcasting, Government of India.

The Editor of the Royal Military Calendar. (2007). *The East India military calendar: Containing the services of general and field officers of the Indian army* (Vol. II). East Sussex.

Edmunds, A.J. (1913). A forgotten victory of the American Revolution. *The Pennsylvania Magazine of History and Biography*. University of Pennsylvania Press. *37*(1) pp. 89-93.

Edney, M.H. (1990). *Mapping an empire: The geographical construction of British India 1765–1843*. University of Chicago Press.

Ellis Jr., J.F. (1993). Maritime Asia. 1500–1800: The interactive emergence of European domination. Review. *The American Historical Review*. *98*(1) pp. 83-105. https://doi.org/10.2307/2166383

Enclosing the land, UK parliament. https://www.parliament.uk/about/living-heritage/transformingsociety/towncountry/landscape/overview/enclosingland/#:~:text=Overall%2C%20between%201604%20and%201914,to%20some%206.8%20million%20acres.

Estelle, E. (2007). *Introduction to Irish history and civilisation: Texts and documents on Ireland*. Presses Universitaires de Limoges.

Feiling, K. (1966). *Warren Hastings*, Macmillan.

Fetters, B. (2016). Pivotal and puzzling: The Indian boy in *A Midsummer Night's Dream*. *The Alpha Chi Journal of Undergraduate Scholarship*. Vol. 1(1) pp. 2-9.

Ford, Col. L. (1910). *Lord Clive's right-hand man*: *A memoir of Colonel Francis Forde*. James Nisbet & Co. Ltd.

Forrest, G.W. (1767). *Selections from the letters, despatches, and other state papers preserved in the Bombay secretariat-Maratha Series* (Vol. I), Bombay Castle 18th November. Thomas Hodge etc.

Fry, M. (2004). *The Dundas Despotism*, John Donald Publishers Ltd.

Fullerton's Hircarrah system. Home Misc. 84ff. British Library, London, pp. 11–23.

Gardyne, C.G. (1903). *The life of a regiment*: *The history of the Gordon Highlanders from 1816 to 1898 including an account of the 75th regiment from 1787 to 1881* (Vol. II). The Medici Society Ltd.

Gascoigne, J. (1998). *Science in the service of empire*. Cambridge University Press.

Gense, Rev. G.H., & D.R. Banaji. (Eds.). (1934). *The third English embassy to Poona, comprising Mostyn's diary. (Sep. 1772–Feb.*

*1774) and Mostyn's letters (Feb.–Nov. 1774).*Taraporevala and Sons.

Glamann, K. (1958). *Dutch-Asiatic trade, 1620–1740*. Danish Science Press.

Gleig, G.R. (1841). *Memoirs of the life of the right hon. Warren Hastings* (Vol. 2). Internet Archives: new.dli.ernet.in/handle/2015/53324

———. (1848). *The life of Robert, first lord Clive,* J. Murray.

Glete, J. (2000). *Warfare at sea, 1500–1650: Maritime conflicts and the transformation of Europe.* Routledge.

Gordon, S. (1993). *The new Cambridge history of India. The Marathas 1600–1818.* Cambridge University Press.

Goodenough, Simon. (1981). *Sailing ships*. Albany Books.

Goodman, H. (2009). The formation of the Bank of England: A response to changing political and economic climate, 1694. *Penn History Review*,Vol.17 (1) Article 2. pp. 10-30.

Gottmann, F. (2013). French-Asian connections: The Compagnies des Indes, France's eastern trade, and new directions in historical scholarship, *The Historical Journal*.

Guilmartin Jr, J.F. (1995). The Military Revolution-Origins and First Tests Abroad. In J.R. Clifford (Ed). *The Military Revolution Debate: Readings on the military transformation of early modern Europe*, Westview Press, pp. 299-333.

———. (2002). *Galleons and galleys*, Cassell & Co.

———. (2007). The earliest shipboard gunpowder ordnance: An analysis of its technical parameters and tactical capabilities. *The Journal of Military History,* pp. 649-669.

Habib, I. (Ed.). (2001). *State and diplomacy under Tipu Sultan*: *Documents and essays*. Tulika, Karnataka, India.

Hakluyt, R. (1904). *The principal navigations, voyages, trafiques & discoveries of the English nation made by sea or overland to the remote and farthest distant quarters of the earth at any time within the compasse of these 1600 years* (Vol. 7), MacLehose and Sons.

Hatalkar, V.G. (1958). *Relations between the French and the Marathas (1668–1815)*, University of Bombay.

Headlam, E J. (1929). The History of the Royal Indian Marine. *Journal of the Royal Society of Arts*, 77(3985), 519-540. www.jstor.org/stable/41358199.

Holden, F. (1976). *Rival empires of trade in the orient, 1600–1800*, University of Minnesota Press.

How did Britain come to rule the waves? (2010, February 23). *History Magazine*, 23.

Hunter, Sir W.W. (1900). *A history of British India*, (Vol. II), Longmans, Green and Co., London.

I.O.R. Home Miscellaneous Series, Vol. 809, f364 et seq. British Library.

Joppen, C. (1907). *Historical atlas of India*, Longmans, Green & Co.

Johnson, S. (1889). *Rasselas: Prince of Abyssinia,* A.C. McClurg and Co.

Joshi, V.V. (1941). *Clash of three empires: A study of British conquest of India with special reference to the Maratha people.* Kitabistan, Allahabad.

Kantak, M.R. (1993). *The first Anglo-Maratha War 1774–1783: A military study of major battles*, Popular Prakashan Pvt Ltd.

Keay, J. (1991). *The honourable company*: *The history of the East India Company,* Harper Collins Publishers.

Keegan, J. (2002). *Intelligence in war*, Vintage Books.

Kenny, K. (Ed). (2004). Ireland *and British empire:.The Oxford History of British Empire Companion Series*, Oxford University Press, Oxford.

Kessel, E. van. (2020). The inventories of the Madre de Deus: Tracing Asian material culture in early modern England, *32*(2), 207–223.

Khan, Y.H. (1936). *Nizamu'l-Mulk Asaf Jah.* Basel Mission Press.

Kimmel, M.S. (1988). *Absolutism and its discontents: State and society in seventeenth century France and England.* Transaction Books.

Kochar, R.K. (1992). Science in British India. I. Colonial tool. *Current Science, 63*(11). pp. 689-694.

Koehn, N.F. (1994). *The Power of commerce*. Economy and Governance in the First British Empire, Cornell University Press.

Konstam, A. (2008). *Sovereigns of the seas: The quest to build the perfect Renaissance battleship*. John Wiley & Sons Inc.

Kroef, J.M. van der. (1948). The decline and fall of the Dutch East India Company. *The Historian. 10*(2). pp. 118-134. https://doi.org/10.1111/j.1540-6563.1948.tb00452.x

Kulke, H., & D. Rothermund, (2004). *The History of India* (4th Ed.), Routledge.

Lenman, B. & P. Lawson.(1983).Robert Clive: The "Black Jagir" and British politics. *The Historical Journal, 26*(4), pp. 801-829. http://www.jstor.org/stable/2639285

Love, H.D. (1913). *Indian records series: Vestiges of old Madras. 1640–1800* (Vol. II), Asian Education Service.

Mackenzie, C. *Marches and encampments of the Grand Army commanded by Major General Medows*. From Art Collection/ Alamy Stock Photo.

Macleod, J. (1996). *Highlanders: A history of the Gales*. Hodder & Stoughton.

Malcolm, Sir J. (1836). *The life of Robert, Lord Clive: Collected from the family papers communicated by the Earl of Powis*, Bibliolife.

Malleson, Col. G.B. (1885). *The decisive battles of India: From 1746 to 1849 Inclusive,* W.H. Allen Co.

———. (1899). *Rulers of India. Dupleix and struggle for India by the European Nations*. Oxford Onlinebooks.library.upenn.edu>book>lookupname.

Marshman, J. C (1863). *The History of India, Part 1.From the earliest period to the close of the eighteenth century*. Serampore Press.

——— 1867). *The history of India from the earliest period to the close of Lord Dalhousie's administration* (Vol. II), Longman Green.

Martin, E.J. (1944). An engineer in the Mysore War of 1791–1792. *Journal of the Society for Army Historical Research. 22(*92). pp. 324-338 https://www.jstor.org/stable/44228373

McGinty, A.B. (1946). Anglo-Dutch rivalry in India. *Current History, 11*(63).

McKillop, A. (2007). Continuity, Coercion and Myth: The Recruitment of Highland Regiments in the later Eighteenth Century. *International Review of Scottish Studies, (26).* pp.30-55. DOI:10.21083/irss.v2610.210

McLynn, F. (2004). *1759: The year Britain became master of the world*, Jonathen Cape.

Mehta, J.L. (2005). *Advanced study in the history of modern India 1707–1813,* New Dawn Press.

Mileham, P. (1988). *The Scottish Regiments (1633–1996)*, Spellmount Ltd.

Mill, J. (1858). *The History of British India* (Vol. III), Baldwin, Cradock and Jov.

Mitra, R.C. (1951). Some light on the Third Anglo-Mysore War from French sources. *Proceedings of the Indian History Congress*. Vol. 14. (pp. 232-238).

Murty, V.K. (2007). *A brief history of Indian Mathematics-eSamskriti.* www.esamscriti.com

Muthiah, I.S. (2008). *Madras-Chennai* (*A 400-year record of the first city of India—The land, the people and their governance*), Palaniyappa Brothers.

Nadkarni, R.V. (1966). *The rise and fall of the Maratha Empire,* Bombay Popular Prakashan.

Narayanan, M.G.S. (2006). *Calicut: City of truth revisited*, Publication Division, University of Calicut.

Oak, M., & A. Swamy. (2010). Commitment and conquest: The case of British rule in India. Department of Economics working papers 2010–08. Department of Economics, Williams

College, Massachusetts. www/.williams.edu> economics> oakswamycommitmentandcare. (pp.1-31)

Padfield, P. (1973). *Explorations by the Atlantic nations, inguns at sea*, Hugh Evlyn Ltd.

———. (1979). *Tide of empires: Decisive naval campaigns in the rise of the West. Vol. I. 1481–1654*, Routledge & Kegan Paul Ltd.

Panikkar, K.M. (1953). *Asia and western dominance: A survey of the Vasco da Gama epoch of Asian History*, George Allen & Unwin Ltd.

Parker, G. (1991). *Europe and the wider world, 1500–1750: The military balance in the political economy of merchant empires*. Edited by J.D. Tracy, Cambridge University Press.

———. (Ed.). (1995). *The Cambridge Illustrated History of Warfare: The Triumph of the West,* Cambridge University Press.

———. (1996). *The Military Revolution: Military innovation and the rise of the West 1500–1800*, Cambridge University Press.

Pearson, M.N. (1991). Merchants and states. In James D Tracy(Ed). *The Political Economy of the Merchant Empire. State power and worldtrade 1350-1750.* (pp. 41-116), Cambridge University Press.

Pearson, R., and Richardson, D. (2019). Insuring the Transatlantic trade. *The Journal of Economic History*, *79*(2), pp. 417-446. DOI: https://doi.org/10.1017/S0022050719000068

Philips, A., & Sharman, J.C. (2020). Company-states and the creation of the global international system. *European Journal of International Relations*. 26(4), 1249-1272.

https://doi.org/10.1177/1354066120928127

Philips, C.H. (1940). The secret committee of the East India Company. *Bulletin of the School of Oriental Studies*, University of London, 10(2). pp. 299-315 http://www.jstor.org/stabl/608393

Pingree, D. (1978). Indian astronomy. *Proceedings of the American Philosophical* Society, *122*(6). pp. 361-364. www.jstor.org/stable/986451.

Poonen, T.I. (1958). A chapter in the history of Kerala. *Proceedings of the Indian History Congress*. Vol. 21. pp. 618-625. https://www.jstor.org/stable/44145270

Prebble, J. (1982). *The highland clearances*, Penguin Books Limited.

Ramaswami, N.S. (1984). *Political history of Carnatic under the nawabs*, Abhinav Publications.

Ramusack, B.N. (2004). *The New Cambridge history of India. III. 6. The Indian princes and their states*, Cambridge University Press.

Ray, N.B. (Ed.). (1937). *Poona residency correspondence, Vol. III, The Allies' war with Tipu Sultan 1790–1793*. Bombay, The Government Central Press.

Records of Fort St. George. Diary and consultation book. Madras. 1931, Duke University Libraries. Records of Fort. St George.

Regani, S. (1988). *Nizam-British relations 1724–1857*, Concept Publications.

Reports & c. (East India Company) First Part. Vol VII. Minutes of evidence taken before committee of the Whole House and the select committee on the affairs of the East India Company. Oxford, 1813.

Roach, J. (1958).The 39th regiment of foot and the East India Company, 1754–1757. *Bulletin of the John Rylands Library*, *41*(1):102–138. www.manchester.ac.uk/library.

Robson, M. (2016). *A history of the Royal Navy—The Seven Years War,* I.B. Tauris & Co Ltd.

Rodger, N.A. (2004). *The command of the ocean. A naval history of Britain 1649–1815.* Penguin Books.

Saldanha, A. (2011). The itineraries of geography: Jan Huygen van Linschoten's 'Itinerario' and Dutch expeditions to the Indian Ocean, 1594–1602. *Annals of the Association of American Geographers.101(1).* pp. 149-177. http://www.jstor.org/stable/27980165

Sardesai, G. S. (Ed). (1936). *Poona residency correspondence, Vol 2, Poona Affairs 1786-1797(Malet's embassy).* Bombay, Government Central Press.

———. (1946a). *New history of the Marathas. The expansion of Maratha Power (1707–1772).* (Vol. II). Digital Library India.

———. (1946b). *New history of the Marathas* (Vol. III), Phoenix Publications.

Sarkar, J.N. (1950). *Fall of the Mughal Empire* (Vol. IV), M.C. Sarkar & Ltd.

Sauer, C.O. (1966). *The early Spanish main.* University of California Press.

Schmidt, K.J. (2015). *An atlas and survey of south Asian history.* Routledge.

Schwarz, G.R. (2008). *The history and development of Caravels, a thesis,* May 2008. http:///www.Anthropology.tamu.edu/papers/ Schwarz-

Scott, W.R. (1911). *The constitution and finance of English, Scottish, Irish joint-stock companies to 1720.* Cambridge.

Seavoy, R.E. (2003). *Origins and growth of the global economy: From the fifteenth century onwards*. Prager.

Sen, S.N. (1959).Origin of the first Anglo-Maratha war. *Proceedings of the Indian History Congress, Vol. 22.* Indian History Congress. pp. 400-402.

Sen, S.N. (1928). *The military system of the Marathas*.Orient Longman.

———. (2007). *Textbook of Indian history and culture.* Macmillan India Ltd.

Sharman, J.C. (2019). Power and profit at sea: The rise of the West in the making of the international system. *International Security.43 (4),* pp.163-196. https://doi.org/10.1162/isec_a_00346

Shejwalker, T.S. (1946). *Panipat: 1761.* Deccan College Monograph Series Deccan College Poona.

Inikori, J. (2000). The Slave Trade and the Atlantic Economies, 1451-1870. In Shepherd, V. A. and Beckles, H. M. (Eds.), Caribbean *Slavery in the Atlantic World* (pp. 290-308). Ian Raandle Publishers Limited.

Singh, A. (2020). Early modern European mercantilism and Indian Ocean trade. In Strootman, R. van den Eijnde & van Wijk,

R. (Eds.), *Empires of the sea: Maritime power networks in world history*. www.jstor.org/stable/10.1163/j.ctv2gjx041.14.

Spear, P. (1975). *Master of Bengal—Clive and his India*, Thames and Hudson Ltd.

Spence, R.T. (1995). *The privateering earl: George Clifford, 3rd Earl of Cumberland, 1558–1605,* Alan Sutton Publishing Ltd.

Stanley, H.E.J. (1869). *The three voyages of Vasco da Gama and his viceroyalty;* From the Lendas Da India of Gasper Correa. Accompanied by Original Documents. Translated from Portuguese with Notes and an Introduction by the Hon. Henry E. Stanley. London. Printed for the Hakluyt Society.

Stone, L. (1980). The results of the English revolutions of the seventeenth century. In Pocock, J G A. (Ed.), *Three British Revolutions, 1641, 1688, 1776*. (pp. 23-108), Princeton University Press.

Subramanyam, S. (1977). *The career and legend of Vasco da Gama*. Cambridge University Press.

Tate, W.E. (1967). *The English village community and the enclosure movements*, Victor Gollancz Ltd.

The East India military calendar containing the services of general and field officers of the India Army.By the Editor of the Royal Military Calendar Vol II, The Naval and Military Press, England. 2007, Reprint in facsimile from Original 1824.

Thomas, H. (1997). *The slave trade: The history of the Atlantic slave trade, 1440–1870*, Picador.

Thompson, E. (1943). *The making of the Indian princes.* G.B.W. Forrest, Selections from the State Papers of the Governors-General of India, Warren Hastings, Oxford University Press.

Thorton, J. (2000). The birth of Atlantic world. In Shepherd V.A. and Beckles H.M (Eds.), *Carribean slavery in the Atlantic world.* (pp. 55-73), Ian Raandle Publishers Limited.

Tibbles, A. (Ed.). (2005). *Transatlantic slavery against human dignity*, Liverpool University Press.

Varma, S.P. (1956). *A study in Maratha Diplomacy (Anglo-Maratha Relations 1772–1783),* Shiva Lal Agrawala & Co.

Wadia, R.A. (1955). *The Bombay dockyard and the Wadia master builders,* R.A. Wadia.

Walrasaid. (2014, October 27). Outward journey of 4th Portuguese India Armada (Vasco da Gama, 1502), showing also the side-trip of Pedro Afonso de Aguiar to Sofala. Wikipedia. www.wikipedia.org/wiki/4thPortuguese-India-Armada.

Weststeijn, A. (2014). The VOC as a company-state: Debating seventeenth-century Dutch colonial expansion. *European Journal of Overseas History*. 38(01), 13-34.

Weatherford, Jack. (2004). *Genghis Khan and the making of the Modern World.* Three Rivers Press. New. York.

Wibulslip, P. (2012). *"I am Nawab of Arcot": Reconsidering political history of the late 18th century kingdom of Arcot through the eye of Nawab Muhammed Ali Wallajah.(r. 1749–1795).* openaccess.leidenuniv.nl>bitstream>handle> I am Nawab of Arcot.

Wickwire, F., & Wickwire, M. (1980). *Cornwallis, the imperial years*. The University of North Carolina Press.

Williams, E. (1994). *Capitalism and slavery*. The University of North Carolina Press.

William, H.R.A. (1793). *Travels in India during the years 1780-1783*. London, Archives.

Wilson, W. J. (1882). *History of the Madras army* (Vol. II), Madras.

Wood, William (1718). *A Survey of Trade.* Part III, London.

Wylly, Col. H.C. (1922). *The Life of Lieutenant General Sir Eyre Coote*. Compiled by Col. H. C. Wylly. Oxford. Archive.org>stream 59-78.

Index

F

G

H

I

J

K

L

M